GUNNER'S GLORY

By Johnnie M. Clark

GUNS UP!
SEMPER FIDELIS
THE OLD CORPS
NO BETTER WAY TO DIE

GUNNER'S GLORY

UNTOLD STORIES OF MARINE MACHINE GUNNERS

JOHNNIE M. CLARK

BALLANTINE BOOKS • NEW YORK

A Presidio Press Book
Published by The Random House Publishing Group

www.presidiopress.com

ISBN 0-345-46389-7

Manufactured in the United States of America

OPM 9 8 7 6 5 4 3 2 1

First Edition: December 2004

As I was writing the dedication for this book, I received a phone call telling me that the legend, Col. Mitchell Paige, had died. America has lost one of her great sons. My sadness is tempered with the knowledge of where Mitch is right now. Semper fi, Marine.

To Nancy, Shawn, and Bonnie Kay, my love and thanks for putting up with a husband and dad who sometimes drifts into the "bush." To my friends, Professor George Leonard and Pastor Phil Engleman. To my editor, Ron Doering, for a ton of work. To Pastor Danny and the gang at Cavary Chapel.

To Smitty, my old A-gunner from Colorado, guns up! I hope you are fat and happy, Buddy. To Doc Turley—see you in heaven, Doc. To the heroic Marines of A 1/5, from Hue City to An Hoa, please forgive an eighteen-year-old machine gunner for those times he screwed up.

I dedicate this book to Jesus Christ for His mercy and grace. To the Corps, Semper Fidelis.

ACKNOWLEDGMENTS

I need to give my thanks and proper credit to the heroes that I have written about in this book. It is not my story, it is their story and they deserve the credit, the praise, and the eternal thanks of all who call themselves American. Their sacrifice cannot be measured in days or years. Those who have been there know that. Their sacrifice was life-ending, life-changing, or lifelong. These men joined the United States Marine Corps. No one forced them to, and they are the first to proudly state that fact.

Ted Eleston's story came from Cpl. Ted "Eli" Eleston. Photos, too. When the folks at Haslam's Bookstore, one of the oldest and most respected in the South, heard that I was writing a book about Marine machine gunners, they contacted me. They told me I had to meet one of their favorite customers. He was an old Marine Raider machine gunner. "As a matter of fact," they said, "Old Ted just knocked some young punk out cold down on Central Avenue for insulting a lady."

"How old is this guy?"

"He's got to be about eighty-three!"

I knew this was one of my Marines. After we met, I asked him why his knuckles were all messed up. "Oh. It's nothin'. Had to square something away." We've become great pals and throw back a shot of brandy together when it's necessary. Getting the story out of some of these guys has not been easy. They don't brag much; if anything, they understated everything until I had to drag it out of them. I'm using Ted as my example, but they're each the same kind of man in one very specific way: Marines. When I found out Ted had not told me about killing enemy soldiers with a knife after running out of ammo, he said, "Oh. I thought I told you that, Johnnie. Say, I still got that knife back here in the closet, want to see it?" I said yes. It was still stained with blood. I ribbed him about not cleaning his weapon. "Angry blood won't clean off, John." This was the blood of that faceless man that still comes at him out of the blackness in the middle of many nights. Ted is a God-fearing Christian who absolutely honors and loves the Lord Jesus Christ.

Col. Mitchell Paige and his lovely wife Marilyn gave me his story through interviews and e-mails, but the majority of this American legend's story came right out of his own mouth and his own book, titled *A Marine Named Mitch* by Mitchell Paige (Wylde & Sons). The photos are with permission from his book. His legend will continue as long as we have a Corps. Mitchell Paige is one of the finest patriots I've ever had the honor of speaking with. He's as brilliant as he is brave. He honors the Lord Jesus Christ in the way he lives and the way he speaks. I pray that God will bless our country with more men like Mitchell Paige. When he spoke with me about his own personal miracle on Guadalcanal, I was touched to my very soul. He told me he was hesitant to even tell the other men what had happened for fear that they would think he was nuts. He and Marilyn told me the story so that God would be honored and people would know the truth about what happened to this hero on Guadalcanal. Mitchell Paige spoke the humble truth, and his story is a blessing to anyone who hears it.

Cpl. Melvin Cruthers gave me his story with such genuine fellowship that I feel as though I've known him for years. He's a humble, caring man who has gone through life with an attitude that few able-bodied men could ever match. There is no malice or bitterness in this man, he's still very proud to have served as a United States Marine machine gunner. Mel makes me ashamed to gripe about anything.

I met Win Scott years ago when I was writing *No Better Way to Die*. It was in Mississippi at the christening of the

USS *Chosin*. I got to meet many of the famous "Chosin Few," the heroes of the battle of Chosin Reservoir. Win and his wife Kay went out of their way to help me with that book. As Win directed me to men who had wonderful stories, he humbly downplayed his own incredible fight for life at the Chosin. I believe he fought and bled through one of the greatest feats in military history. He gave me his time and his memories by phone, letters, e-mail, and hours of tapes.

Dan Bogan received the Silver Star in Korea. He was a hero at a place called Bunker Hill. A lot of our kids don't even know what the Silver Star is. Parents, teach them. I hope Dan's family and friends will read his story and be proud. For me, Dan represents thousands of Marines and soldiers who fought in Korea. I don't think their sacrifice was forgotten, I think it was ignored. I think we have a couple of million young South Koreans who need to read Dan's story and Win's story. When I see South Koreans marching in protest against America, I'm amazed at how short the human memory can be; maybe they're eating too many french fries. Dan feels great pride in his Corps and his service to his country. My hope is that our children will not ignore or forget places like Korea or shell-pocked mountains of mud like Bunker Hill.

PFC Melvin Newlin could not tell me his story. His buddies did. Some of those buddies didn't even know him that well. They probably know him better now. He was a hero, a Marine who died among brave men. He sacrificed his eighteen-year-old life to save a lot of brave men. Cpl. Bob Bowermaster told me he didn't have much of a story and that I should contact Thom Searfoss because Thom was a hero at Nong Son and remembers every moment. He was partially right. Thom remembered amazing details, as did Cpl. Roger Hug and L.Cpl. Ray Alvey and Michael Harris and all the others. Where Bob was wrong was his part in the story. Bob Bowermaster forgot that he is a hero. We will never know how many enemy soldiers he killed that night, even after being shot through the lung and stabbed. Thom Searfoss is a hero. He ran through fire to save other Marines. He paused three times going uphill into the middle of the enemy attack to give Bob mouth-to-mouth, saving his life three times. When I asked Thom, "Why did you carry Bob to the top of the hill, into the center of the battle?" he said without hesitating, "We're Marines, where else would we go?" Every man in this story is a hero. They got Purple Hearts and that says it all, but the Marine Corps is really stingy and really slow about giving out medals. Roger Hug and Dean Johnson and Michael Harris and Don Rouzan and nearly every Marine at Nong Son and those running to their rescue through a pitch-black jungle were heroic. They gave me their stories by interview, phone, e-mail, letters, and photos. If you know any of these Marines, give them your thanks.

Jack Hartzel gave me his story, first through his own writing entitled *Reflections of My Past,* published by Greatunpublished.com, then through his friendship. He shared through letters and e-mails and photographs. Jack contacted some of his buddies to help with photographs. My thanks to Cpl. William Underwood for the use of his personal photographs. When I asked Jack if he would give me his story for this book on Marine gunners, his first reaction was, "I don't know if I belong in such company." Jack, you belong. Guns Up!

My thanks to the National Archives for photographs of Marines on Peleliu, Guadalcanal, Korea, and Vietnam. My special thanks to Patrick Clancey, Executive Directory, HyperWar Foundation, and to *History of U.S. Marine Corps Operations in World War II* for maps vital to the telling of these stories. Thanks to the United States Marine Corps History and Museums Division for their help with maps on Vietnam. My thanks to Ballantine Books–Random House for the use of maps from my own books, *No Better Way to Die* and *Guns Up!,* both published by Ballantine Books. My special thanks to Patrick Smith for the maps he created for this book.

CONTENTS

LIST OF MAPS

INTRODUCTION

The life expectancy of a machine gunner in Vietnam was somewhere around seven seconds after a firefight began. There are a couple of reasons why that startling statistic is accurate. Every good army is taught to knock out the machine gun first, the firepower and the heart of an infantry platoon. A battle at night is a black world with white muzzle flashes that are gone as quickly as they appear. At night the machine gun is usually the only visible target. Every fifth bullet in a belt of machine gun ammo is a tracer round. When a weapon is firing 550 or 600 rounds per minute, those tracer rounds turn into a bright orange or golden arrow that allows the gunner to see where his fire is hitting. It points out enemy targets for the infantry and pinpoints enemy positions for pilots above. With that gun you lay down a wall of lead to cover Marines on the move or to protect a corpsman helping a wounded man. The machine gun can stop an onslaught or begin the assault. A machine gun can cut down a tree or blow holes through concrete block buildings to kill hidden enemy soldiers.

That golden arrow of tracer rounds that is so vital is the same arrow that points right back at the machine gunner pulling that trigger. While rifles flash on and off like lightning bugs in the night, never giving away their position for more than an instant, the machine gunner is not only the one visible target but the most important. You know that truth every single time you pull the trigger. You know every enemy soldier will see your position the instant you open fire. The gunner knows that the enemy will throw everything they have at him—mortars, rockets, artillery, grenades, satchel charges, rifle and machine gunfire. I served as a gunner with the famed 5th Marine Regiment. During my tour with the 5th Marines, I knew of no machine gunner in the regiment who was not killed or wounded. Many were wounded more than once. It was the same for every Marine gunner no matter which war they were fighting.

This is a book of true stories about Marine Corps machine gunners in combat. Fighting for their lives and their country. Battling not only the enemy's best troops but battling the mud, heat, rain, snow, mountains, and jungles of the world. Carrying the heavy gun and as many belts of ammo as humanly possible through the toughest terrain on earth. Sometimes making the single most significant difference between victory and defeat. Their tenacity changed the outcome of battles so important that they very possibly changed the outcome of entire wars. These are real Marines and their stories are not always pretty. They will be the first to tell you that they knew what they were getting into when they joined the Corps. They will be the first to tell you that a Marine is an absolute professional at his job, and his primary job is to kill the enemies of The United States of America, understanding the risk of death, and accepting it. They will also tell you that the dangers of being a machine gunner were no secret in the Corps.

Their sacrifice will make you cry and make you laugh, but most of all I hope it causes you to pause and thank God for blessing America with such men. You'll wonder how they could remember such distant, minute details in the midst of absolute chaos, and you'll equally marvel at how a mind can go so blank as to not remember even one moment out of weeks of brutal combat. Those who have been there will understand, and those who have never lived through such combat may never grasp the reality, but you'll know it's true. Guns Up! and Semper Fidelis.

GUNNER'S
GLORY

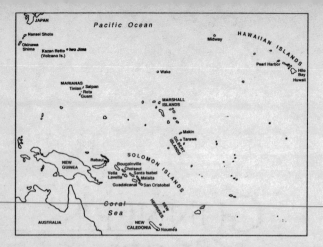

Map by: Patrick A. Smith

Map by: Patrick A. Smith

1

CPL. TED ELESTON

I fell exhausted onto a white stretch of Virginia Beach, not white with sand but snow and bone-aching cold. I looked over at Platoon Sergeant Hinkle. We had been training hard at Quantico. We lived in these rubber boats, making landing after landing after landing. Day landings, night landings, cold landings, and blazing hot landings. Col. "Red Mike" Edson had taken over the 1st Battalion, 5th Marine Regiment. President Roosevelt was being hounded by politicians and even Winston Churchill to form up a new unit like the British Commandos. Marine commandant Thomas Holcomb was not impressed and reminded the world that Marines were Marines and ready to fight any enemy, anywhere and at any time, better than any fighting force on earth. Under pressure from the president, the commandant brought in the legendary jungle fighter, Col. Red Mike Edson, and gave him the pick of the litter of the famous 1st Battalion, 5th Marine Regiment. He flatly refused to call Marines commandos. For a while we became the 1st Separate Battalion. Still under political pressure, the commandant himself finally named us the 1st Marine Raiders.

Red Mike knew what these new Marine Raiders were in for against the Japanese. He was making sure we were ready. Some of us thought Edson was crazy. We would force march in full combat gear faster and longer than any other outfit and then double-time just to keep up this pace of seven miles per hour. We did it all and we did it often. That's why I didn't think it was unusual that Sergeant Hinkle looked so bad at first glance on that ice-cold beach. We were all exhausted, but his ashen face and fatal stare indicated more than fatigue. The men called him Hink for short. He was fiddling with this little gold wedding band around his neck on his leather dog tag strap. Hink's beautiful new bride had died on their wedding night that summer of '41 when we took over New River, later to become Camp Lejeune. He wasn't the same after that, but there was a war to fight, and if he took a leave now he might not be able to stay with the Raiders, so he stuck it out. I rolled onto my side and tried to sound upbeat, as his low emotional state was obvious. "How ya' holdin' up, Sarge?" My words came out like smoke signals in the cold air.

Fatigue and pain stared back at me through ice blue eyes. He fingered that gold ring again and looked me square in the face.

"I'm going to get killed in this war, Eli."

The guys called me Eli. It wasn't the first time or the last time I heard a Marine voice the thought of not making it. You had to just wave it off, so that's what I tried to do. "Ahh! Don't say stuff like that, Sarge! We're going to kill these Japs and come home and have a beer."

"No," he said, appearing to stare through me and at something beyond. "I'm going to get killed in this war."

I was speechless. He was serious, and I didn't know what to say to him. Then he sort of held out the little gold ring to show me. "I want you to put this on my pinkie finger after I die." He looked straight into my soul. "Will you promise me, Eli?"

"Yeah. Okay. Sure."

The 1st Marine Raiders hit Tulagi in August 1942. It was rough. The Japs counterattacked that first night. Jap grenades rained in on us out of the pitch-black night, their fuses sparkling as they whirled in from all directions. Explosions rocked every part of the ridge we were holding; I lost my bearings from the concussion and I lost my machine gun squad. I searched around on my hands and knees for the light .30-caliber machine gun, but it was gone. It was blown away, and we didn't find it until the next day, at the bottom of the hill. I pulled this piece of shrapnel out of my right ear; it was sticking in my skull and it hurt. In spite of that I could hear my gunner moaning, wounded, but I couldn't see him. I crawled around in the brush, feeling with my hands until I felt something wet, then I touched a body. I got his arms over my shoulders and carried him on my back, up this wagon trail toward the top of the ridge where the CP was. I knew there was a corpsman there.

"Halt!" A familiar voice barked and I froze. It was Capt. Lew Walt. Of course no one knew it then, but Lew Walt would go on to play an important role in this war, and in Korea and Vietnam. "Corporal Eleston, guns! I lost my gun and the whole squad, sir!"

He pointed me up the trail. "Get your wounded up to the CP, move it!"

I took off with my gunner over my shoulder, he was bleeding all down my back. About twenty yards up that trail I saw nothing but grenades and muzzle flashes ahead. The CP was being overrun! Mortar rounds started dropping. I heard Marines yelling to get down. I slid over the side of the slope and right into a bunch of wounded Raiders, and I spent the night down on one side of the ridge huddled together with my gunner and the other wounded. Soon we heard another shootout near the CP. Word came down that the old man himself, Red Mike Edson, had charged back into that building with his .45 blazing and helped clean out the Japs when the Marines retook it.

That morning I got my gunner to a corpsman and was still in a fog when I passed all the dead Marines laid out on the trail under ponchos. They were getting them ready to boat them out to the APDs. I didn't really want to look, it wasn't just morbid curiosity, I had to force my eyes down. I had to know who they were. I lifted a poncho and there was Hink, his leather dog tag strap still around his neck and that little gold band on it glistening in the hot sun. I stood there for a long time just staring down at him, that gold band blinding me, my eyes frosted up. I just couldn't do it. I couldn't put that ring on his finger like I promised. I hurt inside over it. I hurt deep into my gut. I regret not doing that for him.

To kids today, 1928 probably sounds like a thousand years ago, but it wasn't a thousand years ago to me. It feels like early yesterday. I woke up each morning to the shudder of the cavalry going past my bedroom window. Those huge horses clopping past, their hoofs resounding off the gravel road outside. I jumped out of bed to watch from my window. Soldiers wearing brown leather cavalry boots in the stirrups of hardworking and well-trained horses. Pack animals snorting under the weight of heavy gear and weapons like a living train of blood and muscle. Sometimes they sounded almost like giant men marching down that hard white gravel road.

Dad was a soldier and I grew up in a military family that had a long military history. I guess you could say it went all the way back to the Spartans on my father's side of the family. I used to listen to the stories about my family members having to fire on the Black Watch Highland Infantry and actually killing their own cousins during the Revolutionary War. Mom's first cousin was in the 7th Cavalry and died with Custer. My grandmother, my mom's mother, was a first cousin to Gen. George Armstrong Custer. Her name was Bertha White Huff. Her maiden name, White, was changed from Whyte, one of the original early colonists. They changed from Whyte to White because of their anger toward England.

Dad was a sergeant major and fought against Pancho Villa in Mexico and then the Kaiser in World War I. Dad was badly wounded by shrapnel in France while attacking and destroying a German machine gun nest. He was also wounded by mustard gas and spent months in the VA hospital in Chillicothe, Ohio. Me and mom and my sister lived at Camp Sherman. When dad healed up, he left the army and started a chicken farm in Toledo, his lifelong dream. Mom had put her foot down and said, "No more moving!"

I have this strange, God-given ability to sense danger. I'm no psychic, I just sort of feel that something is wrong and find out later that something was wrong. One night on the chicken farm, I just shot up out of bed and knew something was real wrong. I got out of bed worried, then I started looking around. I looked out my bedroom window and started yelling for help. I guess, other than combat, that was one of the worst moments in my father's life. It was a simple fire that became a terrible fire, it destroyed the chicken farm. It killed twenty thousand chickens. Dad was utterly broken-hearted and went back in the army after that and stayed in for life.

My father had the equivalent of a university degree at the age of thirteen and expected the same out of me. My grandfather was a Greek Orthodox priest in the old country. He was extreme about education. One day my dad was late for a class and my grandfather strung him up with ropes inside a barn and beat him so badly that he was hospitalized for two weeks. Not long after that, my father's older sister left home and took my dad to America, and he never saw grandfather again until grandfather's visit in 1936. That visit was shortened because of the war. Grandfather and my dad's two brothers were killed by the communists in 1945 just after World War II ended. Few people know or care about that time in history but it was painful for many. The communists kidnapped thousands of Greek children, many taken by Tito, the leader in Yugoslavia. They put these kids in communist indoctrination schools for years, then sent them back to Greece at the end of the war in hopes of turning Greece into a communist country. If people only understood how evil communism is. It is as satanic as any false religion.

My parents taught us to read as soon as we could talk, or almost. I was the only boy and the oldest. I had four sisters eventually. At the age of seven I could read as well as many grown-ups, and getting to that Sunday paper first was important. We had no such thing as television, so the paper was a big deal for us. It was a beautiful Sunday morning when I dived into that newspaper all alone at the kitchen table. The headline was MARINES BATTLING SANDINO. Nicaragua was the big news, and I couldn't read enough about the Marines fighting the Sandinistas in Nicaragua. It was a jungle war, and the Marines were being led by the legendary jungle fighter Red Mike Edson. He was ahead of his time in so many ways. Edson really invented the strategy of vertical envelopment before anybody knew what it was. In Nicaragua, he put a Lewis gun on a ring mount and fixed it under an autogyro (that's like a primitive helicopter, one rotor) in 1927. The gun had these big one-hundred-round drums. He'd fly that thing over the Sandinistas and just wreak havoc and chase them right into his waiting Marines. As I read about these men called Marines, I made a decision right then and there to become one of them. At seven years old I think I understood that these men were different. They were America's Spartans. They had one job and one purpose and that was to kill any enemy of America, even if it meant sacrificing their own life.

At fifteen I quit school and ran away from home with an orphan boy that lived with us. I guess I was being a little rebellious, but I wanted to join the Marines. We ended up joining the nearest military outfit we could find. I was big, about full grown. I ended up being six-foot-three and 215 pounds, so I managed to lie my way in okay. It wasn't that long before dad tracked us down, though. He was not happy. He and mom wanted me to finish high school and go to West Point. Dad's close friend was the attorney general of Ohio, Roland B. Lee. Dad was a sergeant major at the time, so he had some pull even without Mr. Lee, but he worked out a deal with the attorney general that allowed me to be stationed in Toledo with the National Guard Machine Gun Troop 107th Cavalry Regiment. I agreed, but my heart was already set on joining the Marines. That was in 1935.

Being a student and a soldier was no easy chore. While most of my friends were working summer jobs in stores or on farms, I was learning to work with some mean horses and mean machine guns. Both could kill you if you made a mistake. I found out real quick that these animals weren't the family plow horse, by God. They were wild mustangs! They could break loose if spooked and kill other horses and the men around them. The massive packsaddle was padded leather, canvas, and steel. Gun straps and steel clamps held the heavy, water-cooled .30-caliber machine gun in place on one side of this big, wild animal. The trunnion block and tripod were strapped to the other side to balance things off.

Now, as the gunner, I'd ride one horse while holding a thick rope known as the halter shank, which controlled the packhorse carrying the gun, trunnion, and tripod. I had to hold tense to my own bridle, but the trick was to keep the reins and halter shank of the packhorse tight with his head right at my right knee, working in unison with my horse. Of course, your legs played a big part in keeping you in the saddle. If I didn't keep that packhorse's head on my right knee and under control, it could spell serious trouble.

We would train to attack in column or on line with those horses and pack animals. We had to work as a unit and form up when the command came, and that meant your animals better be under control or somebody could die. There were some terrible accidents. During a pass-in-review at Fort Knox, Kentucky, I saw an awful accident. The horse soldiers were slowly being phased out, and the 1st Mechanized Cavalry was being unveiled with much pomp and ceremony. With forty thousand troops taking part in the maneuver, nothing was simple, but we didn't expect any problems during a routine pass-in-review. We rode in formation, trying to keep our eyes on the platoon guidon, the small red flag with the white letters MG TROOP. The MG stood for machine gun. Suddenly a violent commotion up ahead was followed by a lot of shouting and agonizing screams as packhorses broke loose, then panicked. I watched helplessly as men and horses alike were trampled to death.

Though training with horses was sometimes dangerous, it was far better than packing that heavy machine gun over my shoulder. It was no job for weaklings; even the strongest of men found it a daunting task during a forced march. I'd rather strap it on that horse than on my back anytime.

Finally I turned eighteen, and I just couldn't wait any longer to be a Marine. My mom knew she couldn't stop me once I was of age, so she gave in and without Dad's permission drove me to Cincinnati to enlist in the Marines. There was a big group trying to enlist. They chose only four of us.

That's where I met Timothy and Tasker Bliss. Twin brothers.
They got turned down because their shoulders were too
broad. They were mad about being turned down. Their dad
owned a big gambling joint in St. Louis right on the Mississippi. They ended up going out to San Diego and joining up
on the other coast. The cutoff for Parris Island was the Mississippi. A Marine named Jesse Davenport was one of the
four chosen along with me. My adventure had finally started.
My heart was in my throat as I boarded that train for South
Carolina and headed for that ominous little dot on the map
called Parris Island. We rolled into Yemassee, South Carolina, in the middle of a hot, foggy night. It was just me and
the three other fellows that got off there. We boarded this
small whaleboat and this navy coxswain told us to start row-
ing, so we rowed out into the wet fog until we came to a dock
with a couple of lanterns hanging on posts. There were river-
boats docked there, filled with cotton.

About the first thing I saw was this redheaded corporal
named Scott. He had been an "old China hand" for eight
years before becoming a drill instructor. He was this tough
Southern cracker, and he started cussing us out of that
whaleboat and somehow I ended up in the water. From the
instant I stepped on that dock, I already knew that the Marine
Corps was different from anything I had ever experienced.
Things were hard and simple. My drill instructor noticed that
me and this other recruit named Pvt. Paul Boone didn't see
eye to eye a few times. He settled it Marine Corps style. The
cure was immediate.

"You lads form a circle!" came the bellowing, no-nonsense
order. "You two! Get in the middle!" Well, I started looking
around like, "Who, me?" Well, he meant me all right. So me
and Paul Boone step into the center of the circle of Marines
and come to attention. "You two got a problem with each
other. Fight it out! Now!" And we did, and that's the way the
Corps worked. This was a tough outfit, and each man found
out real quick that there was no time or patience for stupid-
ity. I busted Paul's lip and he bloodied my nose, and once we
both drew blood and took the measure of each other we were

all right. We ended up becoming great friends, and Paul's brother Frankie Boone became my good friend, too, when he came into D 1/5 FMF (that's Dog Company, 1st Battalion, 5th Marine Regiment, Fleet Marine Force) out of boot camp in the summer of '39.

After boot camp, I got stationed at 8th & I in Washington, D.C., with Paul Boone. We made about twenty greenbacks a month. Paul and I discovered the Eulien Arena, where they held boxing events on Saturday nights. We signed up for the preliminary matches, four rounds, and got ten dollars per fight. Earning half a month's pay just to knock somebody's block off was a good Marine Corps deal. The 8th & I detail was spit and polish all the way and all the time. We were supposed to be the most squared away Marines in the Corps. We had to drill and drill and drill. We drilled for various dignitaries or any special occasion. On top of that drill, I had to do four or five burial details a week at Arlington.

The Queen of England came in one time. She was a beautiful woman. Her skin was like silk. They made me her bodyguard of sorts. I had to stand at attention in back of her at all times. I was to let no one get too close. She was a remarkable woman. After about six months of this spit-and-polish stuff, I approached the company commander. As a private I was taking a chance approaching the CO like this, but I wanted out of there. "Sir, I'd like a transfer to the real Marine Corps."

"What do you mean, real Marine Corps, Private!" the CO snapped.

"I'd like to transfer to China, sir. I want to be with the real Marines. I want to train and fight."

The scowl on the captain's face said more than any words. For a moment I thought I was on my way to the brig. My orders were cut that day. D Company, 1st Battalion, 5th Marine Regiment, at Quantico, Virginia. Weapons Company included machine guns and 81mm mortars and demolitions with the famous G.Sgt. (Gunnery Sergeant) Lew Diamond commanding.

Almost overnight I found myself surrounded by legends.

The "plank owners" of the most famous regiment in history. The 5th Marine Regiment. "Plank owners" was an old navy term to describe the original crew for a newly commissioned man-of-war. These were tough men who had no time or patience for new recruits. Matter of fact, they looked down on those new kids who wanted to join the Corps for a hitch and get out. They were professional fighting men and had chosen to do this for life. Most of these men had seen years of combat in the Philippines, Haiti, Nicaragua, Mexico, and the Great War. They wore the French Fourragère award given to the regiment by the nation of France after the battle of Belleau Wood. An incredibly brutal battle, much of it hand-to-hand combat. That battle saved Paris from being taken by the Germans. One day this old gunnery sergeant shipped in from China, he was like a kid coming home when he joined up with the 5th. He just kept saying, "I'm home with the 5th, God bless it I'm home with the 5th." He was one of the survivors from Belleau Wood in 1917 and felt a love for the regiment that I was just beginning to understand.

D Company was a machine gun company, heavy weapons. I was already an accomplished machine gunner, so it gave me an edge. I made PFC in 1940 and made corporal in 1941. This was really moving up fast in the Corps, as there were Marines who had been PFC for eight or nine years. I was made a machine gun squad leader. Frank Boone, Paul's brother, was in my squad, and so was Robert Youngdeer, a full-blooded Cherokee Indian. His brother was a Marine, too, and both would be seriously wounded on Guadalcanal. Robert Youngdeer, after a thirty-year career in the Corps, became the principal chief of the Cherokee nation.

I also became friends with one of the great legends of the Corps, G.Sgt. Lew Diamond. You'd hear a lot of bad scuttlebutt about Lew and a lot of it was true. He was mean and drank heavy, but he was all Marine when it counted. Lew Diamond had joined the Marine Corps in 1914 and was a hero in World War I. He was another survivor from the battle of Belleau Wood. He was hated by some of the men and feared by some, but when the shooting started he was respected by all.

G.Sgt. Lew Diamond was from my hometown of Toledo, Ohio; we hit it off right away. On weekends Lew would buy two cases of beer and two bottles of whiskey and put 'em under his rack. Then he would commence to drink it all, but somehow when that bugle blared reveille, old Lew was ready to fight. I was with my machine gun team standing on this ridge near Lew, it was our second day on Tulagi with the 1st Marine Raiders. This was a few days before we moved over to Guadalcanal. This Jap submarine surfaces and starts shelling the crap out of us with its deck gun! Colonel Edson comes running right up to Lew Diamond and yells, "Sink that sub, Gunny!" Well, Lew grabs this 81mm mortar and turns it around toward the sea and commences to guess at the range. He puts a round right on the bloody deck of that Jap sub. The very first round. Some Marines aren't made, they're born. Lew was a special breed of man, he was a Marine. I think he and Edson came out of the womb with a piece of leather around their necks. Well, it didn't sink that sucker, but that Jap submarine submerged and got out of there quick. We don't know if it sank later or not. Gunny Lew was some Marine. I was there to bury Gunny Diamond years later.

During the summers leading up to the war, we would get these reserves coming in to train. Of course you can understand what professionals thought of these ninety-day wonders. In spite of that, there were some remarkable young men that showed up and would later become fine Marines. I met a few German lads who joined the Corps. One was seventeen and swam on the German Olympic team. His father was a German second lieutenant during World War I. His father knew that Hitler was a madman and sent his son to America to join the American Marines, those Devil Dogs. He told his son he had fought them in France and that they were the fiercest fighters on earth. So here he was, a German in the U.S. Marine Corps under orders from his father.

I became sort of a big brother to a Jewish kid from Germany named Pvt. Werner Heuman. His mother had awak-

ened him in the middle of the night; it was the *Kristallnacht*
("crystal night"), when Hitler's Brownshirts burned and
looted Jewish businesses throughout Germany. She knew the
Nazis were going to start killing Jews. She got him up that
night and started walking until they walked all the way to
Bremen, got aboard a ship, and fled to America. She promptly
signed the kid up for the United States Marines at seventeen
for one purpose, to fight Hitler.

In 1924 the war room of the Marines planned a worst-case
scenario. In that scenario the Marine Corps stated that the
United States would be attacked on a Sunday, probably at
Pearl Harbor by the Japanese. Now remember, that was in
1924! So the old salts figured it was just a matter of time,
and the way things were playing out in the world, they were
looking like prophets. Many old China hands had already
been introduced to the Japs in China, so they knew what was
coming. It would be an island-after-island campaign in the
Pacific.

I helped build the base in Guantanamo, Cuba. We trained
a lot in the Caribbean. The 1st Marine Brigade shipped out to
Puerto Rico for three months every year to practice amphibious landings with the navy at Culebra. We attacked Vieques
in rubber boats and the old Higgins boats. These ended up
being pretty important maneuvers as we were to discover
later. Once I was aboard the USS *Arkansas,* a battleship. I
got liberty in San Juan and when I came ashore there were
Ducky Klein and Jimmy Green from Tennessee. They were
old pals and stationed down there at Roosevelt Roads Naval
Base in San Juan. Marines called it Rosie Roads. We steered
immediately for this "bucket of blood," that's what Marines
called the slop-chutes there. It was just another dive, and we
started in drinking rum and Cokes at 10 A.M. I'm not sure
when we decided to take a cab, but right along the dock we
saw all these open-air taxies parked just for the purpose of
making a buck off the men getting liberty. We were just pri-
vates, but we decided to play it big and hire a taxi. It was this
old, four-door touring car, a Buick. The driver took us to a
few more slop-chutes, and we ended up parking in front of

the Hotel Escabron in Rio Piedras. We walked in and right away knew it was a good bar, better than the "bucket of blood" places we'd been in since I got liberty. I ordered a rum and Coke and so did the other guys. That naturally led to more than one drink. I wanted to be nice to our driver so I started buying him drinks. Jimmy bought him a couple, then Ducky bought him a couple, pretty soon he was as drunk as we were, and he was drinking free. I thought this cab driver would be grateful.

I ordered another round, then we took off for Bayamón Village, about twenty miles from Rosie Roads, and ended up in some bucket of blood. We had a couple more drinks and laughs, then I decided it was time to go back to Rosie Roads. I had liberty til only 2200 hours and had to be back aboard the *Arkansas*. I looked at my watch. It was already 2400 hours.

"Hey, you guys. My liberty is already over. I have to get back."

"Sure, Eli. Finish another round. We'll saddle up," somebody said. I slugged down my drink and we paid up and headed outside the bar. We were all pretty well lit, but not incoherent. We walked out to the street, all in a pretty good mood, then our taxi driver stops on the sidewalk in front of his taxi and looks real belligerent.

"Rosie Roads! Fifty dollars!"

I stepped up in front of him and asked in a cordial way, "What do you mean, mate?"

"Fifty dollars! You pay me fifty dollars to drive back to Rosie Roads!"

I was starting to get annoyed with this guy and starting to remember how many rum and Cokes we bought him. "You cheap bum. Get in that car and shut up and drive."

He cussed at me, but I wasn't sure what he said except that it ended with, ". . . American Marines . . ."

"You ain't getting a dime, gook! And you better get in that cab and drive."

He started shouting and cussing real loud about American Marines. Before we knew it, there was a small mob gathering on the sidewalk and they were obviously leaning toward anti-Marine sentiment. The taxi driver suddenly took a swing at me. I parried it and decked him with a pretty good shot to his jaw. He went real limp before he hit the concrete. That was it! The melee was on! Ducky Klein and Jimmy Green and me started swinging and knockin' the stuffin' out of all these Puerto Ricans. I felt fists bouncing off me but we were dropping these guys left and right.

I wasn't sure who hit the last guy but the fight ended when one of them ran away. The sidewalk in front of the bar was just a mess. Blood and unconscious men. A couple were still conscious but the best they could do was moan.

"Hey! Where's our driver?" Ducky yelled.

"I decked him," I answered.

"We better find him, you think?"

I nodded. Ducky and me rolled some guys over. We searched through the pile for our driver. He was under a couple of guys and out cold. We picked him up and heaved him into the backseat of his taxi. We had to decide what to do, so we requisitioned his cab and him, and I drove us back to Rosie Roads.

A few more slop-chutes got in the way before we finally got back, and things were a little hazy. We were outside San Juan, right next to the police station. I could swear that I heard somebody yell my name. "Hey, Eli!" I looked around and there was Pvt. Stanley Yellowchan standing in the middle of the road bleeding from his nose and mouth. Stanley and I were going to go into the Paramarines together at one time. He finally ended up being a Paramarine. He was a real handsome character; Stanley Yellowchan had the whitest teeth I ever saw.

"Chan! What's going on?"

"Lend me a hand here with these guys, Eli." He pointed over at this slop-chute where this group of locals was standing; a few of them were bleeding. I headed on over and without any real signal, the two of us made a rush toward the bar. The guys standing in front of the bar lit out; they ran through the bar and out the back door. When I got inside I stared at the wreckage in bewilderment. I couldn't believe that one Marine could do so much damage. The place looked like a hurricane had just gone through, chairs and tables knocked over everywhere, three or four guys on the floor bleeding, one or two who looked out cold. I couldn't believe that all this had gone on right across from the police station and they never even came over to look. Ducky and Jimmy strolled in and we all ordered drinks and laughed with old Stanley Yellowchan. It was late and I knew I was in trouble, so I got the guys to saddle up and move out again.

We dumped the taxi and the driver in Columbue Circle. I checked on that driver and then Ducky checked on him, and that guy was still out cold but we were sure he was alive. Somehow it was already 0500 Sunday morning. We were a mess, blood on our uniforms and drunk as can be. Everything started becoming blurry. I remembered finally lying down.

I woke up feeling horrible and I was inside a tent. I was in Rosie Roads. I looked around and couldn't believe it, but I was in a tent at Rosie Roads, with Ducky and Jimmy lying there out to the world. There weren't any barracks or anything, the base was relatively new and the Marines lived in two-man tents or under shelter halves. I knew that there was only one way out to the naval base; you had to take a boat. I sat up real slow, trying to figure out how in the world I had ended up inside a tent on Rosie Roads. I had an insufferable headache and thought I was hearing things. Some broad was screaming all kinds of profanity about the Marines and mingled with her screeches were the voices of a couple of men shouting, too. I crawled out of the tent and on all fours I focused in on this small boat going back and forth in the water about fifty yards from the Marine tents. I sort of recognized this gal, and blurred memories of giving some young lady a genuine 14-karat fake gold bracelet came snaking back into my foggy brain. I shook my head a couple of times and moaned. She must have discovered it was fake and was really ticked off about it. I wondered how she knew where I was when I wasn't even positive myself.

It was 1700 hours Sunday afternoon when I made it back to the *Arkansas*. I climbed up the ladder looking pretty rough. This ensign was the officer of the deck. "Permission to come aboard, sir!" I shouted as I came to attention and saluted.

"Master-at-arms!" he barked. This bosun's mate stepped forward. "Escort this man to the brig!"

The first sergeant took me from the bosun's mate and wanted to know what happened to my uniform. I told him I fell down the hatch. His response was not friendly. I was not thrown in the brig but restricted to my bunk and scheduled for "captain's mast" the next day. That's where they literally hold a trial with a desk at the base of the ship's mast. I sweated it out; that twenty-four hours felt like a week, especially with a hangover. The time came and I marched up to the desk, and Captain King, he was the captain of the fleet, he barks, "What's the story, Sergeant Major!"

The sergeant major was a good man and an outstanding Marine. I didn't know what to expect from him. He was at attention. "Sir. He's a machine gun squad leader for the brigade landing at Vieques tomorrow, sir. We need him for tomorrow, sir."

The captain gave me a hard look and I didn't know what was coming my way.

"Restricted to ship, Marine! Fifteen dollars per month for three months. Fine is forty-five dollars. Right face! Forward! March!"

I made thirty-one dollars per month, so this was a serious chunk of my pay, but I marched away from that mast feeling really lucky. Some months later though, when I stood in front of Col. Red Mike Edson as a volunteer for the 1st Marine Raiders, I was worried that this little misunderstanding might keep me out of the Raiders.

After Pearl Harbor the only good news for America was a small Marine detachment on Wake Island holding out and beating up the Japs for the first time in the war. It was in the newspapers every day as long as they held out. The enemy finally took Wake, but it cost the Japs plenty. It was the first time they had met Marines and the leathernecks gave them a real bloody nose. There was very little good news though; America was just unprepared for war. We needed something positive. Each new defeat generated more calls for some kind of commando unit like the Chinese and the British had. Churchill wanted President Roosevelt to form up units based on the British idea, using the Marines. Commandant Holcomb even got a letter from Roosevelt's son, Marine captain James Roosevelt, asking to form up units like the British Commandos and the Chinese guerrillas.

Well, the commandant got real irritated and reminded 'em that Marines were Marines and that's what they did and they didn't need any of this commando bull! The name Marine meant a man was ready for any duty at any time! Marines had been doing that stuff since Tuns Tavern! That's what Marines do on a daily basis, and they didn't need or want to be called anything but United States Marines. If you were a Marine, that said it all, by God!

They kept putting pressure on the commandant, even President Roosevelt. Commandant Holcomb finally agreed to take the 1st Battalion of the 5th Marines and train and organize it for quick amphibious raids against enemy island positions. Not the full amphibious assaults a division of Marines would handle, but surprise raids. So right after Pearl Harbor, December 14 or 15, the commandant designated 1/5 as the 1st Separate Battalion. It was no surprise when Red Mike Edson was given command of this 1st Separate Battalion. He had come back from China and had been in command of the 5th Marines and the 5th was filled with legendary fighting men throughout the outfit. Of course, every man had to volunteer for this Separate Battalion and many of the old "plank owners" said "No" when they found out it meant giving up the right to wear the 5th Marine Regiment's Fourragère. A lot of the old salts didn't like it one bit and refused to leave the regiment.

No one seemed satisfied with the name of the outfit. It wasn't until February 14, 1942, that the commandant finally ended up naming us the 1st Marine Raider Battalion. On December 7 we were 1/5 and about a week later we were the 1st Separate Battalion under Colonel Edson's command. Then we were the 1st Marine Raiders.

When you volunteered for the Raiders you had to be interviewed by Red Mike Edson himself. I know he asked me more than one question, but only one stood out. "Can you slit a man's throat and move on to the next one?"

"Aye, aye, sir. No problem."

Of course, any man who was in the Marines already understood what Marines did, and it was brutally simple. Edson and many of the other old salts had served in China with the 4th Marines and they had been observing the Japanese closely for years. He told us that the Japs had a love for edged weapons and Edson knew that these Marine Raiders were going to be mixing it up in hand-to-hand combat with bayonets, knives, and Samurai swords.

One day Edson brought in Colonel Biddle. He was this old retired Marine, a thin, rather frail, wiry old guy about sixty-five to seventy years old. He had fought alongside Edson in the banana wars. It was obvious that Red Mike held the man in great esteem, and that spoke volumes to us. We were in the big field across Barnet Avenue, where we did our snapping-in and bayonet training. They lined us up and introduced this old gentleman to us. He looked at one of the Marines and said, "I want you to come at me." The Marine walked forward and Colonel Biddle barked, "No! Come at me with your bayonet!" The Marine looked surprised at first, then lowered his Springfield and came forward with his bayonet in the scabbard. "No, Marine! Unsheathe your weapon, Marine! Now come at me to kill me!"

Well, I knew this old guy wasn't there to entertain us, and I didn't take him lightly from the moment he showed up, but I didn't expect him to take out these big, tough Marines the way he did. No one touched him! He parried away every effort and was never touched. He was impressive, I mean he had an eloquence about him and was a patrician, a gentleman, from a bygone era. After that he started working us over with just knives, not rifles and bayonets. Lots of hand-to-hand.

Colonel Edson brought in another Marine named Lieutenant Warner. He had lived and trained in Japan and China since childhood. He was a master in jujitsu and judo. He could tie his hands all the way back in either direction. He walked out onto the field with his hands tied completely backward, looking like he didn't have hands. Then he unraveled them and straightened them out as normal as could be. He had big hands, too. He singled out a Marine and said, "Okay, take hold of my hand." He pointed at me. I grabbed his hand and it would sort of collapse and bam! He had you in a hold you couldn't get out of. We learned a lot from him, but I think I really started getting the hang of hand-to-hand combat when we started training with the FBI men at Quantico. The Japs tried that stuff in hand-to-hand combat throughout the Pacific and the Marines kicked the crap out of them.

We finished up training at Quantico and went to San Diego for about a week. We were getting ready to ship out, and everybody, officers, NCOs, enlisted, the whole outfit, was getting blasted. I mean drinking like it was the last chance, and for many it was. I ran into this good-looking gal, beautiful. She was older, like thirty-five. I was only twenty-two. There was this dance hall and she was there with another gal; we started drinking and dancing and I made a date with her for the next night. I don't remember how I got back to base, but I was so drunk I decided to lie down in the grass and the sprinklers came on. That woke me up in time for reveille.

That next day I got two bottles of Johnnie Walker, Red and Black. I went to her place. It was a nice place, elegant, finely furnished. I pulled out the two fifths of Johnnie Walker and she started making us drinks. I began looking around and saw this photograph on the mantel of the fireplace. It was a naval officer.

"Say, who's this guy?"

"That's my husband."

I wanted to put a fist through her head. There were ships

still smoking at Pearl Harbor and her husband was at sea right now defending our country. I snatched up my whiskey, stuck them in the blouse pockets of my dress greens, and gave her the stare that she deserved. "You whore!" I slammed that door behind me.

Somehow during that night I drank nearly all of that booze and ended up in the Coronado Hotel. Things were blurry and I had no good grasp on exactly what took place. The next day I was pretending that I didn't have a hangover, and guys kept coming up to me and asking me where I got all those women.

"What women?" I kept asking.

Then the lieutenant walked right up to me. I came to attention. He returned my salute and grinned. "Hey, Eli, I hear you were handing out women to every Marine in the Coronado last night."

"Sir?"

"Did you get hurt throwing all those sailors out of the hotel?"

"Sir?"

"Did you get injured? I heard you were throwing all these sailors out of the hotel."

"I guess not, sir. I don't remember throwing anyone anywhere."

He looked at me and chuckled. For the life of me I could not remember throwing those sailors out of the hotel, but everyone swore that I did it.

That very morning we shoved off. Now as the machine gun squad leader, I would not tolerate any Marine getting too drunk to perform his duty. I didn't care how drunk a Marine got, but at 0500 you'd better be stiff and straight, and if you couldn't handle the booze, you'd better not drink it. That was something I didn't tolerate from any Marine, including myself. I climbed aboard that transport with a headache but ready to fight.

We were under way and Corregidor hadn't surrendered yet so we figured that was where we were heading. I had buddies with the 4th Marines. That was the old China Regiment. The 4th had been sent to the Philippines. Jesse Davenport and

Tasker Bliss were with the 4th. We got word at sea that Corregidor had fallen and the Japs were moving on the Samoan Islands. I found out later that Tasker and Jesse got killed on the death march. God, I was angry and it hurt.

We started getting things ready on board ship, and the sailors were real interested in Marines. They would circle around sometimes and watch us as we worked out or took weapons or gear apart and put them back together. One day we were putting together some bangalore torpedoes and we borrowed a hammer from one of the "swab-jockeys." Well, I started hammering this gelignite into shape. Gelignite is a plastic explosive, like a hard putty. These sailors watched us, just fascinated as we started hammering the stuff into the metal tubes and piecing them together. One young, round-faced sailor finally couldn't stand it anymore and stepped up and tapped me on the shoulder. "What the heck are you jarheads doing with those pipes? And what's that stuff?"

I held up a chunk of gelignite. "You mean this?"

"Yeah."

"Gelignite."

He looked around at the other squids for help, then asked me, "What's gelignite?"

I sort of smirked along with all the Raiders nearby. "Well, you know what TNT and dynamite are, don't you?" All the sailors around us started to look a little worried. I saw a need to explain. "It blows things up, boy. We shove these bangalore torpedoes into Jap caves or bunkers and we blow 'em to hell."

His eyes got big as baseballs and he pointed at the gelignite. "You mean that's an explosive? You're hammering dynamite on deck?"

I didn't hear the bugle, but it was like a call to retreat. Those sailors took off like bees were after them. We eventually became shipmates with a lot of those swab-jockeys, but there were major differences between Marines and every other branch of the service. One day some of those same swab-jockeys were watching us work out. We trained all the time, we were professionals at what we did. I finished off a set of twenty-five push-ups, Marine push-ups. A Marine push-up is when only your chest touches the deck and your body is ramrod straight. They started asking us about this or that piece of equipment and then this one sailor says, "You only do twenty-five of those push-ups?"

"I can do another twenty-five."

"Like those? Bull."

"You got any money to put on it?"

The squids started digging into their pockets and laying down bets. I pumped off another twenty-five perfect push-ups. That seemed to naturally lead to another challenge and another twenty-five push-ups. Somebody said, "You can't do fifty of those." That went on until I won nearly four hundred dollars. I could do a couple of hundred push-ups! Marines did push-ups so often I think I could fall asleep doing push-ups. I didn't tell them that, we let them find out for themselves.

We pulled into port at Pago Pago in American Samoa. I was checking the machine guns when I heard Marines aboard ship whistling and shouting the way hungry Marines do only when excited by women. I ran to a place on deck that had a view and quickly discovered that the women in Samoa didn't wear tops. They're island people and not the least bit ashamed, nor should they be; we were invading their culture, they weren't invading ours. But that being a given and all vantage points being equal, still, a shipful of Marines coming ashore after a long voyage and going to war, well, all of these beautiful topless women, this was just an outright gift from the Lord God Almighty.

We had a first lieutenant named Warner on board when we got there. He was big and scary. There were no cupcakes in the Marines, but this guy just looked very dangerous because he was very dangerous. Well, we wanted to enjoy the scenery, and suddenly he went ape as we came into harbor. I don't know what happened to cause him to go ape, but he went crazy and it took about seven or eight of us two-hundred-pounders to pin him down. We finally got him in a strait-jacket and brought him ashore. Before we left Samoa, they put him on a ship in the harbor to take him back to the States, and he broke away and dived off the fantail of the ship. I heard the scuttlebutt later on that Warner got squared away and rejoined his outfit but was killed in action.

The training was nonstop whether aboard ship or on land. The old man wanted to keep us in shape and ready to fight at night. He wanted the Raiders to be able to do everything at night. Some of the marches were brutal, the mountain trails on Samoa were treacherous. A Marine or two died when they fell into ravines. We tried to retrieve the bodies without success. The natives brought them in later. One night I was laboring along a mountain trail with my machine gun squad and the ground just disappeared beneath me. I didn't have time to think or yell, I just fell and the Lord decided it wasn't my time. I landed in a tree on the side of a sheer drop that went down hundreds of feet. The guys managed to pull me back up to the trail, but I knew how close I had come to being dead before ever seeing the first Jap.

At one point on Samoa I started itching. Not just a little itching but I mean I was going nuts. Finally I went to the corpsman and he tells me that I have the crabs real bad. There's no telling where or how you get the crabs, but it's awful. They sent me to sick bay and ordered me to shave my whole body! That's hard to do. So I'm in my tent sitting on my sack stark naked when Maj. "Jumpin' Joe" Chambers comes storming in, screaming for me to get a weapon and follow him. I managed to grab my helmet and put on my pistol belt and .45, and I took off running, thinking I'm going to kill Japs. Not a stitch of clothes, just helmet and weapon. I piled into the back of the major's jeep, and he drove me out in the middle of nowhere to inform me this was a drill. I thought he was a jackass and still do.

We shipped out of Samoa to Noumea, New Caledonia, then Fiji. We loaded onto an Australian cruiser out of the Fijis. A couple of days later we met up with the American fleet. Those Aussies couldn't believe their eyes. They were hanging onto the ship's rail pointing and shouting that it must be the whole American navy. The number of ships was truly impressive and seemed to trail back over the horizon. We pulled up to the USS *Eliot,* an American troop transport, off-loaded down the nets and into Higgins boats, and then went up the cargo nets of the transport. We spent the next three days preparing our weapons, sharpening our K-bars, and praying. On August 6 we were told that a lot of us would probably be dead tomorrow. We were professionals and expected that would be the case.

D day on Tulagi was August 7, 1942. The Japanese were caught by surprise. They woke up that morning to discover Sealark Channel filled with ships while F4F Wildcats and SBD Dauntless dive bombers ripped back and forth over the island. The Raiders landed on Tulagi and the division established a beachhead on Guadalcanal. Guadalcanal with Henderson Field as the main prize was like having an unsinkable aircraft carrier that would allow our planes to dominate the Solomons and stop the Japs from advancing on Australia. This was the first step in a six-month battle for Guadalcanal and the islands around it. In many ways it was a turning point in the Pacific war. Every bit as much as the battle for Midway.

Of course, we weren't thinking about the next six months, we were thinking about the next six seconds as we climbed down the nets to the Higgins boats. As Raiders we had trained long and hard in the rubber boats for night landings, but that didn't happen at Tulagi. Using the rubber boats in a daylight attack would have gotten us all killed before we made it to the beach. Merritt Edson had gone over aerial photographs of Tulagi and seen that most of its defenses were toward the north coast, so he brought us in the back door. These were the old Higgins boats. No ramp, you just climbed over the gunwales and into neck-level water holding your weapon over your head. The boats couldn't get within more than a couple of hundred yards of the beach because of the coral. We had to wade all the way to the island. I could hear the firing but don't know if they were shooting at our boat.

I had seven men in my machine gun team. I was the squad leader, and though each man would take turns carrying the light .30 or its tripod sometimes, as the machine gun squad leader I packed the Reising submachine gun. Some Marines didn't like the Reising, but I loved it. It fired a twenty-round clip of .45-caliber slugs. We made it ashore okay, didn't take any casualties. I came out of the water and walked up on a beach, and there was Red Mike Edson. He looked at me and pointed.

"Move up that wagon trail, Eli!"

"Yes, sir," I said, and my machine gun squad started sloshing up this old wagon trail. We reached a point where the wagon road sloped down to a couple of white clapboard buildings.

"Hey! What are you doing here?" someone yelled.

I looked around and saw Maj. Ken Bailey coming toward us. He was one outstanding Marine. Another one of those legendary Marines that everyone admired.

"Hold your squad here, Eli. Cover me."

He took off down this slope toward the two wood buildings and a few minutes later we heard him blasting something. He waved us on our way and we continued on. Bailey was one brave Marine. Later that day Major Bailey's men ran into a built-up emplacement that had them pinned down. He charged it, kicking open the peepholes and firing ports. He threw in grenades, then used his Reising gun to blow away the rest of the Japs that stormed out of there. He got shot in the leg but continued leading his men. After that he led a bayonet charge on the next bunker and caught a slug in the stomach. He and our CO, Maj. Jumpin' Joe Chambers, were both evacuated. I didn't like Chambers. I had thought he was a jackass ever since Samoa. The scuttlebutt I heard was that he wouldn't listen to his mortar crew. They told him he didn't have clearance under this tree and he wouldn't listen. He threw down a round that hit a tree limb above them. The explosion broke both of his wrists and wounded several other Marines. He lived and later won the Medal of Honor on Iwo Jima.

Everything goes pretty smooth until we reach a Japanese line that runs from the wharf to the eastern tip of this long ridge. The Japs have Nambu machine gun positions covered by snipers in the tops of trees or in caves. We reach this open area, which could have been the golf course that was on Tulagi. The Gunny sees these Japs running in the open about a hundred yards away and opens fire. We set up the gun and start blasting. I can hear a lot of firing going on all over the place. We move out. Our objective is Hill 208.

These were Japan's best troops, the Rikusentai of the 3d Kure Special Naval Landing Force. Japanese Marines. It would be America's best against their best. We had a lot of old salts who had seen the Japs in China. They knew their tactics and we knew what to expect, but that didn't make it any easier. They liked to fight at night, and we were told to expect them to come out of their caves and holes to counterattack that first night. What no one really expected was the Japanese commitment to *gyokusai*. The Japanese would fight to the death or commit suicide rather than surrender. This *gyokusai* mentality is one big reason the war in the Pacific was not the same as fighting in Europe. You had to kill every single man. There were no mass surrenders of entire divisions or regiments. Every Jap had to be killed in every tree and every hole.

The Kure Rikusentai on the island of Tulagi used Arisaka .25-caliber rifles, Nambu light and medium machine guns, and hand grenades. They also used a 50mm, lanyard-fired trench mortar. They were good with that Arisaka rifle. We lost a lot of men to head shots in the first few hours of the battle. And of course, machine gunners were a favorite target. We lost a lot of machine gunners. That first day we reached what had been the British colonial government buildings. There were three or four white clapboard buildings. They were white with tin roofs, had shutters over the windows, and sat near the King George V soccer field. The Japs had taken over the buildings as their headquarters. Six months earlier these buildings had housed the British and Australians who ran the coconut plantations for the Procter & Gamble Company.

We moved in on the first building, with my machine gun covering our riflemen. Most of the Japs had pulled out, but a few snipers tied into trees had to be killed along the way. We started checking out the first building. This private named Thomas found a box with five thousand American dollars in it. There was a note on the box with some lieutenant commander's name and designation on it as paymaster in the Philippines. Private Thomas was later killed. We started searching through the first building and found these incredible British historical documents. There were quite a few of these big, old leatherbound ledgers. Nobody was shooting at us so I started reading one of them and couldn't believe my eyes. It was a trial document about a case where a Solomon Islander had to kill another man for having sex with his sister. The tricky part of it was that by Solomon law he was required to kill the man, but by British law it was a crime. Some of the entries in these ledgers were signed by Capt. James Cook. Right there in the middle of my first real life-and-death battle, I had a genuine desire to sit down and read through those amazing documents. That desire evaporated with the rising cacophony of enemy fire. I put the ledgers down and picked up my Reising gun.

We had to set up a position for the machine gun. I handed my Reising gun to one of my men and pulled out my .45-caliber pistol. I left my squad behind and moved into the second building. It was a two-story white clapboard building, and somehow I ended up securing it with a Marine carrying a BAR (Browning automatic rifle). I don't know where he came from or who he was; we did not have any Brownings in my squad, so I knew he was from a rifle company. We hit the first floor, my .45 in hand and him with his Browning. We found nothing and went up a stairwell to the second floor, which was one big room with polished wood floors. The stairwell opened into the middle of the second-story room. I went to a window to look for a good position for the machine gun, no glass in any of these windows, just a shutter.

Suddenly we heard this big commotion below. Japanese were shouting. The Marine with the BAR ran to the stairwell, looked down those stairs, and cut loose with a twenty-round clip. I saw his body recoil from return fire and he was dead when he hit the deck, his blood splattered everywhere. I ran to the stairwell and slid like a man on ice in all the blood until my boots hit a dry spot and I managed to catch my balance. The BAR man had piled up a bunch of Japs at the foot of the stairwell; some were still moving but most were dead. At least two were still standing, and I took aim with my .45 but got nothing but a click. I chambered another round by pulling back the slide and pulled the trigger, again and again it misfired. We were using this old World War I ammo, and a lot of it was bad. The Japs returned fire and I knew rounds were hitting all over, wood splintering everywhere. I jacked back the slide again and this time it fired. I dropped two of the Nips and kept firing until I emptied the clip. At that moment I heard a lot of firing going on outside the building, and when I went downstairs I saw that one of our patrols had killed the rest of the Japs outside.

It was a running firefight all day and a lot of it at point-blank range. Some of it was long-range though. Every Marine was a marksman, but some were exceptional. At one point we spotted some Japs in open terrain a good 250 yards away. We had this G-2 officer, who was an FBI man now in the Corps. He had this .44 Magnum pistol and could hit anything with it. He ran forward and took aim and popped off a couple of Japs with that .44 at nearly 300 yards distance. It was the best shooting I ever saw in my life with a handgun. We paused in awe for a moment, but we were Marines and there was no time for applause.

By the end of my first day of battle I felt like an older man. It was far from over and we finally settled in along this ridge-line. The Japs were caught by surprise that first day and most retreated into caves along this big ravine. We were warned about their tactic of probing our lines at night. We knew they would make a lot of noise in an effort to locate the machine gun positions, so no machine gun would open fire at night unless it was do-or-die. It was up to the squad around the gun to return fire with rifles. We found out right away that the best way to fight at night without giving away our positions was with grenades. We put men on listening posts, and if they were about to get overrun, they would beat it back to the lines. We had call signs filled with every "L" syllable you can imagine because the Japs had a tough time pronouncing "L." Lola, lollipop, lily, that sort of thing. In spite of using the correct code words, a couple of Marines were killed by friendly fire in the chaos that night.

My gunner's name was Cline. That first night Cline would elbow me awake and I would elbow him awake. We'd had very little sleep and I was finding it nearly impossible to stay awake. From our position on the ridge we overlooked China Town. It wasn't much of a town, just some more of those clapboard buildings with thatched roofs and a dock area along the water. Everything was on fire. Just across Tulagi Harbor was Florida Island not more than a couple of hundred yards away. You could almost wade over to Florida Island in some spots. I knew I was dozing off but I just couldn't help it. Cline elbowed me awake. He pointed toward the water be-tween Tulagi and Florida Island. The fires burning in China Town and the dock area were still blazing from the day's bat-tle. In the glow of that blaze I saw what Cline was pointing at. Japs swimming over to Florida Island. We were fifty or sixty feet up and looking down. I took careful aim as Cline did the same. It was a turkey shoot. We started popping them off. Not with the machine gun, because we couldn't give our position away. I aimed and squeezed off a round. I sited in on another and squeezed off another round. I guess I killed about three of them. Don't know how many the other men shot. Some would scream.

One big ravine was dotted with caves filled with Japs. The ravine sort of paralleled the Marine lines. We were on the ridge with the machine gun. On one side of the ridge were Marine positions and on the other side was the seacoast and a lot of caves beneath us. By the second night the Japs came out of those caves in well-organized attacks. I was sitting and staring into the black night and ready to shoot anything that moved. Suddenly I saw what looked like a bunch of fireflies buzzing through the air. I didn't have a clue what they were until they went off. They were the fuses of Jap grenades sizzling and sparkling in circles as they whirled through the black sky. One or more must have landed right on top of us. I was lifted up into the air by the concussion. My mind was shaken. I could hear Private Cline groaning somewhere nearby and I knew I had to help. I started crawling around, feeling for him in the darkness. I finally touched a wet human. The backside of him was gelatinous, warm blood ran between my fingers. I crawled around looking for the rest of my squad but I couldn't find a single man. Then I tried to find the machine gun but it was gone. I decided to throw Cline over my shoulder and get him to a corpsman. Everything was chaos, firing everywhere and grenades going off all over sending shrapnel, rocks, and white-hot light out in short harsh blasts. I carried him up the ridge trail until I was challenged, "Halt! Who goes there?"

"Corporal Eli! I got a wounded Marine here."

"Take your man on up to the CP, Corporal." By now I realized that I was talking to Maj. Lew Walt, who would go on to play a big role in Korea and Vietnam. Of course, at the time he's just another Marine to me and he's in my way. "Where's the rest of your squad, Corporal?"

"I don't know, sir. I couldn't find any of them. I couldn't even find the machine gun. I don't know if they're dead or blown over the ridge."

With that he motioned me on toward the CP. Colonel Edson had set up the CP inside the residency building. I made it up that trail about fifty yards when mortar rounds started dropping all over the ridge. I didn't know it at the time, but Gunny Lew Diamond was dropping those mortar rounds in on us because he had gotten some bum dope on Jap positions. He almost killed us. We took cover down one slope of the ridge with a rifle company. Everything was going off all over. I heard a lot of firing in the direction of the residency. I found out later that the Japs had hit it pretty hard. One of my best friends, Gordon Giffles, was inside with Col. Red Mike Edson and a couple of intelligence officers. Giffles dived out of a window and right into a hail of Japanese fire and was killed immediately. Big "Stoop" Palonis jumped out of a window in that attack and survived. Palonis was another legendary Marine, enlisting as a private and rising to lieutenant colonel. I was Colonel Palonis's first squad leader long before he was a colonel. Red Mike and big Stoop Palonis and a couple of other Marines organized and went back in blazing, killing the Japs and retaking the residency.

I spent the rest of the night on that slope trying to stay alive and treat Cline for his wounds. The next day I found my machine gun about fifteen feet down the slope, off of the ridge. Every man in the squad was wounded except me, but I think they all lived through that night. Gunny Fetchko had been wounded, too. I saw him some months later on the *Solace,* a hospital ship.

The next day was much the same, a nonstop firefight. Shooting snipers out of trees and trying to eliminate Nambu machine gun positions. Everyone was exhausted. We spent the night back on that ridge waiting for the Japs to come out of their caves with our machine gun overlooking the beach because we were expecting the Japs to counterattack us with a beach landing. We could hear the battle raging over on the island of Gavutu, where the 1st Marine Parachute Battalion had landed. The initial landing went badly, and the Paramarines took horrible casualties. I could hear that battle and it was loud and constant. Torrential rains struck us with thunder and vicious lightning. Marines were engaged in firefights all over Tulagi as the Japs probed our lines. The enemy movements were nearly impossible to hear through the storm. Their attacks weren't as bad as the first couple of nights, but there were still plenty of them sneaking around, searching out machine gun positions. My machine gun squad was nervous and so was I. Suddenly the natural thunder seemed to be overwhelmed by man-made thunder.

The Japanese fleet from Rabaul surprised the Allied fleet. We found ourselves with grandstand seats for a massive naval battle taking place around Savo Island. Savo Island was only a few miles from Tulagi. It was an awesome and terrifying sight and I could literally feel the concussion from the giant guns. When a ship was hit the entire sky lit up, and even through the storm the white-hot explosions from those ships sent shock waves across Tulagi. I heard my gunner say something, then the rest of the squad started mumbling "Eli!"

"What's going on?"

"Hey, what is that?"

I couldn't answer at first. I was in a state of total alert and my senses were on overload with all that was going on around us. We had had no sleep for three days. At first I couldn't believe what I was feeling and I couldn't answer my squad. I finally realized what was happening. It was an earthquake! The whole ridge was moving beneath our feet. I just started thinking that this was it, God was going to finish off the whole insane world. Right then in the middle of this new form of terror, in the middle of about as much insanity as I had ever been in, I suddenly felt an abnormal dread that the Japs were coming up on us. I told my squad to shut up and stay still as I moved over to the backside of the ridge. There was no way to hear or see anything, but I couldn't shake the overwhelming fear that the enemy was in that blackness below us. I pulled the pin on a grenade and tossed it down the slope, then quickly repeated it. The grenades went off and I went back to my position near the .30-caliber machine gun.

"What's going on, Corporal?" my gunner asked.

"I don't believe it, but it's an earthquake."

"You got to be kidding me."

"It's an earthquake all right." Few if any of Edson's Raiders were from the West Coast and I don't think any of us had ever felt an earthquake before. It was a surreal night in so many ways, but throwing an earthquake into the mix was absolutely unbelievable.

"Why are you tossing grenades? Did you hear Nips down there?"

"No."

He didn't bother asking any more questions. The squad probably thought I was nuts or just scared out of my mind. We sat dead still, just staring out at the awesome sea battle. For God's own reasons I felt that same sensation a little while later, that the Nips were coming up on us. I passed the word that I was moving so no one would blow me away by accident. We were on the reverse slope, there were no foxholes, and we were fully exposed. I crawled out and moved to the edge of the ridge again and listened, but with a naval and ground battle going on plus the thunder storm, it was impossible to hear anything. I pulled the pin on another grenade and tossed it down the slope. I waited for the explosion. It melted into a hundred other explosions going off. I pulled the pin on another grenade and tossed it into the dark night below, then crawled back to my machine gun. About an hour later that feeling came over me again. I passed the word, then crawled to the edge of the ridge and tossed two more grenades into the night.

When that night was over we all breathed a big sigh of relief. Watching the sun come up was always a great feeling. For one thing, you knew you had made it through another night alive. By that fourth day the men were really starting to look bad. Most had not slept in four days and their eyes showed it. The sun came up hot. By noon it was scorching. We broke open C rations. All these green flies were buzzing around everybody's food, and we knew what that meant. Dead bodies would bloat up real quick in the heat and draw these stinkin' green flies. I think everyone in my squad wanted to see if I had been throwing grenades at ghosts all night. I took a patrol down off the ridge and searched the area where I had thrown the grenades. I don't know who was more shocked, me or my squad, but sure enough I had killed about a squad of Japs at the bottom. There were eight to twelve bodies scattered about. Some were already starting to bloat in the heat. All killed by shrapnel. It was sort of spooky. They would have killed us for sure if they made it up that slope undetected. My squad was impressed or baffled, but I knew that those strange forewarnings and my reaction was a gift from the Lord God.

Later we discovered that the Allied fleet had taken dreadful losses. The American navy had suffered the worst defeat in our navy's history. Three heavy cruisers and an Australian cruiser, all lost. We didn't know it, but this meant that Admiral Turner had to withdraw the fleet because there was no protection for the supply ships. Most of the supplies had not come ashore yet because the battle was still in progress. Those were our supplies withdrawing and soon we'd be starving.

That day we made a raid on Savo Island, and when we came ashore we saw the awful mess left over from the sea battle. The black oil sludge on the beaches was a foot thick. We picked up a few prisoners, and on the ride back to Tulagi one of the Marines kept his foot on this Jap's neck to keep him still in the boat. There weren't many prisoners. Out of the 350 Japs on Tulagi, we killed all but three. We got a few on Florida Island.

The CP was now in a cave. I was outside of that cave giving one of the prisoners a drink of water when word spread about the slaughter of Lt. Col. Frank Goettge and his patrol of Marines. The Japs had sent word to the Marines on Guadalcanal through some of the island people that a group of them wanted to surrender. The Marines sent word back and a meeting was arranged. When the Marines came ashore to bring them back safely, they were ambushed and butchered, the wounded hacked to pieces with samurai swords and machetes. Only one man got away, and his reports of the Japs hacking the Marines to pieces on the beach went through the division like an angry knife. A Marine came out of the cave after getting that message and told me to get away from that Jap. He lifted his rifle to shoot him right there. We jumped up and stopped him from killing them all, but we understood. We had all learned something about the kind of enemy we were fighting that day.

Cpl. Robert Youngdeer and Cpl. Stanley Yellowchan ended up taking the prisoners over to Guadalcanal. Tulagi was secured, and on August 30 we boarded ships and made the twenty-mile passage to Guadalcanal. It was one very dangerous journey. Many ships and thousands of men were already at the bottom of these deadly waters, already named Ironbottom Bay. Two out of our precious six aircraft carriers, the *Wasp* and the *Hornet,* were sunk. The *Saratoga* had been torpedoed but made it back to the States. The *Enterprise* had been bombed northeast of Tulagi and was out of action. So out of six carriers, we had four sunk and two out of action. The navy was in a bad way, and holding Henderson Field on the Canal was absolutely critical, maybe as dire as any battle America had ever been involved in.

Tense Raiders searched the sky for aircraft and the sea for submarines all the way across Sealark Channel. We made it safely, and immediately after hitting the beach on Guadalcanal we set up a bivouac in the "Coconut Grove." It was a plantation and the trees were in long, neat rows. Dog Company Raiders had just come ashore from the USS *Calhoun* when Jap bombers appeared out of nowhere and hit the ship and blew it in half. We spent a lot of time on those APDs and got very close to our navy shipmates. We lost a lot of good friends when the *Calhoun* went down.

The place was getting clobbered every night. On August 31 the Japs shelled the field and hit a plane that was parked there and it blew up. The fire spread and set off an ammo dump. That was a nightly occurrence, shells from surface ships or bombs from Washing Machine Charlie, a Jap plane that flew over every night about the same time just to keep us awake with a few bombs. And it worked. It was hard to sleep. Many of the men were coming down with malaria and dysentery. I had both but I didn't think it was severe yet. We didn't have much food since most of our supplies never got to shore after the fleet had to withdraw. I was losing weight due to dysentery and hunger.

By this time I had three of my original squad back after losing all of them on Tulagi. I got replacements and put another man on the machine gun since Cline was gone. In the Raiders we had four rifle companies, A, B, C, and D Company. Easy Company was a weapons company, and the machine gun squads or platoons were being taken out of Easy and attached to rifle companies as needed. On Tulagi, Baker Company's machine gun platoon had been demolished. Almost every gunner and machine gun squad leader had been killed or wounded. So my machine gun squad went to B Company on the Canal.

Around September 4 they put Baker Company and Able Company on two of our remaining APDs, the USS *Little* and the USS *Gregory*. We got word that the Japs were landing in force on Savo Island. We landed on Savo, working our way through a foot of oil and sand, then circled the volcanic island. Able Company was going one way and Baker the other until we met up. There were no Japs, just lots of debris from the big naval battles that had floated ashore, and it gave us all a glimpse of just how serious those battles were. We boarded the APDs and headed back to Guadalcanal. I didn't know it at the time, but evidently Colonel Edson had ordered us to stay on board the ships for the night so we could make another raid on Cape Esperance in the morning. By the time word got to the CO it was too late, and most of the men were already back in the Coconut Grove. It was really a miracle. We were that close to losing most of the Marine Raiders. That night both of those APDs were sunk by Jap destroyers. We lost more good friends. We had become very close to the crews of the APDs.

I was determined to not sleep in that stinking mud hole that night and was naked as a jaybird under some mosquito netting when the shelling began. The Jap destroyers that came by every night to shell us had just started blasting the crap out of the Coconut Grove as I got comfortable. I was up and running for my foxhole. I had never experienced anything like a naval bombardment. I huddled in a hole just terrified. The shells really did sound like freight cars from a train coming in, and I sat naked and trembling. I wanted to fight back, but there was no way to fight; all I could do was try to survive. Suddenly the Japs stopped blasting us. They spotted our APDs anchored out there and turned their fire on them. Not all of the Raiders had off-loaded yet, and a few were still caught on board those ships. I watched but it was

pitch black for the most part. All you could see were the big
flashes when the Japs opened up. They poured hundreds of
shells into our APDs. The *Little* and the *Gregory* didn't have
a chance, they were totally outgunned.

I had a good pal from Easy Company, a machine gunner
named Nick Marcelino, who was still on the *Little* when it
went down. He was an Italian kid from Brooklyn, wavy
black hair, a real handsome guy. He was belowdecks when
the *Little* was badly hit and going down. Nick tried to find a
way out but the ship was sinking fast. The water started coming in and he took a deep breath as it washed over him. He
was fighting for his life, now underwater and inside the APD.
By nothing short of a miracle, he spotted a light above and
worked like mad to get to it while he and the *Little* were
heading to the depths of Ironbottom Bay. He fought with all
his strength and with his last gasp of air until it seemed hopeless, then he popped up out of the water like a cork. The light
he had seen was a raging fire, but he managed to swim away
from it. He watched the Jap destroyers running over the survivors and machine gunning them in the water. They missed
Nick. That was the kind of enemy we were fighting. We
started seeing them as subhuman. Marines on Guadalcanal
rescued a couple of hundred sailors and Marines, but a lot of
men died.

Raid on Tasimboko

We moved our base camp from the Coconut Grove to
the ridge that formed a natural barrier between the rest of
Guadalcanal and Henderson Field. Tasimboko was about
eighteen miles from the Marine perimeter guarding the field.
It was a deserted village along the coast, and scuttlebutt said
that our scouts and the islanders had reported that many
Japanese troops were staging for an attack around there. At a
place called Taivu Point, Jap ships were bringing in troops
and supplies at night, and then they were moving into this
abandoned village. We knew the Japs were landing troops

there to stage an attack on Henderson Field. Red Mike lob-
bied to the upper echelon to use his Raiders for what they
were trained for. He wanted to raid the Japs in a surprise attack before they could move on Henderson Field.

Our biggest problem was a lack of ships. Two APD destroyer transports were left, the USS *McKean* and the USS
Manley. They were not big enough to move the six hundred
Raiders and couple hundred Paramarines up the coast to
attack Tasimboko. The 1st Parachute Battalion had taken
heavy casualties on Gavutu, and these two hundred or so
Marines were men from that shot-up battalion. Red Mike noticed a couple of old tuna boats working in the harbor and
requisitioned them. We got the word to draw ammo and move
out. It was a few miles to the seashore and the transports.
As gunners we had to carry a heavier load and it took a toll
on you.

I got put on one of those California tuna boats. We squeezed
about seventy men aboard and set off on a miserable sea ride.
It was the YP-346. It got shot up by Jap planes and sank a
few days later. It was crowded and men were throwing up
everywhere. Cpl. Robert Youngdeer was on board. He was
another machine gunner that had been in my squad at one
time. He had a brother with the Paramarines. We moved up
the coast on the night of September 7 and anchored about
a thousand yards off Taivu Point somewhere around 0500
hours on the eighth of September. We went ashore in Higgins
boats instead of our rubber boats because they wanted to get
more men on shore as fast as possible. It was crucial to form
a beachhead in case we were attacked right away, and it was
crucial to get machine guns set up to cover the landing. The
Higgins boats dropped us off and did a twenty-minute trip
back to the transports and the tuna boats to bring another
load of Marines ashore. As soon as we hit the beach, some of
our guys stumbled upon hundreds of Japanese packs laid out
in neat rows. This left little doubt that a lot of Japs were very
close by. We got those guns ready quick.

The sun came up and we started catching incoming fire.
All of a sudden there was a commotion, the men pointed out

to sea, and every eye strained to see what terror was coming our way. Off in the distance I saw a convoy of ships coming straight at us. Some of the guys started mumbling that we were in real trouble, that we were caught between two forces and they both outnumbered us. The Marines still aboard the transports were plenty worried, too. They were sitting ducks out there. We didn't know it at the time, but the Japs were seeing this same convoy of ships coming and they thought we were part of a major invasion. Soon the word came that it was an American convoy heading for Guadalcanal and every man took a deep breath and thanked God.

That breath didn't last long. I heard this familiar voice yell and I jumped up and moved. "Eleston! Get that gun into action!" Col. Red Mike Edson screamed right at me.

I jumped down behind the .30 and shoved the gunner aside, and Colonel Edson dropped down beside me as my A-gunner. He was pointing at these Jap barges down the coastline that were off-loading troops. I opened fire and he clicked the .30 down and left until I was filling those barges with so many holes that I knew they were no longer seaworthy. It was a turkey shoot, there was no place for the Japs inside to hide, and the hulls of their barges were so thin that I started seeing light as my .30 blew holes clean through both sides. I fired a couple of hundred rounds or more. I kept firing until the colonel slapped me on the shoulder, satisfied that we had killed as many as we were going to get. Almost immediately we were up. The men were moving, then running, at least as close to an all-out run as our squad could do in the jungle terrain with the ammo, tripod, and a .30-caliber machine gun.

Lieutenant Key had been killed on Tulagi, and Captain Sweeney took over the platoon that my machine gun squad had been attached to in Baker Company. Our platoon moved through the jungle fast. Here and there a Jap would pop up out of a spider hole and you had to be quick to kill him before he killed you. I saw one appear and shot a burst into him before he got off a round. Snipers tied themselves into trees so they could protect the Nambu machine gun positions. It got so I was looking up and down and blew away anything out of the ordinary. I took a step forward, looked up into a tree. I sprayed the top of the tree with my Reising submachine gun. A rifle fell to the ground, then this Jap just slid out of the top, limp, and fell with a thump. I didn't have time to check any bodies because we were moving and moving fast. Marines up ahead started shooting. An instant later I heard this horrific crack and a round exploded in front of us. I hit the deck along with everybody else, and an instant later another round hit just behind us. Dirt and rocks covered us. I figured it was mortars and the next one would be right on top of my machine gun squad so I yelled at the men, "Get up and move to the right!"

My gunner pulled on my shirt. "We didn't get any orders to take the gun in that direction, Eli."

I thought for a second and nodded, "Yeah. You're right. Stay where you are, men!"

A moment later another round hit exactly where I had told the squad to run to. It ripped off part of a tree limb and I heard Marines screaming. I thought it must have killed most of the squad that was over there. Cpl. William Carney was killed instantly, he was a squad leader. I still thought it was mortar rounds. We attacked forward again, mortars or no mortars. We waded across the Kema River and found a 75mm artillery gun just sitting there. It was a Jap 75mm firing at us almost point-blank. When a 75mm howitzer shell comes straight at you slapping through the jungle brush, ripping off tree limbs like they're twigs, it'll make even a Marine piss his pants.

Another Jap 75mm opened fire. A Marine screamed for a corpsman. One of the 75mm rounds blew Corporal Pion's arm nearly clean off. It dangled by some skin. We had a couple of outstanding corpsmen. Corpsman Cleveland and another wonderful corpsman named Coleman from Kentucky made their way to Corporal Pion and did an amazing job. Cleveland took a penknife and amputated the dangling arm, then took the skin and wrapped it around the stump and bandaged Corporal Pion up. Corporal Pion lived. After Guadalcanal, corpsman Cleveland put in to be a navy pilot. Marines hate to lose a corpsman who's that good, but he always wanted to be a pilot. He finally made it, too, but I heard that he was shot down in aerial combat and killed later on.

I knew one thing for sure, we couldn't stay there and take point-blank shots by artillery, so we moved forward. The gunner threw the .30 over his shoulder and the assistant carried the tripod, both with .45-caliber pistols ready. I heard shots up ahead. I broke through some brush and stared at a 75mm field piece sitting there with one dead Jap behind it bent backward. Blood from two holes in his chest squirted up in the air in quick spurts like a little fountain, as his heart was still pumping. Two Raiders stood over him arguing about who was going to get the dead Nip's campaign ribbons. Another Jap was on the ground with a clean shot right through his forehead. They had plugged two but a third got away. I ran up to them and for a moment I thought about knocking both of them out cold with the stock of my weapon. I let loose on them. "You idiots! Get movin' or I'm putting my boot up your . . ."

We moved on. We came under fire again and crawled forward. This Marine ahead of me shot off a grenade with his rifle. It didn't explode. He was trying to knock out a Jap machine gun nest with his grenade launcher. He fired another grenade with his rifle but it didn't go off, either. He started cussing something awful. I kept staring at him and then at his rifle and then it hit me. The moron isn't pulling the pin before he fires. I rushed forward and grabbed him hard by his neck and put my face in his and screamed, "You have to pull the pin, you recruit!" He looked shocked, then absolutely embarrassed. He calmly pulled the pin and fired another grenade and this time it exploded on target. Pieces of that Nambu machine gun and the gunner behind it went in different directions. "Move out!"

"Hey, Eli! We got that reporter with us," somebody in my squad yelled. I looked around and sure enough I had Richard Tregaskis with my machine gun squad. He was a reporter for INS, International News Service. There was another correspondent with the Marines named Miller. They were both well known. Tregaskis wrote *Guadalcanal Diary* soon after the battle and it became a movie. I couldn't help thinking that for a civilian, the guy had guts just being there. It took us hours to get to Tasimboko. We crossed at least one river and it took time. Each time we ran into a Jap machine gun, it would be guarded by Jap snipers in the trees. We had to take them out one at a time. No one knew for sure how many Japanese troops we were about to run into. They were unloading troops nearly every night by barges and destroyers to build up for the attack on Henderson Field, so I figured there must be thousands of them out there somewhere.

Holding Henderson Field was do-or-die. The small squadron of planes we had on Guadalcanal called themselves the Cactus Air Force. They were these old F4Fs and P-39s, there were only a few of them, and because the Japs bombed or shelled the airstrip every day and night, it was very difficult for our pilots to get off the ground. They were outstanding pilots, but their planes were outclassed by the Jap Zeros. In spite of the odds they did a remarkable job. A lot of Japanese barges filled with troops never made it to Guadalcanal because of those great Marine pilots.

We were getting near the village but kept getting held up by snipers and machine guns. It wasn't that far from the beach to Tasimboko, but we'd been fighting our way along for nearly five hours. It had been a long day and no head calls. I had to take a dump and bad. I was standing amidst these big banana leaves by this tree and I just couldn't wait any longer so I squatted. *Bam!* Right where my head was before I squatted, this small tree is blown in half. If I hadn't squatted to take a dump at that very second my head would have been blown off my shoulders. I was shaken but I let no one know.

We moved forward again and at one point Colonel Edson, Richard Tregaskis, and this Australian coastwatcher named Clemens were standing beside my machine gun squad discussing something about Tasimboko. All of a sudden all these natives under the command of Clemens just seemed to appear. I mean they just popped up out of nowhere. It was spooky. I had heard they could scale trees and take eggs from nesting birds without spooking the nest. I now believed it. They were great scouts. The most famous was a man named Sgt. Maj. Jacob Vouza.

While the Raiders were on Tulagi, the rest of the 1st Marine Division was fighting on Guadalcanal. The Japs captured Vouza and tortured him, then bayoneted him a few times and left him for dead when he refused to tell them where Marine positions were around Henderson Field. Somehow he survived and made it back to Marine lines. He warned the Marines that the Japs were coming and actually led a patrol back into the jungle after them. The Japs that tortured Vouza were part of Colonel Ichiki's detachment. The Japanese high command thought Ichiki's assault troops would clean the Marines off Guadalcanal in a few days. Ichiki's detachment was slaughtered by the Marines and Jacob Vouza played a role in it. He was later knighted by the Queen of England for bravery. Colonel Ichiki committed suicide. That's when they sent in Kawaguchi and thousands of fresh troops. Tasimboko was Sergeant Major Vouza's home village, and the Marines allowed him to come along on the raid even though he was still recovering from all the bayonet wounds. I felt honored to meet him.

The men were starving. Once we knocked out the last Nambu machine gun nest, we finally made it into the village of Tasimboko. The village consisted of about twenty crude buildings with thatched roofs for the most part. It was abandoned when our machine gun squad got there; the rifle companies were searching the jungle for the last defenders hanging around. Every so often you'd hear shots as they found one. We didn't know it then, but most of the Japanese troops Kawaguchi had left behind to protect his supply dump had taken off when they saw the convoy of ships. They thought it was a major invasion. We found hot meals on boards on the ground and knew we had interrupted their breakfast. I found some big cans, maybe quart size, and knifed one of them open. It was food. I started eating. It tasted wonderful! The can was in three layers, the first layer was grape leaves rolled around some sort of fish. The second layer was rolls of tuna or some white meat that tasted like tuna with grape leaves, and the third layer was delicious baked beans. I ate until I couldn't eat anymore, then I stole as much as I could carry. It was the best food I ever tasted in my life. It must have been the officer's mess because the food was outstanding.

This raid really hurt Kawaguchi's troops over the next few months. Tasimboko was the main supply depot for the entire attacking force trying to take Guadalcanal. They lost most of their heavy weapons, including forty or so crew-served weapons. That alone may have saved us from losing the Battle of Guadalcanal a few days later on Edson's Ridge. We destroyed all the food and supplies we couldn't carry and took all of their medical supplies. Many of their wounded would never survive because of this. We poured gasoline on everything and set the whole place on fire. Richard Tregaskis, the reporter, was nosing around too and found some enemy documents. He found what ended up being Kawaguchi's battle plan for the attack on Henderson Field. It ended up making a difference later on when we were trying to defend the field against overwhelming odds.

I found some sake, and the squad decided right away we weren't letting the officers know about it. They would have taken it for themselves. It was like Christmas! Our guys found a huge supply of mortar rounds. We formed a line and there's no telling how many hundreds of mortar rounds we threw into the water. We dragged their 75mm field pieces into the ocean behind our Higgins boats after we split the blocks on them.

It was one of the most successful raids of the war. Two Marines were killed in action during the raid: one of our squad leaders, Corporal Carney, and one of our machine gunners, Buddy Smith from Ohio. That corpsman got the Navy Cross. We got out of there around 1700 and I went back to the Canal on an APD. It took a couple of hours. It was probably around 2300 hours, maybe midnight, by the time we got back to the Coconut Grove. We knew that we had a few thousand Japs coming toward Henderson Field at that very moment. It seemed that no one was sure where they would attack the Marine lines, except Red Mike Edson. He had already looked over this ridge that paralleled the Lunga River and sloped down to the airfield. It was the high ground overlooking Henderson Field. The jungle was thick and vicious. We knew we wouldn't see the Japs until they were right on top of us. Red Mike Edson and Col. Jerry Thomas had been trying to convince Gen. Alexander Vandegrift, CO of the 1st Marine Division, that the ridge was where the Japs would strike. The general wasn't so sure, and we had about a ten-mile perimeter to cover. They could hit us coming down the coast along the beach or by way of the Lunga River or the Matanikau River, but old Red Mike was convinced that the ridge was a perfect funnel coming out of the jungle from the south.

On September 10 we moved to the ridge along with the depleted Paramarines and engineers. My machine gun squad was put at the southwest foot of the ridge. The first thing I noticed was how thin we were spread out, and I didn't like it. They tried to tell us we were getting a rest because the ridge was more open and wouldn't get bombed as much by the Bettys, which always targeted the airfield and Coconut Grove. Right away we were ordered to start digging in and laying wire. I put out wire about twenty yards in front of the machine gun. We laid the wire in a "V" shape with the gun at the bottom point of the "V." Then we laid two more rows of wire parallel to the first wire, with about twenty yards between the first and second row of wire. This would funnel the Japs into our field of fire, and when we opened up they wouldn't be able to run left or right without getting caught up in the wire. We put up aiming stakes and tried to dig in with our e-tools and bayonets.

The ridge was long, made of hard coral and rock. Digging in was nearly impossible. We were spread out way too thin. Forward observers (FOs) showed up and started plotting for the artillery. The 11th Marines' artillerymen were going to play a big role in the next few nights. They had their

105s turned our way and under camouflage to hide from the bombers. It was sometime that morning when Maj. Ken Bailey came back to the Raiders. He was just an outstanding Marine. One of those billboard Marines. He looked like a matinee idol but he was tough as nails. I got the scuttlebutt straight from those who knew that Bailey had gone AWOL from the hospital back in New Caledonia and somehow made his way back to Guadalcanal. He was still badly wounded. He'd been shot a couple of times, once in the stomach, and he probably had no business being out of a hospital bed. He brought all this back mail with him and man it was wonderful. We had not gotten any mail for months. Sgt. Wallace Bergstrand was my gun squad sergeant and a good friend of mine. He was from Wausau, Wisconsin. I called him Bergie. When that mail came, brother we were in heaven. Bergie got this package of cigars from his sister. We were going to open them later because we still had wire to lay.

I jumped into my own mail and found this official letter from the Book of the Month Club. It was attached with some kind of summons to appear in court. They were suing me for back payment on books. Well, that went through the Raiders pretty quick, the fact that old Eli would have to take his leave from the battle for Guadalcanal because he was to appear in court on charges of defrauding the Book of the Month Club. I didn't put much hope in Colonel Edson giving me a liberty so I could go back to Ohio and clear up the misunderstanding.

Everything seemed to indicate that we were in for it. My good friend Sgt. Frank Guidone and another sergeant named Floeter were called up by Gunnery Sergeant McGlocklin. He told them that one of them had to go on a patrol into the jungle and try to make contact with the lead elements of the Japs coming our way. We had to know what was out there in that jungle in front of us. Just taking a patrol out was dangerous. Guadalcanal was hazardous with or without the Japs. Just to wash off some of the filth by taking a bath in the Lunga River, we first had to set up snipers to pick off the salt-water crocodiles before they attacked. They were very aggressive. Between the poisonous snakes, malaria, dysentery, and lack of food, everything was hard and dangerous.

Sergeant Floeter and Sgt. Frank Guidone looked at each other and decided to flip a coin to see who had to take their squad out on the patrol. My buddy Guidone lost. Sergeant Guidone got his squad saddled up, and they headed down the southern slope of the ridge past us and on into the jungle while we were stringing our wire. That was sometime before noon on the twelfth of September.

Around noon we heard that miserable drone of bombers coming our way. All eyes were staring up. Sure enough a flight of Japanese Betty bombers could be seen in formation, flying straight at us. Everybody sort of assumed that they would pound Henderson Field as usual, but this time they hit the ridge instead of the airfield. I don't know how many sticks of bombs they dropped on us, but it seemed to shake the world. A five-hundred-pound bomb can kill you with the concussion alone, it doesn't have to kill you with shrapnel. Our wire was being blown to bits on the southern slope of the ridge that led into the thick jungle. I heard a tremendous blast and suddenly I was flying through the air and there was nothing I could do except pray. I landed twenty or thirty feet away in the roots of this giant banyan tree. Everything hurt. My head was ringing and my right ear was burning like it was on fire. It felt like somebody was using it for an ashtray to put out a cigar. I reached up with my right hand and blood was pouring out of my ear. There was a hot piece of shrapnel sticking inside my ear, and it was pretty deep. I pinched it between my forefinger and thumb, gritted my teeth, and gave a big yank. It blistered my fingers. God it hurt, but it came out with a gush of blood. I pulled another scalding piece of shrapnel out of the back of my head. Blood was coming from my eyebrows and I had more shrapnel wounds there. Bombs just kept raining down, plastering our positions all over the ridge. It took me a little while to get my bearings. The blood coming out of my ear was screwing up my equilibrium.

At that same time Sergeant Guidone's patrol ran into lead elements of Japanese troops in the jungle. They were exchanging fire as sticks of bombs saturated the ridge. Many of the Jap bombs landed in the jungle surrounding the ridge. Some landed in the jungle at the south end of the ridge where Sergeant Guidone's squad was in a firefight. One bomb hit nearly on top of Guidone and blew him up into the air. He was shaken but he lived. That was the end of that patrol; they broke off contact with the Japs and made their way back to the ridge to report that the Japs were right outside of our perimeter. The bivouac area was blown to bits when they got back. A couple of dead and a lot of wounded. When Guidone and his squad straggled back up out of the jungle, he found Sergeant Floeter sitting up against a tree stump, dead. It's just the way things went. When I heard about it I realized it was just the flip of a coin, heads instead of tails, and Floeter would not have been on the ridge when the bombs struck. Only God knows your allotted time on earth.

The sun dropped away and I knew things were about to get real bad. My machine gun squad was at the foot of the southern end of the ridge along a footpath. We were spread so thin that there was no contact with the next Marine positions on our right or left. At 2130 hours a Japanese navy cruiser opened fire on the ridge. The naval bombardment was awful. One of the Jap ships out in the channel put this giant spotlight on the ridge. It was eerie. Soon three Japanese destroyers opened fire, too. Shells ripped the ridge apart. One hour, two. There was nothing you could do except hunker down and pray you weren't under one of those shells when it hit. We knew all this shelling and bombing was a prelude to an attack and everybody was scared but ready. When the shelling finally stopped, I started hearing machine gun fire at different locations around our 1800 yards of perimeter.

Grenades started popping everywhere with sharp blasts and bursts of light. I strained to see anything. Jap mortars thumped in the distance, then landed with sudden explosions that you couldn't get ready for. The firing became intense but died out. I knew what the Japs were doing and I guess every Marine there knew it, too. They were probing our lines all over to try and get a fix on our positions, especially our machine gun positions. Our fire discipline was strong. Every Marine knew to use his weapon as the last resort so as not to give away his position. Especially the machine gun squads.

We stared into the pitch-black night hearing noises everywhere and expecting them to hit us at any moment. I was on my stomach gripping the Reising gun beside our .30-caliber machine gun. There was some sharp fighting going on, but none of it had hit us yet. We were spread out right along this trail, more of a footpath really. I could hear men moving and it was terrifying not being able to see except for those flashes of light after an explosion. Suddenly I heard footsteps and we all froze stiff. The foot of a Japanese soldier stepped right on my face. They wore these rubber-and-canvas two-toe shoes, almost like a tennis shoe with a place for the big toe to fit. Sort of like a canvas-covered sandal, so there was no doubt it was no Marine foot in my face. He just walked right on past, along with probably a squad of them. They were moving fast trying to find our positions.

I don't know why or how I didn't crap my pants, but I wanted to. It happened too fast for anyone to throw a grenade. We couldn't open up with the machine gun unless we had a lot of sure targets in a killing zone. The rest of the night went by one second at a time, and each second seemed to last longer than the one before. Fighting was going on in different areas, but I never fired a shot that first night. There was a brutal fight happening somewhere on our right flank. You couldn't do anything except watch the machine gun tracer rounds and listen. The Japs overran some machine gun positions. They captured some wounded Raiders and were torturing them out in the jungle, making them scream as they cut them to pieces. Hearing Marines being tortured made me want to kill every Japanese on earth.

Charlie Company took the brunt of it, we heard later. Some of my buddies from our machine gun company, Easy Company, were in the thick of it. Machine gunners Sergeants Frank Boone and Neil Champoux were both hit. They lost a lot of gunners that first night. Champoux was killed as his squad was overrun. Frank lived through that initial attack along with another good friend and former member of my machine gun squad named Cpl. Robert Youngdeer. Youngdeer got shot right through the mouth when he tried to rescue a wounded Raider. The shot blew away some of his teeth and jaw. Frank was Paul's brother, the Marine I had fought with at Parris Island. Two days later they put Frank Boone in a truck and tried to get him and some of the other wounded back to a safer location to be worked on by the doctors. The truck didn't even make it to the airstrip. A Nambu machine gun raked it over and killed Frank and Major Brown and the corpsman who was driving. Major Brown got part of his hand blown away trying to throw back a Jap grenade. He didn't want to evacuate. He was ordered to go back with the wounded. If he had stayed he might still be alive. We lost some real fine Marines.

I didn't know much about what was going on except in my own little hole. We knew this could be face-to-face at any time, so I cut the flap off my .45 pistol holster so that I could get it out quick. I had written my dad a letter asking him to ship me my hunting knife, as I didn't have a K-bar. I fixed my .45 holster so that I could place that hunting knife inside of it right with my pistol. That knife looked very similar to a K-bar, about the same size. I also had a small K-bar that could fix on the end of my Reising gun as a bayonet.

That second day, September 13, was so hot that some of the men got heatstroke. The men higher up on the ridge had no shade and we didn't have any to speak of at the foot of the ridge. We spent the day digging deeper and trying to spread what wire we could scrounge up. My machine gun squad was still attached to Baker Company and the CO got heatstroke and word was that he had to be evacuated. The sun beat down on us that hard and the heat factor was serious. Captain Sweeney became the company commander.

Scuttlebutt was that we had lost a lot of machine gunners during the night. Besides the wounded and killed, we were taking a lot of casualties from malaria and dysentery. I knew we were spread real thin on the southern slope of the ridge, and we had only 115 men in the company. Scuttlebutt was never an accurate science, but the word was that there were thousands of Japs in the jungle facing us. We just had to pray it wasn't true, but this time the scuttlebutt was true. The platoon sergeant showed up and spread us out even thinner before nightfall. I didn't like it one bit. I found myself all alone and couldn't even see another Marine in our machine gun squad to my left or right.

It was painfully obvious that 115 men were not going to stop thousands of Japs, even if that 115 were Marine Raiders. If Colonel Edson was right and this was where the main attack would come, it was clear that our job was to slow them down by killing as many as possible while giving the rest of the battalion time to react and reinforce where needed. It was a dirty job, some guys griped out loud, but every Marine knows what he's signing up for when he joins the Corps. We cursed every officer in the Corps at that moment, but that was normal and we all knew it might come to this from the moment we joined the Marines, it's as plain and simple as that. No one ever misled us into thinking our job was anything else. We knew from day one that it might come down to a situation exactly like this, and we were expected to fight and die like professionals. Like United States Marines. It was a deadly serious profession. No one forced any of us to join the Corps. Lying there staring into that black jungle was a very reflective time for all of us.

I relied on my ears as much as my eyes. The normal jungle noises, everything from frogs to crocodiles, started their nightly serenade. Soon I could hear other noises. Troops were moving out there and my heart was pounding with fear and adrenaline. Some of our company was spread from the slope out into the jungle. When they got hit, it was a sign for our artillery to open up. If they couldn't make it back to the ridge in time, they'd be killed by our own guns.

Daylight seemed to disappear suddenly, as suddenly as the battle started. Shots rang out from those positions in the jungle. After a sharp exchange, some of those guys tried to get back to the ridge. Not long after that we started getting pounded by Jap ships. I found out later that as many as six Jap destroyers opened fire on us. I started throwing my grenades at the Japs in front of me when they were close. I didn't want to open fire, one flash from my muzzle and that would be the end of me, I figured. Soon enough any worry over a muzzle flash was gone as the jungle lit up like a light show. People were screaming as if all the abyss had been opened and the demons unleashed. I kept waiting for it to slow down, but it didn't slow down. Explosions silhouetted the onrushing Japanese. We mowed them down with everything we could throw at them. Our machine guns chopped them to shreds.

I couldn't judge time. It just went on and on. I killed everything that moved in front of my position, reloading the submachine gun with clip after clip and firing at every muzzle flash that fired at me. I could hear my machine gun team firing like mad and I knew we were knocking down a lot of Japs, but we were all running out of ammo and time. I wondered about time and wondered if the sun was even close to coming up. I reached for another clip of ammo and found only one left on my cartridge belt. I patted my .45, then felt for more grenades but there were none. At that instant the Japs overwhelmed our machine gun position and were just coming right through our scattered lines. I stood up knowing I had to go get more ammo and grenades. This faceless form, a man, just came out of the blackness, we clashed, he was shorter than me but stocky and strong. It was knees and elbows and the melee was all around but the war was just me and him for that moment. I was elbowed and punched, all the time striving to get to my .45 pistol. I grabbed for the pistol but my hand came up with my hunting knife. I started stabbing him and killed him. I don't know how long I was fighting with him or how many times I stabbed him. I fell into a strange daze but I knew I was still fighting. I was fighting with that knife.

Marines were using their rifles like baseball bats. It was bayonets and K-bars and horizontal butt strokes. I couldn't tell what was going on around me, it was utter chaos, shouting and shooting and explosions and screams and groans.

Our 105s started pouring in like mad. The arty guys had plotted perfectly, and the Japs were being mauled by continuous artillery fire. Some of our squads that were farther out into the jungle were in the middle of our own artillery barrage.

I had to get ammo. I don't know how long it was before I ran back up the slope of the ridge for more ammunition, but somehow I made it up the path to the ridge. It felt like I was running around in a nightmare, the kind of nightmare where you aren't sure what is happening. Then suddenly something would be clear. There was Bull Sterling! A communications man. One of the wire stringers for our radios. He was shouting at me.

"I'm going back to the CP for ammo!"

He was off with those words. I hunkered down gripping my Reising gun. I knew this was it if we didn't get more grenades and ammo. There was no way to hold on against the constant onslaught of Nips. The artillery barrage was saving us. Their attacks were being broken up, so they came piecemeal, groups at a time. Our machine gunners were doing a great job, firing short deadly bursts just like we were trained to do, and being careful to save depleting ammunition while making it harder for the enemy to zero in on the tracer rounds. Then *wham!* Machine gun tracers streamed at the Japs from all directions, crisscrossing the battlefield with enough lead to build a Sherman tank.

I heard a noise and looked back at Bull Sterling pushing, dragging, and hauling machine gun belts and two boxes of grenades. I loaded up and brought gun ammo to our machine gun squad and started throwing grenades. The battle subsided for a few moments as the Japs regrouped. Our 105s whistled overhead continuously, and I knew the Nips were taking heavy casualties, but the shells were landing closer and closer to our own lines. The enemy was getting so close that soon we'd have to call in arty on our own positions. Jap mortars started dropping all over the ridge and shells from the Jap destroyers sitting offshore whooshed overhead like freight trains going by. It seemed like the naval gunfire was sailing high and striking their own troops.

Soon another wave of Japs attacked. I threw grenades until my arm was sore. The insanity seemed to go on forever. The 11th Marines never stopped firing their 105s. The artillery rounds just pounded the Japs right in front of us all night. They were dropping the rounds so close to us that I'm sure some of our men must have been hit by our own artillery, but there was no choice to be made. The fighting went on and on. I knew that if I lived, it would be the longest night of my life. I sat staring wild-eyed at the first shafts of sunlight peeking over the horizon, but I was too drained to recognize it. Marine artillery finally eased up. Somebody said that the 11th Marines had fired three thousand arty rounds during the night. I had no trouble believing it.

When the sun came up, I was sitting behind the machine gun with Bergie facing me. I don't know how or when I ended up there. We had a foxhole with the dirt piled around it like a parapet about six or eight foot square. Our machine gun position was along this path that came out of the jungle, but we were facing away from the path. My back was to the ridge and Bergie faced me with his back to the path. There was a lull in the fighting. That's the way it went, we'd kill a wave of Japs and they'd crawl back into the jungle and regroup and hit us again, but there would be fewer than before.

The terrain was rugged and covered by kunai grass and rocks. There were crevices in the slope behind me from years of water runoff, like big cracks, big enough for a man to squeeze into. Bergie hadn't opened those cigars from his sister yet and this seemed like a darn good time to do so. I wondered how he had kept them through the night but somehow he did. He gave me one and we lit up. I was still sort of in a daze. I'm sure we all were. Thousands of artillery rounds and thousands of grenades and Japanese naval bombardment and endless machine gun fire had just left everyone numb, almost like we were all drugged.

We smoked a bit, then we started playing cribbage. Sergeant Bergstrand was looking at me. I was completely soaked, covered with Jap blood. I felt terrible, so much had happened during the night that my mind was scattered, I guess. I couldn't remember anything after killing that first Jap with my knife. I did remember Bull Sterling bringing more grenades and ammo, but everything else was sort of foggy. The cribbage board was between us. Bergie said, "It's your move, dumbass." I looked at Bergie puffing on his cigar, then in that moment a Japanese Nambu machine gun opened up from this path along the ridge. Bergie fell forward onto my lap. I don't know how many bullets hit him in the back. He was dead instantly.

Bullets hit everywhere around me. I don't know how they missed me. I rolled Bergie off and turned the .30 toward the Japs to return fire, but it jammed. I cranked the handle but there was a ruptured round in the barrel. Bullets kept slapping the dirt all around. I tried to squeeze into the natural crevice in the slope behind me. I tried to bury myself in it. Bullets smacked the hard ground by my head and I just waited for one to go through my skull and prayed for Jesus to save me. A bullet tore off a chunk of my ear and another grazed my face. I knew I was going to die. Suddenly the sweet-sounding cracks of Springfield '03s and a Marine .30-caliber machine gun opened up from somewhere farther up that path. Our guys got them. The enemy fire stopped. I don't know who got 'em, but I was thanking God. I stared down at Bergie. Sgt. Wallace Bergstrand was about twenty-three or twenty-four years old. He was a good Marine, from Wausau, Wisconsin.

After Bergie was killed, everything went blank. I'm not sure what time of day it was, but I found myself near the Lunga River and I was tearing my clothes off like a madman. This corpsman ran up to me yelling, "You're hit! You're hit bad! Lay down!" I heard me yelling that I'm not hit.

"You're covered with blood!" He shouted right into my face.

"It's Jap blood!" I screamed back and shoved him away real hard and angry.

"Let me check you out, Eli!"

"Get away from me!" I shouted and shoved the guy away.

I ripped my shirt with both hands, I felt crazy. I tore at my clothes like they were on fire. I was drenched in blood and it was making me berserk. I shredded my blouse and trousers, threw away my ammo and cartridge belt and helmet, grenades, pistol, Reising gun, knife, bayonet, boondockers. I threw everything away from me. I knew I was going over the edge but nothing mattered but getting all this Jap blood off me. Once I was naked I ran and just jumped in the river. There were still Japs all over the place but nothing mattered right then. I hit the water and started scrubbing with both hands, trying to get all the blood off of me. Marines were yelling at me but nothing mattered. Then this big log floated up near me. I kept scratching at caked-on blood like a madman, then noticed that log moving. It was like some weird dream. My mind seemed to come back into focus for a moment. In that instant I realized that the log was a great big saltwater crocodile. I panicked and swam like an Olympian to the riverbank. I made it back ashore and don't know why that croc did not attack. The guys reasoned that he was already full from eating dead Japs in the river. That was September 14.

Then I was in the jungle. I felt like I had just woken up in the jungle. I stopped and turned to face the Raiders in column behind me. It looked to be a squad or so of Marines. I was weak with malaria and dysentery, but I knew I was on a trail in the jungle. This squad of Marines behind me all stopped and looked at me. The man closest to me said something but his voice sounded like it was coming out of a barrel, sort of far away. I looked at him and asked, "Where are we?"

He looked at me real strange.

"What do you mean?" he asked.

"Where are we?"

"On patrol, Eli."

"Patrol? Where?" I could tell we were on a trail in the jungle. I felt like I was waking up from being asleep. I had no idea what the crap was going on.

"You're leading the patrol, Corporal!" he said with some quiet frustration, not yelling because we were obviously in Indian country. "The Matanikau River. Guadalcanal."

"What day is it?" I asked.

This Raider looked at me real worried. "I think it's October fifth or seventh. I ain't no calendar. Why? Hey, you ain't all right."

"Where am I?"

"You're leading a patrol, Eli."

Right then I felt utterly confused. I couldn't believe it was October. I knew the battle of the ridge was September 13 and 14. I had absolutely no clue what happened to that period of time after the second night on the ridge. I guess my mind just shut down or something. The Marines in the patrol probably knew that I had shell shock, combat fatigue, or whatever you want to call it. I'm sure it did not give them any sense of security when they realized that the guy leading the patrol didn't know where he was at or what month it was. I sure felt weird.

I sort of knew I was going in and out mentally, but I just went along with the program the way a Marine does. We walked into this big field of kunai grass. It was six feet tall in places and I couldn't see anything clearly. In a flash there was an exchange of fire. Japs were blasting away at us and we were blasting back. I went through a clip on my Reising gun with this Jap closing in. I could hear him in the grass working his bolt. I knew he either had a jam or was out of ammo. He came out of the kunai grass with a bayonet charge at me and I parried it to my left and hit him with a straight butt stroke right above his eyes. The adrenaline shot so much fear and strength through my system that I killed him instantly. I felt his head just cave in. The Reising gun has a solid wood stock, and I drove it real deep inside his head. Then I couldn't pull it out. I had to put my foot on his throat to pull the stock out of his head. I started fumbling for another clip for my weapon. There was hand-to-hand going on in the kunai grass all around me. I didn't know how many Japs we killed or how many got away in that fight. When that patrol was over, I couldn't remember anything about it except all the trouble I had had pulling the butt end of my stock out of that guy's head.

I did not know any of this at that moment, but while I was out of it, Colonel Edson had been ordered to take over the 5th Marine Regiment and Lt. Col. Sam Griffith was now the Raider Battalion commanding officer. We were on this trail with about a company of Marine Raiders. I don't know where exactly other than it was near the Matanikau River, where the Japs had retreated after their defeat at the Ridge. They were regrouping in strength, and the battle for Guadalcanal was far from over.

The Matanikau came down out of the mountains and into Sealark Channel. A big river, it was fast-flowing in places with small trails on both sides of it. Word was the Japs had tanks and thousands of troops upriver. Of course, you never knew what was true or just foolish scuttlebutt, but in this case the scuttlebutt was true as I found out later. I had a good buddy that I had played football with at Toledo. He was a gunner on one of those halftracks with the 75mms mounted on them. I never saw any Jap tanks, but after I was evacuated he was part of a big ambush the Marines pulled on those Jap tanks. Killed an entire column of Jap tanks, killed them all.

To this day I draw mostly a blank for that period of time after I jumped in the Lunga River to wash the Japanese blood off of me. Until I sort of woke up on that patrol. The 7th Marine Regiment had landed behind the Japs. Chesty Puller led the 1st Battalion, 7th Marine Regiment and was hitting the Japs from one direction as the 5th Marine Regiment and what was left of the Raiders were going up the Matanikau. We ran into heavily fortified Jap positions. I remember the word coming back down the trail that Maj. Ken Bailey was dead. It was devastating to every Raider, but the truth for me was that I thought he had already been killed on Edson's Ridge. It was like losing him twice. He was an outstanding Marine. I had been his runner back at Quantico, and I mean the man was all Marine and greatly respected. He was one hard charger. One day at Quantico I was ordered to be his runner. They needed a Marine who was exceptionally athletic to keep up with him, to run messages for him under combat conditions. I played football for the Corps and had a reputation, so he chose me.

Major Bailey was awarded the Medal of Honor. The two big battles of the Matanikau River were evidently very rough. I don't think I was in them, but it remains hazy. Combat fatigue or shell shock or PTSD or whatever you want to call it, is real. Lt. Col. Sam Griffith was shot but lived. We took a lot of casualties. Matanikau II as it's come to be called, the second battle at the Matanikau, was a convincing victory for us. It was the last battle for the Raiders on the Canal. There was some very ferocious hand-to-hand combat, and upon viewing the carnage afterward even the general was overwhelmed with what the Marines had done. For the most part it is all a blank to me. I believe the good Lord protects our sanity like that.

The Raiders were pulled off of Guadalcanal on October 13. My records say I was evacuated on October 15, but I was flown out on a DC-3 with many other wounded. On October 13 the 164th Infantry landed. They were an Army National Guard outfit. I heard that they ended up being an outstanding outfit, too. Once the army was off of those transports, the Raiders boarded. I heard later that the army guys looked at the Raiders like they were from another planet. We looked awful. The Marines were a mess with wounds and disease. I guess more than half of the men had malaria and dysentery. Nearly all had some form of combat fatigue.

We had landed on Tulagi with a battalion of more than 900 Marine Raiders. When the battalion left the Canal there were 555 Raiders left. Ninety-four were killed and over 200 wounded. History books say the Raiders killed 1,100 Japanese soldiers and marines on the Canal, but I'm sure that we killed a lot more than that. We lost many fine machine gunners. The machine gun company took terrible losses, but they played a huge part in winning the battle of Edson's Ridge. And after we left the Canal, machine gun squads would once again play a critical role in holding Henderson Field as gunners like Mitchell Paige and John Basilone brought more glory upon the Marine Corps with incredible acts of bravery, both winning the Medal of Honor.

As the DC-3 lifted off of that stinking island, there was no way to describe the feelings. It was flown by a corporal and the navigator was a private. When we landed in Efate, New Hebrides (now Vanuatu), they put me on this bus to take me to the naval hospital there. Right away I'm looking out the window of the bus and I see Paul Boone. His outfit was in New Hebrides. He was looking for his brother or trying to get word about him from casualties coming out of Guadalcanal. There wasn't anything I could do except tell him, "Frank's dead, Paul. He was killed the second day on the ridge." Paul was devastated.

From New Hebrides, I was put on the *Solace,* a hospital ship heading for Auckland, New Zealand. I had lost about fifty or sixty pounds. The *Solace* was filled with wounded sailors and Marines and I met a lot of my old buddies. It was a great thrill to find a buddy that you thought had been killed on the Canal or Tulagi. I ran into Gunny Fetchko and it was good to see that he was alive. That's the way it was on the *Solace.* Every once in a while you'd see a Raider that you thought had been killed, and it was wonderful to see that they made it out. There were a lot of wounded sailors on board. A lot of them were survivors from the carriers *Hornet* and *Wasp.* Many were badly burned.

I had this navy kid in the rack next to me who was bandaged all over. He was really young. He had been on board the USS *Wasp* when it went down along with the *Hornet* in the savage sea battles surrounding Guadalcanal. He was covered with gauze from head to toe, and each day corpsmen would come by to put water and some solution on the burns. I was very sick with malaria and dysentery, and had shrapnel wounds in the back of my head, ear, and eyebrows, but I was mobile enough to help out and did so. I would hold the kid's cigarette for him so he could take a couple of puffs through the gauze hole that was his mouth, and I'd feed him ice cream. He was young and naturally worried about what he would look like now. I tried to convince him he'd look fine.

There were so many sad or curious cases aboard the *Solace,* and it was hard to see young men in such pain, but one young Marine stood out to me. He was badly wounded and had combat fatigue. He would just lie there near death and keep repeating, "The Lord is my shepherd, I shall not want. He makes me lie down in green pastures; He leads me beside quiet waters. He restores my soul; He guides me in paths of righteousness for His name's sake. Even though I walk through the valley of the shadow of death, I fear no evil; for Thou art with me; Thy rod and Thy staff, they comfort me. Thou dost prepare a table before me in the presence of my enemies; Thou has anointed my head with oil; My cup runs over. Surely goodness and mercy will follow me all the days of my life, and I will dwell in the house of the Lord forever." This Marine would just lay there and repeat the Twenty-third Psalm over and over. I'd sit and listen to him, as did others. There was a strange peace in his tone, even through the pain. It gave the rest of us a sense of peace, too.

We landed in Auckland, New Zealand, and from there we headed Stateside aboard one of those big ocean liners, of the President's Line. We were the first wounded coming back from the Battle of Guadalcanal and it was big news. A lot of people understood just how critical that battle was if we were going to win the war, and Americans were discovering that Marines were literally holding onto that island with knives and bayonets. I didn't know it at the time, but the theater commander had considered the Marines' position so hopeless that he had given General Vandegrift the go-ahead for the Marines to surrender. I felt insulted. Getting killed in action was considered a very real possibility and a risk that every Marine accepted. I don't think anyone in the Marine Corps could spell surrender let alone know how to do it. That's what people just don't understand. That's the job! If you didn't like that job description, then don't join the United States Marine Corps! Of course, civilians or people who are not Marines can't really understand the way Marines operate. They're professionals in a job that is not like other professions.

We landed in the States and it was grand. We were placed in the Mare Island Naval Hospital in Vallejo, California. Once you were up and moving around, you could get liberty or sneak out of the hospital. I was downtown and this car backfires and me and this buddy from the Canal hit the pavement. These civilians started laughing and it almost became ugly, but they knew better. I found myself in a pretty nice slop-chute in Vallejo, and there was this Marine who thought I was trying to take his girl. He decked me with a sucker punch and I guess he thought I'd stay down, but now I was gonna beat the crap out of this guy. He took off before I could get him. I ran outside looking for him and there were these two army sergeants sitting in a jeep outside. They made some crack about my uniform or something and I was already in a rage, so I yanked one of them out of the jeep and decked him. Then I proceeded to beat up the other one. Things went nuts and the whole place turned into a tremendous brawl, spreading all over like a flood. MPs and police came from every direction to stop the melee. A military ambulance was parked there, and I jumped in and told them I was supposed to be in Mare Island Naval Hospital and that they should get me back there quick. I guess they believed me, so I escaped the brig.

Near the end of my time at Mare Island, I was going to make a phone call home. You had to schedule it properly because there was a three-hour time difference. I ran into one of my old machine gunners, Sgt. Nick Marcelino. Nick was the Raider who had gone down with the USS *Calhoun* and lived to tell about it. Nick was making a call to Linda Darnell, the movie star. There was a famous soda fountain at Hollywood and Vine where movie stars would show up sometimes just to treat the troops to a little thrill. Well, ol' Nick met Linda Darnell there, and they were both from Brooklyn. He must have done something right because they hit it off and had a whirlwind romance. He had a ring and they were going to get married. He was calling her that very moment to meet her to get married. It was pretty exciting. He called her up and her maid answered the phone. He asked to speak to Linda, told the maid who he was and that they were getting married that day. The maid told him that Miss Darnell was not there and that she had just gone to Reno or someplace to marry her agent. Nick was crushed. He finally got over the blow and stayed in Hollywood. He had met a lot of movie people and went on to become a pretty famous makeup artist for film and television.

Before I left the hospital I met another old friend, the navy kid who was so badly burned when the *Wasp* went down at Guadalcanal. He came up to me smiling and pointing at his face.

"Look, Eli!"

I looked. He was still badly burned, but a lot of it was covered with a beard now.

"What do you think of my beard?" he asked excitedly.

"It looks great, kid."

"Look at it. The doctors tattooed a beard on me to cover the scars! Look at it, it looks real, don't it?"

"It does!" And it did. It looked like a real beard.

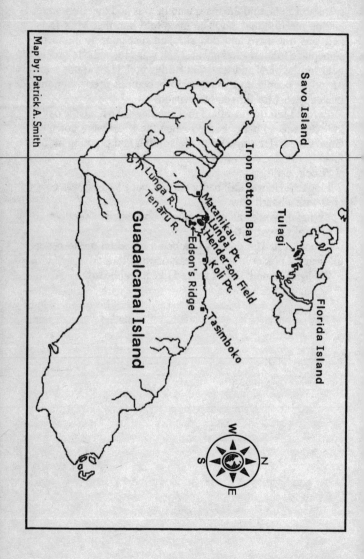

Map by: Patrick A. Smith

2

SGT. MITCHELL PAIGE

Medal of Honor

Rank and organization: Platoon Sergeant, United States Marine Corps. Place and date: Solomon Islands, 26 October 1942. Entered service at: Pennsylvania. Birth: Charleroi, Pa. Citation: For extraordinary heroism and conspicuous gallantry in action above and beyond the call of duty while serving with a company of marines in combat against enemy Japanese forces in the Solomon Islands on 26 October 1942. When the enemy broke through the line directly in front of his position, Platoon Sergeant Paige, commanding a machine gun section with fearless determination, continued to direct the fire of his gunners until all of his men were either killed or wounded. Alone, against the deadly hail of Japanese shells, he fought with his gun and when it was destroyed, took over another, moving from gun to gun, never ceasing his withering fire against the advancing hordes until reinforcements finally arrived. Then, forming a new line, he dauntlessly and aggressively led a bayonet charge, driving the enemy back and preventing a breakthrough in our lines. His great personal valor and unyielding devotion to duty were in keeping with the highest traditions of the United States Naval Service.

I was born in Charleroi, Pennsylvania, in 1918. My dad was a railroad construction worker, so we moved around when the job demanded. My older brother Pete was born in Kentucky, and older sister Millie was born in Indiana. When I was six years old Millie was nine, and we would sit on a bluff and watch Pete jump into the Monongahela River and swim out to play in the wake of the big powerful paddleboats that pushed the heavy barges along. Pete was eleven and a capable swimmer. The barges were filled with coal going to the steel mills. Every time Pete headed into the churning water he would disappear for a few seconds in the white wash near the huge paddles, and Millie would bring her hands together anxiously and pray out loud for him to be okay. When he popped up out of the wake, Millie sighed a thanks to God. Millie was an angel to all who knew her, she even looked the part. Her eyes were big, beautiful, and filled with such sincere compassion that she seemed to touch everyone with God's love.

Millie was a prayer warrior. With any joy or any concern, her first instinct was prayer. One day while picking purple wildflowers together, Millie suddenly spotted a copperhead snake about to strike at me. I didn't see the snake. She told me not to breathe, not to move a muscle until she gave the word to jump and for me to jump backward like never before. I knew it was serious by the tone of her voice. "Now!" she yelled. I jumped over backward like I was shot out of a cannon. When I was safe and we both stopped shaking, Millie looked at me with an expression of fear and thanksgiving. "I prayed to Jesus for the snake not to bite you, Mitch." She seemed to always have such confidence in God, a faith so strong that it overflowed until all who knew her felt that same confidence.

Millie helped foster my love of our country. I'd sit listening to her exciting descriptions of crucial battles and historic moments that made America. She would tell me about the French and Indian War and battles that were fought right near our very home. Just hearing Millie's stories made me want to go to school. I remember that I couldn't wait for September to come. My sister loved sharing those marvelous stories of America's brave history, stories that filled me with a lifelong pride in being an American.

I genuinely liked school. Each day our teacher would lead us in the Pledge of Allegiance to the flag as we stood by our desks. Before sitting she would then read a passage from the Bible. Each day was a different verse but one passage has always remained my favorite. "I will lift up mine eyes unto the hills, from whence cometh my help. My help cometh from the Lord, which made Heaven and earth. . . ." It was the 121st Psalm and it remains my favorite. I had wonderful teachers and we respected them greatly. My teachers were strict, but they taught us faith in God and the Bible. They taught us a love of our country and what our flag stood for and the cost of freedom. They taught us to honor our father and mother. The love of God and country that I learned in the little Camden School always remained with me, even on Guadalcanal.

One beautiful sunny spring day, Millie took her bath, got dressed, then walked out to Kenny's Field to watch us play baseball. The breeze was cool and Millie had a thin cotton dress on. That night she developed a severe cold. The next morning she had a fever. We were all worried. Mother treated her as best she could. Each night an owl would screech in a tree near our house. Mother would look at me with alarm because she said in the "old country" that was a bad omen. Millie became worse and finally a doctor came to the house and said she had pneumonia. She soon went into a coma. Mother sat beside Millie day and night. When I came home from school, Mother and I would sit together at Millie's bed. One night as Mother and I sat there we heard the owl on the porch, then it flew away. A few minutes later everything seemed still and serene when I suddenly heard a distinct flap of wings. After a moment I could hear Mother sobbing as she said, "An angel just came and took our Millie to heaven." We were both on our knees, but I do not recall getting off the chair. Mother was praying out loud as Millie used to do on the hill overlooking the Monongahela River. I missed Millie very much as she was always like an angel to me.

In 1936, I joined the Marine Corps. My mother's parting words were, "Trust in the Lord always." I had tried to join earlier, but after making the two-hundred-mile walk and hitch to Baltimore, Maryland, to the nearest recruiter, I was told that I was too young and too light. When I turned eighteen I tried again, but even then I had to gulp down a dozen bananas and drink several glasses of water to weigh enough. Parris Island was very tough. That's where the backbone of the Corps begins. I left Parris Island by train for Quantico, Virginia, along with a good number of my platoon. I was transferred to H Company, 2d Battalion, 5th Marine Regiment, a machine gun company. We were privileged to wear on our left shoulder the French Fourragère.

While I was at Quantico, Maj. Gen. John H. Russell retired. A new commandant of the Marine Corps came aboard, Maj. Gen. Thomas Holcomb. It was standard for "old salts" to challenge each other on who was saltier. Who had been in the Corps longer. The standard question was, "And how many commandants have you served under, recruit?" Now I was no longer a recruit, and it was at that moment that I knew I had gone from boy to man.

The total strength of the Marine Corps at that time was seventeen thousand men. A private's pay was twenty-one dollars a month. In December 1936 we went aboard a battleship, the USS *Wyoming,* at Norfolk, Virginia. The next morning we sailed out into the Atlantic. This was my first cruise and it was the first step in an incredible Marine Corps adventure. This adventure would be filled with every human emotion, more than anything I could have ever imagined. "Join the Marines and see the world." That was what the poster in Baltimore said, the words emblazoned above a rugged-looking Marine in a campaign hat. It could not have been more accurate in my case.

We made stops at Culebra Island, and San Juan, Puerto Rico, and Guantanamo, Cuba. It was a constant thrill for me as we visited all the places I had read about in the little Camden School that had taught me so much. I saw places that Millie used to speak of in tones of awe. Through the Panama Canal, Central American coast, and Mexico. On February 18, 1937, we were off San Clemente Island when a powder charge exploded in the breech of a five-inch battery that had not been properly closed. At that precise moment, 10:42, Marine captain Edward J. Trumble and five enlisted men were killed. I helped a man to sick bay whose arm had been blown off at the shoulder. It was a horrible thing to see, just the first of many terrible sights I would witness in the next few years.

I went aboard the USS *Chaumont* and we sailed out of San Francisco Bay, past Alcatraz Island, and underneath the new bridge that was being built, to be known as the Golden Gate Bridge. Huge nets were attached to the underside of the bridge to protect the hundreds of workers above. We anchored in Hawaii for a bit, then on the twelfth of June we pulled into Apra Harbor, Guam.

Conditions aboard a troop transport are tough. One canteen of freshwater a day to brush your teeth and wash your face, saltwater showers, and sleeping quarters stacked so high, so deep, and so close together, you never knew whose foot or hand would be in your face. Anyone with claustrophobia would never survive a cruise with the Corps. The chow lines were unbelievable. One continuous line that snaked all around the topside of the ship. After an 0500 breakfast, it was a dash to the head to brush your teeth, etc., and then a mad scramble back to the end of the line to be in time for noon chow. The same procedure for evening chow, then hopefully a movie on deck.

On the nineteenth of June, 1937, we steamed into Manila Bay past Corregidor and into Manila, Philippine Islands, some fifteen hundred miles from Guam. A tugboat eased us into the dock and a loud cheer went up and much laughter. Some Marine had lowered himself over the fantail of the ship and under the letters of the ship's name he had painted the following:

```
C  H  A  U  M  O  N  T
H  E  L  S  A  N  A  R
R  L  L     R  N  V  A
I  P        I     Y  N
S           N        S
T           E        P
            S        O
                     R
                     T
                     S
```

The Corps, having no sense of humor, sent that comical Marine to the brig. Word came down. "Prepare to disembark! All Marines disembarking at Manila for assignment to the Cavite Naval Station." I hurriedly got my gear together and said good-byes to all my old friends who were going on to stations in China. Cavite was my first permanent overseas duty station. I was in the Philippines for the next year and a half or so. I was very happy in Cavite. Many of the Marines here had seen service in Haiti, Nicaragua, or some other "banana war" as they were known. We really had some hard "old salts." The Marine Corps was filled with them, each one a living piece of history and what made the Corps so special. Just one example would be Sgt. Henry L. Claude, our police sergeant. Sergeant Claude had done a three-year hitch in the army, one four-year hitch in the U.S. Navy, and a tour of duty with the French Foreign Legion in the Sahara Desert. He, now, in 1937, had completed nineteen years of service in the Marine Corps.

I saw intrigue, tragedy, and murder during that year and a half in the Philippines. One Sunday afternoon I was walking post number 13, about a mile walk around the beaches at Sangley Point. I spotted someone in a white uniform getting out of an automobile. He stood still for a moment facing the fuel docks with his white hat near his chest. Then he faced toward the six-hundred-foot-high radio towers for a moment, the tallest in the Philippines. As he turned to face the naval hospital, I realized he must be taking pictures, and with that I yelled at him and took off at high port. He heard me and jumped into his car and took off. I got to the fuel docks and the nearest phone and called the corporal of the guard, Corporal Mouchet, to stop the car coming out with a driver in a white uniform. Then I heard a racing motor and heard Mouchet holler to stop. We reported the incident to the officer of the day and feared getting busted.

The intruder was from a Japanese vessel in Manila, and he had presented an authorized pass from the U.S. naval commander. Several nights later on an 8 to 12 watch, I reported a *hanca,* a native canoe-outrigger, and I fired one shot to chase it off. One night after that I had the 4 to 8 watch, and we could not locate the man on the midnight to 0400 watch. The corporal of the guard called the officer of the day, Gunner Derdman, and we made a thorough search of the whole post number 13 area. As dawn approached we spotted something out in the water. It was the Marine that I was to relieve. His hands were tied tightly behind his back with baling wire and his throat had been slashed. We never caught the murderer.

After a year or so, a notice went up on our bulletin board that examinations would be given for promotion to private first class. Me and a couple of buddies noticed that our names were not on the list of eligibles. We went in to 1st Sgt. Jimmie Jordan's office to inquire. "Get out of here, you stinkin' recruits! When you get at least three years in the Corps, you'll be eligible to take the exam."

1st Sgt. Jimmie Jordan was a most interesting character. His shack was across the Paseo from my home at Porta Vaga. The story the old salts told was that in 1922, Jimmie was a sergeant here in Cavite, and one night as he was walking along Calle P. Gomez he saw a house on fire. He yelled to the occupants upstairs to drop the children to him. He caught both of the young girls but tragically both parents died in the flames. Jimmie raised both of the youngsters and was now living with one of them, named Tina. Tina was a dancer at the Dreamland Cabaret in the evenings. Dancers were known as ballerinas. She and Jimmie were constantly fighting. When I heard Jimmie's door slamming shut across the Paseo, I knew Jimmie was on his way out, headed for the bar around the corner. Tina would stick her head out the window and scream, "Jimmie you sonna ma —itch! Come back here! I luv you."

I was assigned choice duty at the old Spanish fort Porta Vaga at the entrance to Cavite Island. There were a total of about ten Marines whose duties entailed military police work and assisting the local constabulary. I got called to help stop a big brawl in the Dreamland Cabaret. When I got to the place, there were about two hundred sailors, Marines, and civilians turning on one another. I started blowing my whistle and pulling sailors and Marines apart, then I felt someone pummeling my back and the back of my head. I swung around quickly. A ballerina flopped to the floor from my elbow strike. I picked her up and deposited her behind the bar and told the bartender to put some ice on her head. I was sure glad when that night was over. I was worried about the ballerina but she was okay. Two years later I was involved in a similar incident in Tientsin, China.

December 12, 1937, the Japanese bombed the American gunboat USS *Panay* in the Yangtze River. We were put on alert to go help the 4th Marines in China. On October 25, 1938, I went aboard ship in Manila and we sailed up to Hong Kong for a few days, then sailed into the yellow waters of the Yangtze. We ended up steaming along the muddy Whangpoo River to Shanghai. I went ashore in Shanghai, where I met many of my old friends at the Fourth Marines Club on Bubbling Well Road. I wanted to see the sights and decided to take a walk along the street adjacent to the park. I saw two Marines battling it out on the grass. Each time one got knocked down, the other one would assist him to his feet. Another Marine came along and said to me, "Well, I wonder who caught who in whose shack with whose girl?"

Over on the other side of the park a group of sailors was also watching this bit of fisticuffs. The sailors started over toward our entertaining Marines. I told my friend that we should ease out to the park, too. He held my arm and said, "Just stand here if you want to see some fun."

The sailors grabbed the Marines to pull them apart and were shouting, "All right, let's knock it off." When the two Marines realized someone was interfering with their private brawl, they turned-to on the sailors. In a few moments there were white uniforms sprawled all over the grass. Having accomplished that to their satisfaction, the two Marines resumed their bareknuckle pummeling of one another. It was one of those Marine moments I just couldn't stop laughing about.

From Shanghai, I went to North China, to Chinwangtao for further assignment to Tientsin, where I arrived on November 6, 1938. Tientsin was a city of many concessions.

The British Concession, the French Concession, the Italian Concession, the Old German Concession, and the Japanese Concession. It was ironic that our Marine barracks was located in the Japanese Concession. Shortly after I had arrived in Tientsin, I was standing watch at the gate. I could see the Japanese sentry on duty at the barbed-wire barricade just a stone's throw from where my post was. There was an opening in the fence through which the Chinese were permitted to go back and forth along the street. There was a mud puddle in the street in front of the Japanese sentry.

One morning as two little Chinese girls dressed in their neat, starched blue-and-white dresses and their arms loaded with books stepped through the gate, that Japanese sentry stuck his foot out and tripped one of the little girls. At the same time he pushed the other one and both girls fell into that puddle. Those little girls were only about eight or nine years old. They picked up their wet and muddy books and started off again. They came by me, their cute little dresses now a mess. They looked up at me with the most pitiful expressions of humiliation in their kind little eyes, seemingly pleading for help. Big tears were running down their rosy cheeks.

After they passed, I came to port arms from my parade-rest position. I took out a five-round clip of .30-caliber ammunition from my cartridge belt and loaded my Springfield rifle. I raised the rifle to my shoulder to take aim at that Japanese sentry, and as I pulled the trigger I felt myself and the rifle going up in the air. Big Corporal Lee Bolander had come up behind me and grabbed me so that the round went high over the buildings. During World War I, Lee had fought the great Gene Tunney for the heavyweight championship of the Marine Corps. I had the 8 to 12 watch and fortunately, Lee, who was with another company, was still at the guardhouse waiting at the gate to see a civilian friend of his when he saw me take aim.

In a flash 1st Lt. Arthur A. Chidester, the officer of the day, came running out, and I told him exactly what had transpired. Bolander told him that he would have probably done the same thing under the circumstances, as he witnessed the incident. Lieutenant Chidester then said, "Let's just hope the old man didn't hear that shot." He told me to forget it and to not mention a word of it to anyone. The old man was Col. William C. James. He had not heard the shot, thank God. I was sincerely grateful to both of them. I very likely would have gotten a court-martial. Down deep in my heart, however, I still felt that the sentry had it coming to him.

Free time in Tientsin could always be an adventure. One night as I sat in a nightclub in Tientsin listening to a Russian orchestra playing, I could see tears rolling down the cheeks of my very good friend, "Big Mary." The violins always seemed to have a certain air of sadness in their strains. Big Mary was a wonderful White Russian girl who wanted to learn to speak English. We had met one evening while ice skating. As we sat enjoying the music, I could hear some nasty remarks directed to all U.S. Marines from a nearby table crowded with Limeys, British soldiers. Suddenly I felt someone pulling my chair and I looked around and saw two big Limeys.

"Aw right, Yank, get to your bloody feet."

"Shove off, mates, no one is bothering you. Can't you see I'm enjoying the company of my friend?" I turned back around but they persisted. Before I knew it, Big Mary had gotten up and grabbed the two Limeys by the stacking-swivels, that's neck in Corps language, and there was a deep, dull thud as she cracked their skulls together. Mary released the two Limeys, who dropped to the deck in a heap. I politely got up and held Big Mary's chair as she sat down to listen to the music again.

For the next year, whenever Big Mary and I were seen in a nightclub or restaurant, word got around quickly, "Don't mess with that bloody Marine, or his friend Big Mary will tear you apart."

On another occasion I was in Annie's Place down on Taku Road one night when I spotted my good friend Ned Clark at the bar alone. I assumed that he and his fiancée Freda, an attractive White Russian, must have had a little squabble. The place was filled with "frogs," which is what we called Frenchmen. I was talking to my buddy Lem Hilmer when we heard a loud commotion at the bar. We could see Ned's fists flying in all directions, and in a few moments nine Frenchmen lay sprawled out on the deck with bloody noses and broken jaws. The rest took off running. Lem and I didn't have time to get out of our chairs, it happened so fast.

Ned Clark was our star athlete. He held the boxing title in North China, was considered the fastest human in North China on the track field, was an amazing pole-vaulter, and an all-around athlete. Ned sat down with Lem and I and gulped down a quart of Five Star beer and told us about his spat with Freda. Knocking out all those frogs didn't even enter the conversation. A few weeks later, Ned and Freda were married after waiting for the necessary clearance through the State Department and Headquarters Marine Corps in Washington. Big Mary and I attended that beautiful wedding in Tientsin, China; as a matter of fact, I was the best man.

I found myself in another brawl one night at Minez's Oriental Café-Restaurant on Woodrow Wilson Road. I stopped in for some sukiyaki though I did not particularly relish that food. There were French, British, Italians, and White Russians enjoying their meals. This group of loud Japanese officers with their ladies came in the restaurant. They'd obviously been drinking a lot of sake. Suddenly the place exploded. Glasses and bottles flew everywhere. Tables and chairs and dishes crashed all around. Fists flew and it was every man for himself. I was going-to with some real gusto, especially on a couple of Japs. At one point I turned around swinging and landed a solid right flush on the jaw of a girl in a bright red dress. She went down like a ton of bricks. I was startled to see that I had decked a girl and was about to reach down to help her when I saw the flash of a Japanese samurai blade trying to impale me. I managed to avoid being skewered and decided that this was no place for a peace-loving Marine like myself. I made a successful escape from the vicious barroom brawl by running outside and jumping into a ricksha. *"Meg wa fu!"* I yelled as the fight was moving out into the street. "American barracks, hurry!"

It was about ninety miles between Tientsin and Peking,

and about every two or three weeks I made a train run to
Peking. When I left Tientsin, I would be locked up inside a
boxcar with supplies and equipment for the Marines and the
embassy in Peking. A quartermaster in Peking would unlock
me when I reached there. It was a miserable three-day journey. In the winter it was so cold that I was afraid to fall
asleep for fear of freezing to death. The Japanese had fifty
thousand troops in China and they were everywhere. Occasionally the train would stop amid Japanese troops. I had to
remain silent. A sneeze and they would have blown the car
open. I usually went on these trips alone, but sometimes I
was accompanied by another Marine.

When I didn't get stuck with this duty, some other poor
slob did. On one of these trips another Marine, Corporal Armonia, did not fare so well. Somehow he had managed to
get his Chinese girlfriend in the boxcar. When the train
pulled into Tientsin, the dock was filled with several hundred
Japanese troops in formation and full battle dress. As the big
door of the boxcar swung open, the Japanese officer standing
in front of his troops in formation nearest the door saw Armonia's Chinese girlfriend. As Corporal Armonia emerged
from the boxcar, the officer blurted out something to Armonia that he didn't understand. The Japanese officer was drunk
from the night before and staggering around in front of the
boxcar. He suddenly pulled out his two-handed samurai
sword and took a wild swing at Armonia's head as the corporal stepped onto the loading dock. Armonia saw it coming.
He dropped to the deck, drawing his Colt automatic .45-
caliber pistol. He pulled the slide back and fired one shot.
The Japanese officer fell dead on the deck. Armonia jumped
to his feet and ran the length of that long station, past all of
those Japanese troops still standing in ranks, and not one
stepped out of line to apprehend him.

Corporal Armonia made it to the Marine barracks. I was
in the guardhouse when he arrived and told me what had
transpired. I went with him as he reported the matter to the
officer of the day. At office hours that morning, Armonia was
confined to the brig for further investigation. The Japanese

embassy immediately sent a message to Colonel Hawthorne to release Corporal Armonia to them for proper punishment. The colonel refused. Armonia was kept in the brig for several weeks until the next navy transport arrived in Chinwangtao. Armonia was hustled aboard without any notice and returned to the States. We learned that upon arrival at Philadelphia Navy Yard, he was given a trial and fined $1.05 and restored to duty. We figured that the dollar and five cents was for the spent bullet. I never found out what reply they gave the Japanese embassy, but I can imagine that they were advised that Corporal Armonia had been tried and executed.

On September 4 the headlines in the Tientsin English newspaper, the *North China Star,* read, BRITAIN DECLARES WAR ON REICH! On the seventeenth of September, 1939, I was transferred to Peking to the American embassy guard. Peking was one of those special places so filled with history that it could never be boring, and not just ancient Chinese history. At one point I found myself actually walking post on top of the ancient Tartar Wall in Peking. On this very wall the immortal Daniel Joseph Daley had crawled to the top under fire, then volunteered to hold it alone until new fortifications could be finished. All night he held the point, shooting and bayoneting the Boxers as they tried to overrun his position. He was awarded the Medal of Honor. G.Sgt. Dan Daley won his second Medal of Honor in a brutal battle in Haiti, where once again he fought against overwhelming odds, attacking, killing, and scattering the enemy. On June 15, 1918, in France during World War I, Daley risked his life to put out a fire in an ammunition dump. Then five days later he attacked an enemy machine gun emplacement alone and captured it with hand grenades and a pistol. Shortly before he was wounded in the battle of Belleau Wood, the wiry little sergeant ordered his men to jump off faster in the attack, bellowing the historic command, "Come on, you bastards, do you want to live forever?" Those words will be repeated as long as there are Marines. He was awarded the Navy Cross. Just to walk where he had fought was an honor. I loved it there, but my fascinating time in Peking finally ended.

I returned to Tientsin in 1940 to rejoin my former organization, D Company, with its machine guns. I had my orders to return to the States. When I left Tientsin for Chinwangtao, a lot of my friends were there to say good-bye. None of us knew at the time that many of them would be captured by the Japanese and interned when the war began. I boarded the USS *Henderson,* known as the "Hendy Maru" to any sailor or Marine who ever traveled to or from the Far East in the thirties or forties. It was named after the fifth commandant of the Marine Corps. The slowest vessel afloat. As I looked back toward the mainland of China toward Shanhaikwan, where the Great Wall made its winding way into the interior, I wondered if I would ever visit again. Those bitter cold winters, scorching dry summers, and red-dust storms off the Gobi Desert were things I could talk about for a lifetime. It seemed like a lifetime on the Hendy Maru before we reached the Panama Canal.

After departing Panama, we continued up the East Coast of the U.S. to Brooklyn, where I was assigned guard duty at the navy yard. A few days later I was granted annual leave and immediately left for home. It was wonderful seeing everyone again. Father was still drinking a lot and Mother had given up hope that he would ever quit. My brother Pete was with the railroad at Camden Hill. Mother wanted to know all about the Far East. I told her that I saw war coming with the Japanese. She read several letters to me that she had received from the "old country." The letters made it clear that they feared war in Serbia. Prince Paul of Yugoslavia was reported visiting with Hitler, and many of the high Yugoslav air force officers were mingling with German officials and military personnel. Mother said that she was certain the country was being sold out to the Germans.

When my leave was over, I was ordered to the Philadelphia Navy Yard. Marines there were charged with security. Each night many thousands of civilian workers left the yard in their automobiles. It became a practice to stop a car occasionally to check the trunk. I could almost sense a suspicious driver as he approached the gate. I made a habit of waving some over to the side, where other Marines would do the checking. One evening I stopped a car that I had recognized on several other watches. The driver was all smiles and even saluted me each time he went out the gate. When we opened the trunk we found dozens of official navy blueprints and other papers, which I confiscated and turned over to the duty officer. Our commanding officer, Colonel Ames, thanked me for a "job well done." I was promoted to corporal on September 10, 1940.

All noncommissioned officers who had past experience in the Orient were transferred to the Fleet Marine Force. I was on my way to Quantico, Virginia. I reported back in with my old organization, H Company, 2d Battalion, 5th Marines, and was given the assignment as a machine gun squad leader. As a member of the 5th Marine Regiment, I was entitled again to wear the French Fourragère, which was bestowed upon the 5th Regiment by the French government for its outstanding service in 1918. It's the only nonissue item any Marine is allowed to wear. A few days later I heard that old familiar order, "Stand by to move out." We were off to Norfolk to board ships for maneuvers in the Caribbean Sea area.

At Norfolk, I had the great pleasure of meeting another Marine legend, Sgt. Louis Cukela. Louis had served with the 5th Marines in France, where he had been awarded both the Army Medal of Honor and the Navy Medal of Honor for the same action in Forest de Retz, near Villers-Cotterêts, France, July 18, 1918. Part of his citation reads: "Sergeant Cukela advanced alone against an enemy strong point that was holding up his line. Disregarding the warnings of his comrades, he crawled out from the flank in the face of heavy enemy fire and worked his way to the rear of the enemy position. Rushing a machine gun emplacement, he killed or drove off the crew with his bayonet, bombed out the remaining part of the strong point with German hand grenades and captured two more machine guns and four men."

Louis was hilarious. He had us in stitches with his quips; his English had a little Serbian touch to it, even though he was born in Austria. There was a famous story about Louis that we all wanted to know the truth about. "Oh yes," he said, when we asked. The story was that Louis had sent this private, who was his runner, off with a message, and obviously the runner got it fouled up worse than a Russian roll call when he delivered it. Louis was fit to be tied. When he finally got hold of the runner, he told him, "Next time I send ——— fool, I go myself!"

From Norfolk we cruised to the Caribbean and made practice landings on Culebra Island. Once we made an emergency run to Martinique, the French island of the Windward Islands group in the West Indies. Martinique had sent many thousands of its men to France when the Germans invaded that country. The local administration had decided in favor of the Vichy government, which was nothing but a puppet government set up by the Germans. A serious uprising was expected as a consequence, but the French puppet government had gold and aircraft stored in Martinique and was backed by the French aircraft carrier, the *Beam,* and naval units. It could have easily been a shootout between us and the French who had turned against their own country, but it didn't happen.

After that our home port became Guantanamo Bay, Cuba. We set up a permanent tent camp. The Marine Corps was expanding rapidly as war clouds began to move across the entire world. The commandant issued mobilization orders to all Marine Corps Reserve units to begin mobilization on November 1, 1940. The first group of Marine reservists started to arrive in Cuba to join us in January 1941. On February 1, 1941, while we were aboard ship in the Caribbean, we were told that the 1st Marine Division had been created. We had been making landings constantly while bivouacked on the island of Culebra. Our 1st Marine Division was unique because it was the first Marine division in USMC history, and it was also the first integrated amphibious striking force of the armed forces of the United States. Since the 5th Marine Regiment was the nucleus of the 1st Brigade, it was split up to form the 7th Marines. Then the 1st was made up of personnel from the 5th and 7th Marine Regiments.

When we returned to Guantanamo Bay, my company

commander was Capt. Michael McGinnis Mahoney. He was considered a rebel by some officers for his frankness and boldness. Sgt. Bill Agee was another "old China hand," and a strong bond of friendship grew between the three of us. I dug a hole in the ground beneath my cot and placed an empty .30-caliber ammo box with its metal liner into the hole. I then placed wet gunny sacks around the box and pushed small rocks and dirt over it, up to the top of the box. I put a few inches of water in the box and then filled it with cans of beer. I put a lid on it and camouflaged it with a thin layer of dirt. Every afternoon the captain and Sergeant Agee would stop at my tent to discuss the progress of our machine guns that we were modifying. We told those who heard the sound of cans being opened that it was the sound of the captain's new loading machine.

In April 1941 we went aboard ship again, headed for Charleston, South Carolina. We were transferred to Parris Island. We moved into a tent camp out near the rifle range, where we continued our training. We had a permanent mess hall, which really beat being in Guantanamo. We would march to the mess hall for each meal, and one morning as we passed someone's quarters, I noticed a Nazi flag on the wall. It was prominently displayed for everyone to see. As far as I was concerned it was an enemy flag. I knew recruits marching past could see it. I told some of the men that if that Hitler flag was up there when we marched by for evening chow, I was going to rip it off that bulkhead.

When we returned to our tents that evening, I could hear some of the fellas up ahead saying, "It's still up there, Mitch." I dropped out of ranks and walked over to the building and knocked on the door. A black maid answered and asked me what I wanted and I replied that I wanted that Nazi flag on the wall. She told me I couldn't have it. I walked past her and tore it off the wall and walked out. A big lieutenant grabbed me from behind and said, "Who the hell do you think you are?" Several of my NCO buddies rushed over and pulled the lieutenant off my back. We went back to our area and I immediately reported to Captain Mahoney. I gave him the flag and told him the entire incident. I also told him I had never seen that lieutenant before.

At 0830 the next morning I was summoned to the company office and Captain Mahoney informed me to get into my best khaki as a staff car would be picking me up in a few minutes to take me to the main station, as the commanding general wanted to see me.

When the adjutant marched me into the general's office, he told me to stand at ease. He slowly opened his top desk drawer and I could see the Nazi flag that I had ripped off the wall. The general then looked up at me as he pulled the flag out of his drawer and said, "Have you ever seen this before?"

"Yes, sir."

He then asked me how long I'd been in the Corps and about my tour in the Orient. In a few minutes he stood up and said, "You know this is a general court-martial offense, breaking into private quarters."

"Yes, sir," I said, expecting that the MPs would be coming in to take me to the brig. The general suddenly raised his head and stuck his hand out to shake mine.

"Thank you for being alert, Corporal."

I shook his hand but I was stunned.

The next morning Captain Mahoney took me off to the side to talk with me. He said the general had also called him and told him that just recently two officers had been apprehended while trying to scuttle one of our warships in the Charleston Navy Yard. They were apprehended while trying to flood the ship's lower compartments. A few days later Captain Mahoney called me to the office and handed me a sheet of paper, then he reached out his hand and said, "Congratulations, Sergeant." I was promoted. May 14, 1941.

On Sunday, December 7, 1941, I was sitting in my tent in New River, North Carolina, when the news on the radio was interrupted by a special bulletin—the Japanese were bombing Pearl Harbor, Hawaii. The Japanese had also struck at all of our other bases in the Pacific and in the Orient. All 16 officers and 178 enlisted men at Tientsin and Peking were interned that day by the Japanese. A short time after the first announcement, Captain Mahoney and Sgt. Bill Agee came charging into my tent. "Well, this is it this time."

The three of us sat on the machine gun boxes in my tent, nervous and excited at the same time. Captain Mahoney looked wide-eyed and ready. "We must have all the guns and everything else checked over as quick as possible."

One of our machine guns was set up inside the tent. The captain was so proud of our guns, as much as Agee and I were. He had every right to be. It was Captain Mahoney's original idea to drill holes through the bolts in the guns in order to lighten them and to speed up the recoil. Then we changed the backplates by using double springs and changed the driving springs in all of our guns to much stronger ones. For the past year in Cuba and on maneuvers, we tested those guns thoroughly, firing thousands of rounds. We had stepped up the cyclic rate of fire from the normal 400 to 550 rounds per minute to 1,300 rounds per minute, enabling us to get better accuracy because of the decreased vibration. We learned at long ranges that there was less dispersion, and we could cut the black out of a target at a thousand yards.

Captain Mahoney paused and gave me a serious look as he tenderly patted the water jacket of the machine gun on his way out. "Let's be ready to move out anywhere on a moment's notice, and be ready to fight. The Japanese are going to feel the sting of these babies soon."

On April 4, 1942, I was promoted to platoon sergeant in the 2d Battalion, 7th Marine Regiment. Our commanding officer was Col. Herman Henry Hanneken, Medal of Honor recipient for extraordinary heroism in Haiti. The CO for the 1st Battalion, 7th Marines was Lt. Col. Lewis Burwell Puller, more affectionately known to all Marines as "Chesty." Chesty had already been decorated with the Medaille Militaire of the Republic of Haiti. In 1930, Chesty was recommended for the Navy Cross. He was awarded his second Navy Cross in 1933. The list of outstanding Marines went on and on. I was very proud to be part of the 7th Marines.

Guadalcanal

We spent time in Samoa and I grew to love it. I even visited the mountaintop grave of Robert Louis Stevenson, the great writer. Just standing by the tomb on Mt. Vaea, overlooking the blue Pacific, it was easy to see his inspiration for the wonderful adventure books that every kid read when I was a boy. *Treasure Island, Kidnapped,* and *Dr. Jekyll and Mr. Hyde.* I had no idea what adventure awaited me on another island not that far away, named Guadalcanal.

We went ashore at Kukum, Guadalcanal, at 0545 on September 18, 1942. There were many old friends from the 5th Marines to greet us. The 5th and 1st Marine Regiments along with the 1st Marine Raiders and Paramarines had been holding on to a cutout landing strip known as Henderson Field since the seventh of August. They looked tired and weary and nothing like the men we had known. They spoke to us as they constantly scanned the sky above. It was obvious that these Marines had been through a terrible ordeal.

This was Guadalcanal, British Solomon Islands, America's first offensive since the day the Japanese struck at Pearl Harbor, and it was absolutely critical that we hold onto it, and we knew it. Suddenly we heard antiaircraft fire all around us. Someone yelled, "Jap Zeros!" I dived behind some crates and glanced up. An American plane ripped by overhead, but it was too late. In that moment we were all sickened. Our guns had crippled one of our own aircraft. We felt awful about it.

That night we moved across a clearing near Henderson Field. I heard Washing Machine Charlie, the Jap observation and spotter plane overhead. He dropped greenish white illumination flares that lit up the area like daylight. A moment later horrifying, red-hot naval fire moved the earth beneath us as Japanese ships in Sealark Channel opened fire. Full-size trees were torn out of the ground and tossed into the air. A weird swishing sound followed by a distinct thud hit inches away from me. It felt like I was lying there for hours with the flares floating down under tiny parachutes and giant explosions everywhere. Washing Machine Charlie seemed to be cruising around so slow that I couldn't understand why our antiaircraft guns had not blasted him out of the sky. I wondered how many of those ships pounding us had been the same ships I had watched in Shanghai and other ports in China.

When the first rays of dawn crept into the skyline, it felt safe to sit up. A few feet from where my outstretched feet had been was a bluish-looking chunk of steel about eleven or twelve inches long and about four or five inches thick. I reached over to pick it up and quickly released it. I was bleeding from the tips of all of my fingers. There wasn't a spot on that shell fragment that I could touch without snagging my skin. It was razor sharp and certainly would have severed any part of my body that it struck.

For the next several days it was foxhole-digging and manning the line. Nearly every day at least one Japanese sniper was shot out of a tree. They would tie themselves in a tree at night and try to pick off Marines during the day. Enemy planes were overhead daily trying to knock out Henderson Field. At night warships would slip into Sealark Channel and try to do the same thing and lob shells into the front lines for good measure. Malaria began to take a toll from the anopheles mosquitoes. At night every shape looked like a Jap soldier. Moving around at night was very dangerous.

One night one of my gun crew got up quietly and went back of the line to relieve himself. As he returned to the line his best buddy turned and fired at point-blank range, killing the man instantly. The Marine who fired the fatal shot went into shock and had to be taken to the battalion sick bay. I knew there would have to be an investigation when the word reached HQ. The men accepted it as fate. Before noon that day, Colonel Hanneken visited our position and questioned me about the shooting. I showed him the exact spot where it had happened. He questioned several of the other men. We were in a very dense part of the jungle and he decided he wanted to look over the area. He told me to get a machete and follow him. We took off through the jungle and I followed his footsteps. The man moved like a cat, putting each foot down softly, then pausing suddenly to stare at one point.

I was wondering where we were going when without any warning, the colonel had his .45-caliber pistol out and fired one round up into a tree. A moment later a black-clad body fell out of a tree just ahead of us. With his pistol still in his hands the colonel eased over to the victim and rolled him over with his foot. It was a Japanese sniper in his sniper suit, including the split-toed cloth sandals.

After the colonel left, several members of my platoon went over the same trail to see the body. We buried the sniper and took his rifle. Berry was detailed to take the Japanese rifle to the beach and trade it for canned fruit, baking powder, and flour. We had a couple of Southern boys who could cook and bake, and from that day on, in between air raids, we had apple or peach turnovers.

On September 27 we counted 53 enemy aircraft in the sky over us. The next day we counted 28 bombers in formation. These raids continued for the rest of the month and for the better part of October. On the seventh of October we moved west toward the Matanikau River area. My machine gun platoon was assigned the mission of setting up on high ground to lend overhead fire across the Matanikau. We set up on the forward slope, just over the crest of a hill, which was the only commanding terrain east of the river. We could even see across the channel to Tulagi and Savo Islands.

I was scanning the far hills when everyone seemed to say "Look!" at the same time. We spotted seven or eight Japs making their way across some open ground. A reconnaissance patrol. They were on hills to the rear of our forces. I guessed the distance to be about 2,000 yards. The belt of ammo was loaded with tracer and ball ammunition with every third round being a tracer. I opened up, the rounds plowed in and around the Japs, and all hit the deck about the same time. I knew that with that belt of 180-grain rounds that we had, I was in at the estimated distance, and the beaten zone at 2,000 yards would be about 55 yards long and about 4 yards wide. With the quick search and traverse, the dispersion was adequate to handle that group. I had no sooner ceased fire when some of our senior officers arrived. One was Col. Amor LeRoy Sims, our 7th Marines commander. They couldn't get over how fast my machine gun was firing. I explained how Captain Mahoney had originally started the bolt drilling and spring concept and how myself and Sergeant Agee had worked on the guns. They were really impressed. My guns were becoming famous throughout the division.

This three-day operation cost the Japanese one thousand dead. On the tenth, with all the other units making their way back to the perimeter, we still hadn't received orders to move out. Major Mahoney came looking for me. He had a new Johnson rifle, which was quite an oddity. All our rifles were the old 1903 bolt-action Springfields. He wanted to give me the rifle, but I talked him into keeping it. He sat down and we gabbed about events. His eyes widened with that look I'd come to know when he had one of his new ideas.

"Pistol Pete has been really giving Henderson Field a going over."

"I know. Our planes can't catch him before they wheel it back inside that mountain, and our artillery can't reach him."

"Listen, Mitch. I have a plan for knocking out Pistol Pete."

"Oh no."

"Yeah. I have an empty Coca-Cola case, and it's got twenty-four little spaces that are just perfect for hand grenades to fit into. I'm going to insert grenades into each space with the pins pulled, the space holds the spoons in. I've arranged with a dive bomber pilot at Henderson to fly me in low, then glide over Pistol Pete's position when they wheel that 150mm out to fire. Then I'm going to personally drop the twenty-four grenades on his noggin."

I started laughing, then pleading with him not to do it. "It's too risky! Besides, I don't think grenades will do much to a 150mm piece. It'll just kill some personnel." I kept laughing and telling him not to do it, but Mahoney was all fired up on his plan as he always was on any project he started.

On October 13 the 164th Army Infantry landed to reinforce our lines. They were greeted with one hot reception. Betty bombers and Zero fighters plastered the beach. Henderson Field was pounded, and one of the aviation fuel dumps exploded with six thousand gallons of precious fuel going up. Another wave of bombers came over, and many of our planes were caught trying to refuel. Then Pistol Pete, the giant Jap artillery piece, opened up from somewhere west of the Matanikau River. The artillery fire continued all day and night. That night the army units were shuffled into the line and Washing Machine Charlie dropped his usual parachute flares. The greenish blue light seemed to be a signal for naval gunfire. This was the biggest stuff I ever had thrown at me. It had to be battleships. These were fourteen-inch shells landing. Huge trees were being cut apart and flying through the air like toothpicks. The shells hit some gasoline dumps, and the island shook like an earthquake was breaking it apart. The crazy Marines around me were shouting out wisecracks throughout the blasting. It was normal behavior for these Marines, but anyone who didn't understand them would think the guys had gone totally nuts.

The mood was dark the next day when we discovered that forty-nine of our planes had been destroyed on the ground. They threw two more heavy air raids at us and more artillery. It was clear that the Japs were trying to knock us out. Pistol Pete lobbed his big shells in all day. That night their ships were back and gave us another shellacking. They fired nearly fifteen hundred more rounds at our positions. We knew this meant only one thing. A ground attack was imminent, either from the thousands of fresh enemy troops that had landed earlier or from an invasion by sea. It looked bad.

I didn't think it could get worse, and then it did. The next day was even more bleak as we watched Japanese warships bring transports into the channel in bright daylight and calmly unload their troops and supplies off Tassafaronga Point. Word came down that old gunny sergeant Lew Diamond had one of his 81mm mortars down on the beach lobbing shells at the enemy out in the channel. Their planes were all over the skies as if they had already taken over Henderson Field and the fighter airstrip. We could see five enemy transports and eleven escorting warships out in the channel.

That afternoon I was ordered to the battalion command

post. I was given my allotment of ammunition and rations for my platoon. I was advised to use it sparingly as this was it. Lt. McC. Pate was visiting the area. He would later become the twenty-first commandant of the Marine Corps. He said there was no more ammo available and no more chow. After my men picked up our last supplies we got more bad news. Word had been received that Vice Admiral Robert L. Ghormley, commander of the South Pacific Area, had proclaimed that due to the extensive damage suffered on our airstrips and the fact that our ships could not come in with additional men and supplies, that the 1st Marine Division would have to fight it out alone as there was no other way. Later we heard that Admiral Ghormley had been relieved and that the aggressive Vice Admiral William "Bull" Halsey had taken his place. A cheer went up along the lines when it was reported that Halsey's message was, "By God, if the Marines can stay, the Navy will stay." It lifted the spirits of the men.

Days went by and the air raids continued. More and more men were stricken with malaria, but most of them would not leave the lines. We bundled each victim up in anything we had when the chills came, and each Marine would sweat it out until it hit again. Then I caught malaria, too. It hit so hard that I couldn't move any part of my body except my eyes. I could only look down, if I moved them up toward my forehead the pain was terrible. If I looked up fast it felt as though my eyeballs had pressed against a sharp blade. I was going through a bad spell when an air raid came over us. I couldn't move. I laid out and tried to keep from moving my eyes up as bombs began to land around us. One of my men came and sat beside me.

"Get into a foxhole, Marine," I ordered with the strongest voice I could muster. It was a Marine named Wilson B. Faust. He ignored me and began to pray for us. I could hear a string of Jap bombs whistling down on us and since my head was flat on the ground, I could tell by each explosion that we were right in the bomb pattern. The explosions were getting closer. Wilson kept praying. A bomb landed just to our right and I knew the next one would be a direct hit on Faust and me. He continued praying out loud and the next bomb dropped into a soggy part of the jungle a few yards away from us. Mud covered both of us as the bomb created a huge crater. I looked up at Faust. "We were saved by your fervent prayer, Faust." He nodded and I asked him to join me in reciting the 121st Psalm together. We did and I felt close to the Lord. I felt that peace that passes understanding.

On October 23, our 2d Battalion, 7th Marines was ordered to move toward the Matanikau River again. One heavy water-cooled machine gun platoon was assigned to a rifle company for support. I was still with Fox Company. On the twenty-fourth, a large body of Japanese troops was observed making its way east toward our perimeter. Colonel Hanneken had given each company commander final orders to stop the enemy at all costs to prevent him from taking our precious airfields. We knew that if Henderson Field and the fighter strip fell to the Japs, the battle for Guadalcanal was lost. Our Easy Company would be facing south and would occupy the portion of the ridgeline farthest west, tying in with the 3d Battalion's exposed left flank. George Company would take up positions tying in with Easy and Fox companies. The positions comprised a very strange line as there were ridges, grassy knolls, dense jungle growth, and very steep slopes bordering on cliffs. Our job as heavy machine gun platoon would be to find the best terrain for a final protective line with interlocking bands of grazing fire, which in this instance was out of the question.

From the time we departed our area before dawn that day near Henderson Field, we were under constant observation by a Jap spotter. Our passage through the dense jungle, onto spiny ridges, back down into thick jungle, then up again to the next ridge was hard on all of us, but it was also under consistent barrages of artillery and mortar fire. As a result of the route we had taken, it took all day. By the time we were able to reach our positions, it was night and pitch black. We trudged along under the weight of heavy water-cooled machine guns, ammunition, personal weapons, and packs, stumbling on tangled roots under an umbrella of tall rain forests. They were lush tropical trees that incessantly dripped rain. The ridge on top was kunai grass, but hard as concrete underneath. Nobody had the strength left to dig a foxhole. Before we were able to set up our guns, the drizzle turned into a heavy downpour.

We were bone weary, wet, cold, and miserable. Visibility was practically zero. I had been ordered to put the guns out front on a knoll. I talked it over with Lt. John Phillips and we agreed that I would take one section forward to that knoll the captain spoke of and he would take the other section of guns to the left and somewhat to the rear of my position. The front line made a big turn between us. I wasn't sure we had even reached the knoll, so I told my men to drop their equipment while I crawled forward with my pistol, praying that I didn't crawl into an ambush or booby trap. I crawled along the ground, groping my way forward until I felt the ridge dropping away on all sides, then returned to my men and told them to set up along the knoll. We immediately set up the .30-caliber water-cooled guns in the best possible spots. We ate chow, and periodically I'd crawl around to whisper their names to make sure someone was on watch.

I moved near the edge of the knoll and lay on my back to allow the rain to pelt me in the face to keep me awake. At about 0200, I stiffened with fear at the low, unmistakable mumbling sounds of Japanese troops. I woke up PFC "Smitty" Smith who was near me. We strained to hear something for a few minutes, then we heard it. *"Da-mah-reh [damare]."* It meant keep quiet; I had picked up some Japanese in China. *"You-kohnee nah-reh [yoko ni nare]."* I caught enough to hear "Lie down." I crawled around whispering the word to my men, telling them exactly where me and Smitty were so they wouldn't kill us by mistake. I crawled back to my listening post and my mind was racing. I had no idea how large a force was out in front of us, or precisely where they were. I knew we couldn't just wait, they might be preparing to charge our lines right now. We couldn't open fire with the guns, it would be suicide to give away the machine gun positions.

I resolved to get it over with right now. I wasn't sure I was doing the right thing, but I knew I had to do something. I pulled the pin on a grenade and held the spoon for a moment before pitching the grenade over the slope where we had heard the noises. As soon as my men heard that click the grenade made when the spoon was released, they did the same thing and a cascade of grenades started exploding below us. Anguished screams mingled with more explosions from the bottom of the slope. Smitty and I were pulling the pins and throwing grenades as fast as we could. Then silence engulfed the knoll and the jungle below and it was over. The tension, fear, and the galling discomfort kept most of us awake all night.

At first light we started cutting foxholes into the ridge. For some reason most of us had dropped our entrenching tools and we had to dig with our bayonets. Several men wandered over from George Company to complain about the noise during the night.

"What are you guys, trigger happy?" a Marine chided. "Are your men a bunch of dumb rookies?"

My men were ready for a fight anyway and this looked like a good place to start it. "Moose" Stansberry and "Big Stoop" Gaston were ready to tear the guy apart. He'll never know how lucky he was to make it out of our position alive. Smitty and I went down the slope and found two dead Japs and pools of blood. At the edge of the jungle, where they apparently had been carried by other soldiers, were fifteen more bodies. The growling and fussing didn't stop until Major Conoley came up the reverse slope from the forward battalion command post to investigate the disturbance. When I explained the matter to Major Conoley, he nodded judiciously and said, "Mitch, you better get your men some more grenades." I felt vindicated. I accompanied the major on a tour of our front lines. We both agreed that no one in their right mind would purposely set up a defense like this. We had no choice in the matter and simply had to make the best of it.

My machine gun position was out in front of both George Company and Fox Company with a little bit of every type of terrain imaginable. The only grazing fire I could produce would be by turning my guns around to the rear and firing to the crest behind me. Just a few yards below that crest was where Major Conoley had his forward command post. We both laughed when he said, "Don't forget, I'm back in that end zone, in the draw." We discussed the denseness of the jungle and steep slope leading into it just a few yards from my position on my left. That line ran back and then around to my left rear where the other section of my platoon was set up. In between my sections, the riflemen of Fox Company were deployed with their automatic rifles and light air-cooled machine guns. A worse line of defense couldn't have been dreamed up.

"This is a pretty bad defensive position, sir. It couldn't be much worse."

Major Conoley was a tall, athletic, powerful, lean, tough Marine. He and Colonel Hanneken were much the same and my idea of a real Marine officer. I had the greatest respect for both and would have gone anywhere with either one as I knew they were leaders and fighters. Major Conoley pointed down through the jungles and slopes and said, "Look, Mitch. There's hardly anything between us here and a straight shot right into Henderson Field. Even Chesty and the army units wouldn't be able to help or even be aware of an attack through here, they're too far south of Henderson Field." For the first time I realized that what looked like a ragged, seemingly impossible-to-defend piece of real estate was in fact absolutely critical if we were to hold Henderson Field, and holding the field meant holding Guadalcanal.

George Company was in a clump of trees about a hundred yards to my right rear. After Major Conoley left, I went over to see Bill Agee, he was in George Company. I found Bill sitting on the ground looking at an overlay. There was a guy standing on top of the skyline looking west through field glasses. Bill looked at me and back at the man standing in the open with the field glasses.

"Who's that, Bill?"

"Oh, that's the skipper," Bill replied in a discomforted tone.

"That's your captain?"

"Yeah."

"Knuckleheads like that my friend will get you killed. You can bet your boots some Jap scout is watching him and I'll bet he isn't standing on the skyline. Doesn't he know the enemy surely has his artillery registered on that hill?"

Bill nodded helplessly. "I know, I told him so, but he's the skipper."

After a few minutes visiting with Bill, I said, "So long, old friend, *fai fai la mu, Tofa!*" Bill and I had learned some of the Samoan language before shipping out to Guadalcanal. It meant "Take it easy, old friend." I returned to my position and grabbed up my canteen. I got a sip down when I heard the first faraway whistle of incoming artillery. I hit the deck with everyone else. I heard the impact and knew it was right where Bill Agee was. I knew that captain must have walked directly down the hill to where Agee and I were sitting. After the artillery fire lifted, I ran over to see Agee. It was a direct hit. My dear friend Bill Agee was dead, so was the captain and several other poor Marines. All victims of a foolish mistake by that captain. I loved Bill Agee and wanted desperately inside to just sit down and cry or get drunk enough to forget the world and the war for a while but none of that was possible. I swallowed the pain and tried to focus on my duty.

Throughout the daylight hours of October 25 we tended our weapons and waited with some apprehension for nightfall. All that day Japanese warships steamed down from Rabaul to shell our installations. Above us there were constant dogfights between Jap Zeros and our Marine Grumman Wildcats. Enemy bombers made their daily appearance and dropped their loads of bombs on Henderson Field and the surrounding area. At one point a loud shrieking sound caught my attention as something heavy was coming out of the sky. An enemy bomber had exploded in midair above us and one of its motors ripped deep into the earth in front of my position. The day was spent checking and rechecking rifles, pistols, machine guns, bayonets, K-bars, and ammunition.

I didn't feel like a storybook Marine. I guess none of us did. We would cheerfully have done without a battle, I suppose, but we were quietly confident that we'd acquit ourselves with honor like Marines. We considered ourselves the best machine gunners in the entire Corps. We were all in top physical and mental condition despite a general prevalence of malaria. All the constant training together in the Carolinas, Culebra, Cuba, and Samoa coupled with the fact that all my guns were equipped with our beloved "Mahoney system" gave us some added confidence. Everyone in the division knew of the work that Captain Mahoney had done with our machine guns and the assistance Bill Agee and I had given him to alter each gun.

I sat nervous and waiting and looking out at our ragged line of defense. To the front the ridge sloped gently down toward a draw covered over by six-foot-high patches of kunai grass. The enemy could easily crawl through it undetected. Beyond that draw, about 65 or 70 yards distance, the dense jungle began. To my left was the heavily overgrown gully. There, the steep cliff sides, some about 50 or 60 feet high, would make difficult climbing for an attacking force, but the tangled dense foliage would provide excellent concealment to the very edge of the ridge. Every Marine knew this was the nearest thing to an indefensible position to be found. The intervening presence of supporting riflemen would prevent us from backing up Fox Company, except for the guns that were placed to the most forward positions. The irregularity of the terrain nullified the possibility of grazing fire, greatly reducing the efficiency of the guns.

I took two of my gunners, Jonjock and Swanek, and crawled out in front of our lines with some wire and empty ration cans. We stretched the wire and tied empty, blackened ration cans on the wire, then put an empty cartridge case in each can that would rattle if a Jap foot happened upon it. We made our way back to our lines, then I requested some artillery and mortar fire but it was denied because the enemy was still in the jungle and the fire would do no good.

As darkness fell over the jungle on October 25, I knew the Japanese were definitely coming. My orders were to defend the ridge at any cost. I knew what that meant. I spoke with each machine-gun team and told each man that we would have 100 percent watch tonight. "Hold all machine gun fire until you actually see a Jap in front of you." The Marines already knew that, but they knew it was my job to remind them.

The first few hours went by with no sight of the enemy, then between 1900 and 2000 hours there was an exchange of artillery fire and we knew that signaled a coming attack. Most of the enemy shells landed somewhere behind the ridge, east of our battalion command post and in our 81mm mortar platoon area. Just before midnight our probing patrols reported a large enemy force moving toward Fox Company's position, our position. These were Colonel Oka's men, in strength somewhat less than a regiment, made up of remnants of the Ichiki Detachment and the Kawaguchi Brigade.

About 0200, in a silence so heavy that men who were placed many yards apart could actually hear each other breathing, I began to sense movement all along the front and deep in the jungle below us and to our left. We could hear the muffled clanking of equipment and periodically voices of Japanese squad leaders whispering orders. Small colored lights began flicking on and off throughout the jungle.

"Mitch," PFC Price whispered. I crawled over to his position. "Am I cracking up? What are all those fireflies?"

"You're not cracking up. Those lights are assembly signals for Jap squads," I said. I then crawled around warning my men what the lights were and telling them not to open fire. We were outnumbered and our muzzle flashes would give away our positions and we would be raked with fire and smothered with grenades. I crawled back to my own foxhole. Manning my number two gun was Cpl. Raymond "Big Stoop" Gaston and Pvt. Samuel "Muscles" Leiphart. Their gun was at the part of our line that bordered on the side where the jungle came up to meet the ridge.

"Mitch, there's rustling in the brush, real close," Big Stoop whispered.

"Hold your fire."

Nearby, Cpl. Richard "Moose" Stansberry had arranged several grenades in a neat row in front of him. He nervously rearranged them with one hand and gripped his Thompson submachine gun with the other. Everyone was straining to hear and see. The bushes rustled and the maddening voices continued their soft, sibilant muttering, but still nothing could be seen.

Then I sensed a dark figure near Gaston's position. I grabbed a grenade, pulled the pin and held down the lever ready to throw it. Around me I could hear the others pulling pins as we had the night before. Suddenly the ration cans rattled and somebody let out a shriek and instantaneously the battle erupted. Grenades were exploding all over the nose of the ridge. Japanese rifles and machine guns fired blindly in the night and the first wave of enemy troops swarmed into our position from the jungle flanking Gaston's gun.

Stansberry was pulling the pins out of his grenades with his teeth and lobbing them down the slope into the jungle. Leiphart was skying them overhead like a baseball pitcher. Insanity engulfed the moment and men started cursing, growling, and screaming like banshees. Japanese voices shouted, "Banzai! Blood for the emperor!"

"Blood for Eleanor!" Stansberry responded spontaneously in a weird tribute to President Roosevelt's wife.

The battleground was lit by arching red patterns of machine gun tracer fire, exploding grenades, and a barrage of Capt. Louis Ditta's 60mm mortar rounds landing no more than thirty yards in front of the ridge. It was a confusing maelstrom, dark shapes crawling everywhere, struggling men falling on each other with bayonets, swords, and all of it filled with violent oaths. After the first American grenades exploded, the wave of Japanese crowding onto the knoll thickened. PFC Charles H. Lock was killed from a burst of enemy machine gun fire.

I screamed, "Fire! Machine guns! Fire!" The guns opened up and with them all the rifles and Tommy guns. Flashing lights came from explosions and I'm not sure what else. I saw a fierce struggle taking place for the number two gun. Several Japanese soldiers were racing toward Leiphart, who was kneeling, apparently already hit. I managed to shoot two of them while the third lowered his bayonet and lunged.

Leiphart was the smallest man in the platoon, weighing barely 125 pounds. The Japanese soldier ran him through, the force of the thrust lifting him high in the air. I took careful aim and shot Leiphart's killer. Gaston was flat on his back, scrambling away from a Japanese officer who was hacking at him with a two-handed samurai sword and grunting out loud with each hack. Gaston tried desperately to block the sword with a Springfield rifle he had picked up off the ground, apparently Leiphart's. One of his legs was badly cut from the blows. The rifle splintered under the sharp force of the sword. The Japanese officer raised his sword for the killing thrust, and Gaston, with a life-or-death burst of maniac strength, snapped his good leg up and caught the Jap under the chin with the heel of his boondocker. It was such a violent blow that it broke the enemy officer's neck with a loud snap. The rest of the attacking Japanese ran past Gaston's gun and spread out, concentrating their fire on the left flank gun manned by Cpl. John Grant, PFC Sam H. Scott, and Willis A. Hinson. Within minutes Scott was killed and Hinson was wounded in the head. Then Joseph A. Pawlowski was killed. Stansberry, who had been near me, was hit in the shoulder, but the last time I saw him he was still firing his Tommy gun with ferocity and shouting, "Charge! Charge! Blood for Eleanor!"

To my right, Corporal Pettyjohn cried out in anguish, "My gun's jammed!" I was too busy to answer his call for help. At the center we were beating back the seemingly endless wall of Japanese coming up the gentle slope at the front of our position. About seventy-five enemy soldiers crashed through the platoon, most of them on the left flank, but the main force of the attack had already begun to ebb. The ridge was crowded with men fighting. I suddenly put up my left hand just as an enemy soldier lunged at me with a fixed bayonet. He must have been off balance, the point of the bayonet hit between my little finger and the ring finger just enough to let me parry it off. As the enemy soldier went by me with his bayonet lunge he fell dead to the ground. I didn't know who to thank other than the Lord and there wasn't time for anything else.

We continued to fire as the enemy melted back down the

slope. Before the Japs were out of sight, navy corpsmen began snaking forward to treat the wounded. At Pettyjohn's gun, James "Knobby" McNabb and Mitchell F. "Pat" Swanek were badly wounded and had to be moved off the line. Stansberry was still around and didn't want to leave. I crawled over to Pettyjohn's gun and grabbed him.

"What's wrong with it?"

"Ruptured cartridge. It won't budge!"

"Move over," I said. I began to fumble with stiff fingers and broke a nail completely off. It hurt but the tension was way beyond noticing broken fingernails. I found a combination tool in the spare parts kit under the tripod and somehow pried the slug out. I also changed the damaged belt feed pawl while Pettyjohn and Faust covered me. We were taking fire from enemy soldiers who had shinnied to the tops of tall hardwood trees growing up from the jungle between the machine gun platoon and Fox Company. They were able to shoot down on us in two directions. Men in foxholes on the crest were especially vulnerable. Bob G. Jonjock and John W. Price were wounded and helped back to relative safety by corpsmen.

I was getting ready to feed a new belt of ammunition into Pettyjohn's gun, but my left hand felt slippery so I rubbed it in the dirt under the tripod, then reached up to hold the belt again. A sharp vibration and a jab of hot pain shot through my hand. I fell back flapping my arm and angry enough to kick the gun over the slope. Then I saw that the gun had been wrecked by Japanese machine gun fire.

At that instant a second assault wave came washing over our positions. Oliver Hinkley and William R. Dudley were wounded. Hinson over on the left gun continued to fire until all of his supporting riflemen were killed or wounded. He put his machine gun out of action and withdrew down around the hill to George Company. That section had been hit hard with mortars and grenades. The men on the spur had been literally blasted off, including Lieutenant Phillips, Bill Payne, and John Grant.

I glanced to my left rear at the Fox Company area, and men were pulling out and disappearing over the crest. I picked up a Springfield rifle and fired a shot at them and screamed for them to hold the line. The Japanese swarmed up that seventy-foot cliff in great numbers, armed with three heavy and six light machine guns, a number of captured Tommy guns, and several knee mortars. I knew that Major Conoley and his small command post were just over that crest. Here was the only grazing fire I could deliver with my machine guns. I quickly found Gaston's gun and swung it around toward our own lines. There was nothing between my gun and the crest except Japanese soldiers. I fired a full belt of ammunition into the backs of crouching Japanese troops who were preparing to go over the crest. The peculiar sound of our fast-firing "Mahoney" guns combined with Marine tracer fire ricocheting over the heads of Major Conoley's command post caused the word to spread that the Japs had captured one of Paige's fast-firing machine guns.

I continued to trigger bursts until the barrel began to steam. In front of me was a large pile of dead bodies. I ran around the ridge from gun to gun trying to keep each gun firing, but at each emplacement I found only dead Marine gunners. I knew then that I must be all alone. As I ran back and forth, I bumped into enemy soldiers who seemed to be dashing about aimlessly in the dark. It was obvious that they didn't know that they were almost in complete possession of the knoll. I found a Springfield and fired it. Then somehow, I stumbled over into the right flank into George Company. I found two men whom I knew named Kelly and Totman. They had a water-cooled machine gun. I told them I needed their gun and grabbed it and took off with it. They jumped up and I yelled, "Follow me!" I ordered several riflemen to fix bayonets and follow us to form a skirmish line back across the ridge. It was near dawn, and I knew that if the Japs saw how much progress they had made, they'd surely send a third wave up the slope to solidify their hold on the knoll.

On the way back to the knoll, I saw the movement of Japanese troops on the ridge just above Major Conoley's position, the exact position that I had raked with grazing fire earlier. I fired Kelly's and Totman's full belt of 250 rounds into that area and once again the rounds were ricocheting over Conoley's head, but they had no way of knowing that I was doing the firing. We advanced back across the ridge. Some of the Japanese began falling back. To my right I saw that several Japs were crawling awkwardly across the knoll with their rifles in the crooks of their arms. My heart froze as I realized they were crawling toward one of my guns, which was now out in the open and unmanned. I ran for the gun. From the gully area several Japanese guns spotted me and swiveled to rake me with fire. Their fire brought more fire as snipers in the trees tried to bring me down. Mortar shells began bursting around me as I ran to that gun. An enemy soldier with a Nambu machine gun saw me coming and jumped up to race me to the prize. I got there first and jumped into a hole behind the gun. The Japanese soldier dropped to the ground with his Nambu machine gun less than twenty-five yards away, point-blank range. He opened fire. I turned my machine gun on the enemy soldier only to realize it was not loaded. I scooped a partial belt of .30-caliber ammo out of the dirt, my fingers bleeding and slippery, and fumbled frantically trying to load the gun. I got the belt in and moved to pull back the bolt.

Suddenly an extraordinary sensation came over me. I tried desperately to reach forward to pull the bolt handle back to load the gun, but I felt as though I were in a vise. The Japanese machine gunner was blazing away at me, but something was keeping me from moving forward. As if some invisible force held me back. In spite of what I know should have been a life-and-death state of hopeless panic, I was completely relaxed and felt as though I were sitting peacefully in a park. I could feel a strange, warm impression between my chin and my Adam's apple, which I knew were bullets. The Japanese Nambu gunner finished his thirty-round magazine at the precise moment that I suddenly fell forward over the gun as if suddenly being released from some invisible hold. I pulled the bolt handle back and swung it at the enemy gunner. I killed him. For the rest of my life I would think about this moment. I never wanted to relate this experience to anyone because I did not ever want to have anyone question it. Jesus Christ and I know exactly what happened.

I found three more belts of ammunition and quickly fired them into the trees and all along the ridge. I sprayed the terrain with the remaining rounds, clearing everything in sight. It appeared that all of the Japanese fire was being directed at me since mine was the only automatic weapon firing from a forward position. The barrage of incoming fire was tearing up the nose of the ridge and made me feel as though the entire Japanese army was trying to kill me. George Company mortar fire laid in on the spur and kept the Japs from being able to move up and envelop my gun position from the rear. Other than the supporting mortar fire, I was still alone and running out of ammunition. I searched the ground around me but there was none to be found. At that moment three men from my platoon ran through the field of fire to bring me machine gun ammo. The first one to reach me fell just as he got to the gun, shot in the stomach. The second Marine was shot in the groin as he reached me. He fell forward wounded, knocking me away from the machine gun like an offensive guard throwing a block. Seconds later Bob Jonjock, who had been wounded earlier, rushed in from somewhere with more ammunition. He jumped down beside me and began to feed in a belt of .30-caliber ammo. I glanced at him just as a piece of flesh was shot away from his neck by an incoming bullet.

"Get back!" I yelled as I sprayed the area with machine gun fire.

"I'm staying with you!"

He was bleeding badly. I turned and yelled again, "Get the hell back, Jonjock!"

"No! I'm staying with you!"

I released the gun and punched him hard enough on the chin to bowl him over. "That's an order! You're gonna bleed to death! Get back!"

Jonjock took off. He made it back to relative safety without getting killed. Meanwhile, Major Conoley at the forward command post had rounded up a ragtag force of stretcher-bearers, wiremen, runners, cooks, and even mess boys who

had brought some hot food up to the front during the night
and stayed just in case. These men, numbering no more than
twenty-four, mounted a counterattack up over the crest line
to retake the Fox Company spur. The same crest line that I
had fired five hundred rounds at. There, they found the Japanese machine guns and several Fox Company weapons, including three light machine guns, all in good working order.
That counterattack found ninety-eight dead on the spur by
actual count.

That was about 0530 or so. Dawn was already breaking. I
was able to watch the progress of that Marine charge because
I was directly out in front. I saw a lot of enemy soldiers
scrambling back into the jungle, but I couldn't fire in that direction. Just watching those crazy Marines make that charge
filled me with an inspiration to join in.

"Stand by to charge!" I screamed at men from George
Company who had fixed bayonets. I yelled out in Japanese,
"Tate!—tah-the, tah-the! Isoge!—ee-soh-geh, ee-soh-geh!"
It meant, "Stand up, hurry!"

Immediately a large group of Japanese soldiers, about thirty
in all, popped up into view. I opened fire with the machine
gun and they peeled off like grass under a mower. I turned
and shouted to Marines nearby, "I'm going to charge over the
knoll and I want every one of you right behind me." I threw
the two remaining belts of ammunition over my shoulder,
unclamped the heavy machine gun from the tripod, and cra-
dled it in my arms. In the adrenaline rush I didn't really notice the eighty pounds of gun, and I wasn't even aware of the
red-hot water jacket of the gun. I fed one of the belts into the
gun and started forward, down the slope, scrambling to keep
my balance while spraying bullets back and forth. There were
still a number of enemy soldiers on the hillside in the tall
grass, pressed against the slope. They were caught by complete surprise and I cut them all down. A Japanese field-grade
officer had just expended the rounds in his revolver and was
reaching for his two-handed sword. He was no more than
four or five feet away from me when I ran into him head-on.
He exploded backward from the powerful .30-caliber rounds.

I could hear the Marines with me screaming out a rebel yell as they followed me over the rim of the knoll. They shrieked and catcalled like little boys imitating Marines. We sounded like a thousand men rather than the handful we actually were. With fixed bayonets, they followed me all the way across the draw to the end of the jungle, where so many long hours ago the Japanese attacks had started. There we found nothing left to shoot at. The battle was over. A strange quiet engulfed the jungle. A surrealistic stillness. If not for the dead strewn everywhere, the silence would have given no evidence of the hours of utter horror that had ended with the suddenness of death itself.

I slumped down, soaked with perspiration. Steam rose from the barrel of the heavy .30-caliber machine gun still resting in my arms. Capt. Louis Ditta, another wonderful officer who had joined the skirmish line for the charge, slapped me on the back and handed me his canteen. "Tremendous! Tremendous! Tremendous!" He kept repeating it as if unable to believe what had taken place. He looked down at his legs and my eyes followed his. Blood was soaking through his dungarees. He had a neat bullet hole in his right leg.

As I gathered up my backpack, I had a question in my mind and heart that I had to have an answer to. I walked over to the body of the Japanese Nambu machine gunner and shoved his body over the bank with my foot. The man who had shot a full load of thirty rounds at my head at point-blank range. Those rounds shaved my chin and throat at that exact moment when I could not move forward to pull back the bolt and load the machine gun, that moment when something held me like I was in an inconceivable, supernatural grip. I laid my pack down and crouched to look through the sights of the Nambu. I saw that there was absolutely no doubt. It was too incredible to understand, and I mumbled to myself, "Lord, he had me dead center. How could he miss me with thirty rounds, thirty rounds that should have gone right into my left ear?" My pinky finger was bleeding badly from parrying away the Jap bayonet. It was nearly severed. I reached over and grabbed my pack to try to find something to wrap my bleeding finger. A small Gideon Bible fell out of it, open on the ground. The book seemed to open, though I felt no wind. I looked down at it. Letters on one page stood out as if they were larger than all the other words in that small Bible. There was still very little light and those words seemed to be larger, almost lit up compared to everything around them. They looked to be an inch larger than the rest of the page. I stared for a few moments in awe. It was Proverbs 3:5–6. Then I read those words. "Trust in the Lord with all your heart and lean not on your own understanding, in all your ways acknowledge Him and He will direct your path." I picked up the Bible and my pack and found a spot to sit and think. My mom's last words to me when I joined the Corps rang out like a church bell, "Mitch, trust in the Lord with all your heart." I believe there is no doubt that this was a word from the Lord God Almighty. I told no one about the incident. I didn't want the guys to think I'd gone nuts. But it is true.

There were hundreds of enemy dead in the grass, on the ridge, in the draw, and at the edge of the jungle. Bloody and ripped bodies lay everywhere. Weapons and body parts were spread in every direction. I don't know if there was an order to do it, but almost by instinct we began to drag as many bodies as we could out of the sun and into the jungle. The sun would bloat them quickly and the stink would be unbearable. We buried as many as we could, then we blasted some of the ridge over them with explosives to try to cover them to prevent the smell that only a dead human can expel in heat. Captain Ditta sent a corpsman over to take care of me. He smeared my whole left arm with a tube of salve of some kind. He cleaned off the bayonet gash, it was filled with dirt, and the bullet nicks on my hands had also filled with dirt and coagulated blood during the fight. He stuck a patch on my back, just below the shoulder blade. In 1955, I had a three-quarter-inch-long piece of steel removed from that spot. The corpsman gave me a last once-over before moving on to other wounded Marines. "You know," he said, "you have some pretty neat creases in your helmet."

"Yeah. Thank God, made in America."

A little later Major Conoley came over to me. We walked

around the area as we had before the battle. We inspected the Japanese bodies on the ridge just above his position.

"Why, hell, look how many of these guys have bullet holes in the back of their heads, their backs, sides, and even through the soles of their feet."

I could only stare, knowing how some of those holes got there. I felt overjoyed that I had done my job. I felt good inside. The next day Chesty Puller came over to see me. He sat down beside me after we shook hands and told me about the attack they had had down at the airport on the night of the twenty-fourth. He said that he had just seen Colonel Hanneken at the division command post before coming to see me. He had just read the report that Colonel Hanneken was preparing, recommending me for a medal. "I'm preparing a report for one of my sergeants, recommending him for a medal. He's a machine gunner, too."

"That's wonderful, sir. What's his name? I might know him."

"His name is Basilone."

"Johnny Basilone?"

"Yes."

I told him that I knew Johnny well. He had served in the Philippines, too. I called him "Doggie Manila John" because he had been in the army before joining the Corps. He called me "Cavite Mitch." Chesty Puller was admired by all enlisted men, and while we were sitting on the ground, PFC Price came up to us, very anxious to meet the great jungle fighter Chesty Puller. Price had been shot through the face the night before and bled so much that it was difficult to determine how serious the wound was. He was bandaged up now and paid no attention to it. Chesty shook hands with him and offered Price some pipe tobacco. A very kind gesture since it was the only thing he had at the time. Price refused because he didn't have a pipe but he never forgot that moment with Chesty Puller. Two years later PFC John W. Price was killed in action.

Now that the enemy's back had been broken, at least temporarily, General Vandegrift believed this was an opportune time to continue the aborted attack of October 7. He believed that we could clean out the enemy from the Kukumbona area. That would prevent the big Jap gun, Pistol Pete, from disrupting Henderson Field. On the first of November the 5th Marines, 2d and 3d Battalions of the 7th Marines, and Whaling's Scout-Sniper Detachment were given the job. With an improved situation at sea and in the air, things were looking better. However, a last-minute situation developed. Data was pieced together from our intelligence sections, the coast-watchers, and reconnaissance flights, and it revealed some alarming information. The enemy was preparing to land a large group of soldiers on the east side of the perimeter, which was the opposite side of Henderson Field.

Col. "Red Mike" Edson's 5th Marines had started their advance west when we in Colonel Hanneken's 2d Battalion, 7th Marines were ordered to prepare to leave for the eastern side of the perimeter. We picked up weapons and equipment and made a forced march to the Metapona River. We had the heavy guns on machine gun carts, which we dragged along or carried across rivers. When we got to the beach road, we boarded trucks. This was a real treat for guys packing heavy machine guns. The trucks dropped us off at either the Ilu or the Tenaru River. We weren't sure because some of the maps our officers had were ancient Australian cartography. We ended up on the west bank of the river. Scuttlebutt had it that Bull Halsey had notified General Vandegrift that Koli Point was the current enemy target.

The next morning we started out on a forced march across rivers and along trails near the beach. Word came back to take a break and we fell out. Someone yelled, "Watch out!" At that moment a huge coconut log dropped out of a tree. One of the men had tripped a vine releasing the ingenious and lethal Japanese booby trap. Captain Foley and G.Sgt. Dusty Rhodes were instantly killed. Another captain and three enlisted men were injured. It tore your heart out to see Marines die like that, but there was no time to mourn, so you got your mind off it and moved on to a job that had to be done at any cost.

It was almost nightfall when we arrived at our destination

along the beach east of the Metapona River, about thirteen miles from the perimeter. Colonel Hanneken ordered the battalion to deploy from the mouth of the river to a spot about two thousand yards to the east, away from Henderson Field. Some units were scattered under the shelter of the trees that bordered the beach. Others were actually dug in, in the sand between the water's edge and the berm or edge of the jungle, in position to fire on any landing from the sea. We were in no position to do much if the enemy landed at any other point along the beach. We left our machine gun carts in the jungle, and I was ordered to set up my machine guns on the beach. My platoon was a bunch of patched-up Marines and some replacements.

Our position didn't look too bad. The beach curved in then out about a mile or so east of us, which would allow us to lay down grazing fire all the way around the curve. I told the squad leaders to have the guns dug-in in such a way that if we had to fire up the beach, we could fire all the guns in echelon. We dug in deep enough so that only the guns' barrels were above the sand, with the tripods practically floating. Each gun could search, and the first gun could traverse if necessary as it was a "free gun." We used seaweed and other debris along the beach as camouflage. Soon we were all sitting in water, eating our C rations, and watching. The rain started coming down hard. Our visibility was limited in the downpour. At about 2230 my heart popped up in my throat at the sight of ghostly looking ships slowly coming into view, as if creeping up on us silently. This was the famous Tokyo Express. We started counting them as they emerged from the black sea. One. Then two more. Finally six.

Suddenly we heard two Japanese voices, then I saw a very small light up the beach flashing on and off. We could hear the unloading of the ships and the first craft coming ashore with troops. Every gun was loaded and ready to fire at nearly point-blank range when the first group landed. The biggest weapons we had were my .30-caliber water-cooled machine guns. We were facing tons of steel and big naval guns. I wasn't sure if they could lower the big guns enough to fire on us, but

I sure didn't want to find out. It was a horrible thought knowing how much firepower they could bring to bear on us. I prayed that no one would accidentally trip a trigger. The first boat landed about three hundred yards up the beach. Others continued to land still farther up the beach. We could hear the sounds of heavy metal splashing and chattering Japanese, who obviously had no concern about Americans being near. We were deep inside enemy territory, which was becoming more evident with each bargeload of enemy troops. No one dared to even whisper as the enemy continued to land troops and supplies.

I sat wondering where Admiral Halsey and our fleet were. Where were our dive bombers and PT boats? These guys were sitting ducks. Something had gone terribly wrong. At about 0200 those ghostly looking ships started to fade away, back out to sea. They had completed their mission. Fifteen hundred troops of the 228th Infantry Regiment had landed right under our noses.

Colonel Hanneken's radio was out and the rain played havoc with our communications. Nothing was working. There was no way to relay information back to our perimeter. In sheer desperation two runners were sent back. They never made it. Both were killed by roving Japanese patrols. I whispered to my men to just be patient. I knew in my heart that being patient was the only choice we had anyway. Waiting for daylight was all that was left for us. I set us up so that the extreme right flank was open so that particular gun could fire into the jungle, up the beach, or out to sea. I got behind the next gun and placed a bayonet in the sand against the water jacket at a point where it could fire up the beach, just clearing the left shoulder of the gunner of the first gun. The gunner knew that no matter what, he couldn't swing his machine gun past that bayonet without hitting our own men. I did the same thing with each of the other guns so that in fact we would be in echelon with each gun being able to fire just to the left of the gun in front of it. Everybody knew the plan and the limitations of the traverse for each gun. I knew these

Marines were professionals, none better, and they each understood their job.

We sat waiting for daybreak, nervous but steady and knowing that there was a very good chance that the Japanese might come down that beach right at us. The first rays of sun brought relief but just as quickly brought evidence of the coming danger. Enemy troops started to wander down onto the beach a few hundred yards away. Straggling at first, walking with their weapons at their sides or over their shoulders, down to the water's edge. We watched in a state of disbelief as slowly but surely they formed ranks in rows of four. It seemed implausible, but the Japanese appeared to be preparing for a march down the beach in formation, long columns of four. We could hardly believe our eyes; this was a machine gunner's dream. We waited anxiously, crouching as low into the surf and sand as humanly possible.

Each second felt like an hour as we lay in wait. Then suddenly a single Springfield rifle went off some distance down the beach behind us, over our heads. Some nervous finger just couldn't wait. The enemy started to break ranks. I screamed, "Open fire!" Every machine gun opened up and not a single Japanese soldier made it back into the cover of the jungle. Our fire was devastating, like a giant scythe cutting down rows of wheat. It was textbook grazing fire on troops in formation. Each machine gun firing at 1,300 rounds per minute was set up for the maximum amount of fire to be delivered into a section of the standing Japanese. All four guns spit out a belt of 250 rounds each. No waste of time or ammunition, it was as though each of the thousand rounds fired in those few seconds hit their mark.

There were piles of dead men on the beach and in the surf. I believe that we killed more enemy troops with our machine guns than any machine gun platoon in Marine Corps history. We were in awe of what had taken place, but there was barely a moment to contemplate it as immediately the sound of a flying boxcar roared through the trees behind us. Then huge explosions shook the earth. We could see the handle and wheels of one of our machine gun carts sailing up through the trees. Then mortar fire started to drop all around us. Word came up the line that the battalion was pulling back immediately. As Captain Rea came running up to give us instructions, a mortar round exploded near him. He was blown into the air and suffered a serious head wound.

We moved back into the brush and started a withdrawal back to the main perimeter. It was fire and move all the way. Our 81mm mortars opened up on the enemy, but it was the only supporting fire we had. Still no American planes or ships. The withdrawal didn't work as planned, but it got accomplished. Scouts reported that a large enemy force was trying to outflank us. We got word that a new line would be established on the west bank of the river behind us if we could manage to make it back to that point. Colonel Hanneken was still trying to contact the main perimeter around Henderson Field, whose personnel still had no idea we had even made contact with the enemy. In the afternoon of November 3, Colonel Hanneken's radio was repaired and we finally got word back to Henderson that we were in a serious fight.

When the first friendly aircraft appeared we were thrilled, then they dived on us with a strafing run. I waved my arms frantically as the rounds kicked sand up all around me. Frank Sawchuk was next to me, I saw Frank go down from the fire of our own planes. Some idiot was waving a captured Japanese flag, and one of my gunners ran at him and clobbered him and took the flag and stomped it into the sand. We figured the pilot must have seen that flag and figured we were Japs. The pilot evidently recognized us as Marines and stopped the strafing run. We heard that General Vandegrift had ordered Chesty Puller's battalion, 1/7, and the army's 164th Infantry to leave the perimeter and reinforce our battalion. The 2d and 3d Battalions of the 164th Infantry were making a forced march up the beach accompanied by some units of the 8th Marines. We would be getting air and naval gunfire support together with our artillery. We were to attack the enemy from east to west. Chesty's 1st Battalion would attack from west to east, and the 164th Infantry would attack from their inland positions, north toward the beach to drive the enemy into a small pocket at the beach.

We crossed back over the Nalimbiu River as the attack moved east to surround the Japanese forces. Our aircraft and artillery were really pounding them. We were operating near the beaches and the 1st Battalion from the west and the army from the north were making a sweeping movement to envelop the enemy. We were gradually driving them into a pocket. About the fifth or sixth of November we were held up by considerable firing just a short distance from my position. It was back in the jungle, we were in a swampy area. Colonel Hanneken came past me, paused, and asked, "What the hell is going on in there?"

"It seems strange that they're carrying army casualties down both sides of this swamp, sir."

"You're right."

"Colonel, those are eight-round clips they're firing!"

"I know," he said, and it was clear that he was thinking the same thing I was. Marines had the old Springfields, and those sure weren't Japanese rifles we were hearing. Those were American M-1s, .30-caliber Garand rifles used by our army. We stood silent and counted the rounds by individual weapon. Colonel Hanneken looked at me. "Can you sneak up that swamp and check this thing out?"

I immediately took off into the swamp as a few rounds went whistling through the trees where I had just left the colonel. I made my way up the small creek with just my head out of the water and soon came to where I thought the firing was coming from. I lay flat watching both sides of the creek. A head peeked up about twenty yards off to my right. About thirty yards away to my left, I saw movement in thick underbrush. It was an American helmet. The rifleman on my right raised for a better look, he was an American, too. All I could think to do was shout.

"Hey, you guys! Don't shoot! This is a U.S. Marine!"

Heads started to slowly pop up all around the area. The skirmish ended there, but tragically there had been casualties. I ran back to report to Colonel Hanneken. He turned and was off in an angry flash. That night that army unit was attached to our battalion.

The attack continued across the Metapona River and we were gradually bottling up the enemy. Scuttlebutt drifted through the ranks that Chesty Puller had been hit that day. He'd been wounded by a grenade. Shrapnel wounds in both legs, but he did not leave the lines until the next day. On the ninth and tenth we made a final push and killed most of the enemy, though a few escaped through a gap in the army line. The few that got away would find it a short relief, as we were now on the offensive. We headed back to the perimeter at Henderson Field on the eleventh. It had cost us 21 killed and 61 wounded. We learned from a pilot at Henderson Field that he had seen the carnage on the beach at Koli Point. He said there were so many dead that they were visible as a large clump of bodies even from the air. Japanese troops were trying to drag as many as possible back into the jungle when he flew over and strafed them.

We moved through the perimeter and were ordered to set up on Edson's Ridge, directly behind Henderson Field. The battle was not over. Enemy bombers appeared overhead and our ships, which had been unloading, started to pull out. This signaled that another big battle was imminent. There were about twenty bombers and forty Zero fighters in the air. They seemed to fill the sky above us. I was on the ground next to one of our guns just watching the show. Suddenly a Zero swooped down right on top of us. I jumped behind my machine gun and fired a full belt of ammunition as he ripped past us and started to climb. Gray and black smoke poured out of that Zero, leaving a trail through the sky until he crashed in the distant jungle. As the bombardment continued, another Zero came in low, straight at our position. Willingham, another one of my gunners, opened up on him. His fire was accurate. The Zero flamed into the jungle and exploded.

That night the Japanese fleet came in and blasted the airport and all the ridges around it, including Edson's Ridge where we were dug in. Being on the receiving end of naval gunfire is an all-consuming form of terror. Nothing in combat compared to it. I clung to the dirt with my fingernails beside Sgt. Bill Payne. Trees were uprooted and splintered into pieces, the earth quaked from the power. My face contorted as shells roared into Edson's Ridge like freight trains coming down out of the sky. The ground under us felt like Jell-O, it literally rolled with each crashing shell. Suddenly, with no hope or chance of reaction, Bill and I were lifted out of our holes and found ourselves flopping on the hard ground in a semi–state of consciousness. Somehow we survived and made it back into our foxholes, only to be lifted into the air again like two dolls thrown away by an angry child. Again we survived and crawled back into our foxholes and tried to cling to our sanity until the shelling finally ended.

When the all-clear signal was ultimately passed that morning, I sat on the edge of my foxhole shaking. I had a tradition of handing out cigarettes to those men near me when the all-clear signal was passed. I didn't smoke so I saved my little C-ration packs for the men who smoked. I heard Bill speaking and looked over at him.

"Boy, what a night! You know it was Friday the thirteenth?"

I found my pack and gave Bill a cigarette. We were both still shaking so bad that it was hard to hand it to him. Bill tried to light his cigarette but couldn't get the match to hold still. We started laughing loud and hard. His hands were trembling uncontrollably. Mine were, too. I pointed at a rock. "Try putting it on that rock to light it." He looked like he was about to start pulling his hair out. We started laughing even louder and the rest of the platoon thought we had cracked up. Bill finally got the thing lit, and just watching him smoke sort of settled me down.

The next day I went down to the airfield to see if I could locate Major Mahoney. All the talk was about the big sea battle off Savo Island. It was still going on somewhere around Guadalcanal. No one seemed to know where Major Mahoney was. I finally found a tech sergeant who had met the major when he brought his Coca-Cola box to the airfield. He was pretty closemouthed about it, and I could tell that something was wrong. I told him that the major and I had been close friends since China days. I finally convinced him that I was safe to talk to. He didn't even want to give me his name because he was afraid of getting mixed up in the ongoing investigation by a board of inquiry.

The tech sergeant started talking slow at first. He didn't really want to speak of it. He began by recalling the day that Major Mahoney and the pilot took off to get Pistol Pete. He watched the dive bomber slowly gliding over the purported position of Pistol Pete, just as Major Mahoney had planned for so long. Tracers shot up from the mountains. The plane was suddenly hit by ground fire. He and evidently others saw a body falling from the bomb rack to the jungle below. The pilot bailed out and parachuted to safety as his plane swerved and crashed into the channel. I felt the loss deep in my heart. The Marine Corps had lost another hero and I had lost another wonderful friend in Maj. Michael McGinnis Mahoney. Mr. Machine Gunner.

As time passed, the perimeter around Henderson Field became more quiet. The Japs had been driven back, though their bombers and ships would still throw a lot of steel at us every chance they had. More and more of their planes were getting knocked out of the air by our gallant little Cactus Air Force. Those fabulous Marine pilots were doing some legendary work in the skies over Guadalcanal. We would watch Col. Harold W. Bauer, Maj. Marion Carl, Capt. Joe Foss, Maj. Bob Galer, and Maj. John L. Smith in action above when we were not in action below. They would dive into formations of enemy planes and were always outnumbered ten or fifteen to one. They would buzz in and out and around, looping and diving and pressing the attack, doing anything to keep the enemy from hitting us on the ground. We actually watched Carl, Foss, Galer, and Smith get shot down and have to bail out of their burning planes. In one instance, Colonel Bauer was shot down over the water and was never seen again. The others would be rescued and jump into another plane to continue the fight. Bauer, Galer, Foss, and Smith were all awarded the Congressional Medal of Honor, and Carl was awarded the Navy Cross. Joe Foss became the ace of aces when he shot down his 27th enemy plane, beating Capt. Eddie Rickenbacker's 1918 record of 26 enemy planes shot down.

Rumors were spreading that all the Marines would be leaving the island as soon as the army took over. Finally, on December 9, 1942, the 5th Marines started to move down to the beach area to prepare to go aboard ship. We knew that we would be leaving soon. It was around that time when we got a batch of new lieutenants. Captain Farrell escorted our new lieutenant to our area. It was in the middle of a driving rainstorm when I introduced Lt. Tom Myers to all my men. We took a liking to him immediately. He was smart and told us he didn't want to change anything, he would just be doing a lot of listening. Captain Farrell in a very friendly manner had warned Lieutenant Myers that he was inheriting Major Mahoney's original "forty thieves."

A couple of days later our platoon was detailed to help unload an ammunition ship that had arrived for the army, in addition to other ships carrying chow and other necessary supplies. When we returned to our platoon area that night, it looked like a commissary. Each man during the day had carefully set aside any loose cans that had fallen out of broken crates. Every Marine hid the cans inside packs or dungarees or anyplace available. Those cans of fruit and other foods were delicacies we hadn't seen for a long time. It was a feast. We were sitting around smelling the bacon frying the next morning like it was perfume, and the smiles on our faces would have normally indicated that there was a beautiful woman nearby. We had not smelled breakfast cooking in so long, we had forgotten how wonderful just the aroma alone tasted. That's when Colonel Hanneken appeared and we knew that someone had reported the pilfering.

"Is everything all right, men?"

"Yes, sir!" we chimed in together and awaited our fate.

"Think I'll sit down here and have some breakfast with you Marines."

After breakfast, he left with no mention of the stolen goods. The men were most grateful, then I reminded them that Colonel Hanneken had been a sergeant before he was a colonel.

Each day we cleaned our machine guns, had gun drill, and helped Lt. Tom Myers get snapped in with us. We went on short patrols around the perimeter and continued to be harassed by Washing Machine Charlie at night. On the fifth of January, 1943, our 7th Marines went aboard the USS *Rachel Jackson,* and the 2d Battalion was on its way to Melbourne, Australia, to rejoin the 1st Marine Division.

A few days after our arrival, I had no sooner settled into my tent than I was commissioned a second lieutenant. I took over the platoon that I had been with since its inception in Cuba, and Tom Myers was moved up to the job of company reconnaissance officer. Our company commander was Capt. Bob Farrell. Replacements were arriving from the States, filling in the ranks of the dead and wounded. They fit right in with the old-timers and quickly picked up the spirit and enthusiasm engendered by our veterans as the best machine gunners in the Corps. We conducted gun drill every day until every man could detail strip and assemble the gun blindfolded and remedy any stoppage that might occur if the gun did not function properly. This was a ritual with our platoon.

Malaria struck me hard and I had to spend some time in an army hospital. One day I was helped out of bed by a nurse who led me to a relatively empty room where a young doctor was standing over some medical instruments. I was too weak to walk by myself. He sat me in a chair, stuffed my mouth with cotton, and stuck me with a needle more than once in the mouth area. "Now lean back," he said. I had little choice. I could sort of feel and hear scissors cutting inside my throat. Moments later something went plop into this metal pan I was holding. Blood splattered up into my face. I looked at the bloody mess in the pan and knew it had to be my tonsils. I was going to grab him by the "stacking swivel" and deck him, but I didn't have the strength. Somehow I made it back to my room and for days I felt like there was broken glass inside my throat.

Time passed easily in Australia. The people were the most hospitable people I have ever met in my entire life. I finally went back to my unit. We were tuning up and looking like Marines ready for a fight. One day the entire camp went on parade. A group of us was assembled on the parade ground waiting for instructions when Col. Chesty Puller came smartly over to us. We came to attention and snapped off salutes. Chesty grabbed me by the arm and said, "Sergeant Paige, you're senior here, oh yeah, now you're a looie." He twisted his jowls to one side and with a warm smile said, "You'll always be a sergeant to me, you know the backbone of the Corps is the noncommissioned officer." Then he turned to Johnny Basilone. "Sergeant Basilone, you will march next to Paige." He then lined up the rest of our group.

The band struck up a march and Chesty marched us up front and center. My spine tingled with pride being with such men. Chesty halted us directly in front of the division commander, General Vandegrift. My citation was read and then the name of the Congress and the President of the United States, and General Vandegrift placed the Congressional Medal of Honor around my neck. After that, I stepped over beside Col. Merritt "Red Mike" Edson and continued to stand at attention as Johnny Basilone's citation was read. The 1st Marine Division Band and all the troops passed in review as General Vandegrift, Colonel Edson, myself, and Johnny Basilone received the honors. All four with the Congressional Medal of Honor and all for Guadalcanal.

Johnny Basilone went back to the States to sell war bonds. Two years later he volunteered to go back into combat. He joined up with the 5th Marine Division. Johnny "Manila John" Basilone was killed in action along with four of his men in a mortar barrage a few minutes after hitting the beach on Iwo Jima, February 19, 1945.

While we were at Mount Martha, I started to develop a new type of hip-firing machine gun. Before I had it perfected, we got the word and the division was off to war again. We landed in New Guinea in September. Both the U.S. Army and the Australians had units fighting in New Guinea when we got there. Nothing changed for the Corps, we drilled and trained nonstop. When we arrived in New Guinea it was easier and more practical to pursue the work on my hip-firing machine gun. The terrain and availability of parts from the large army and air force maintenance shops gave me everything I needed to complete the job.

I used the basic .30-caliber M1919A4 light Browning machine gun, which weighed thirty-one pounds less the tripod, the pintle, the elevating and the traversing mechanism, none of which I needed. The heavy twenty-four-inch barrel could also be lightened by lathing away a portion of the center of the barrel as the entire barrel was covered by a jacket with holes in it to permit the air to circulate around the barrel itself, cooling it off in firing. I cut down the slide plates and drilled holes through the bolt as we had done with our water-cooled machine guns. I then welded sling swivels and used the handle from a Japanese 7.7mm light machine gun on the barrel jacket. I did all this work in a huge trailer at the airport. The armorer there had any parts I needed. When I had it ready to test, a group of Australians was nearby and wanted to see if it worked. I test-fired it and the Aussies immediately named it the "Blitzbanger." The name stuck.

On Christmas Eve, December 24, 1943, we were aboard the USS *Leedstown,* and the 7th Marines had been selected to lead the invasion of Cape Gloucester, New Britain Island. On Christmas Day we rendezvoused in the straits with the other ships. Early the next morning we headed ashore as our planes bombed and strafed the beaches and the jungles while our warships shelled and poured rocket fire into the island. Our planes laid down a thick smoke screen that served only to blind and confuse the landing craft coxswains. The first group finally swarmed ashore at 0745.

There was light resistance. We moved off the beach and into very dense jungle. I was carrying my Blitzbanger. I had taken an old pack and laid out a five-hundred-round belt of ammunition into it. I had the pack strapped to my chest so that the ammo could feed right into the machine gun, so I didn't need an A-gunner, and I could fire straight from the hip. Casualties were light the first two days. On the third day more than a company of Japanese attacked the 2d Battalion, 7th Marines perimeter. We killed 466 enemy. We lost 25 Marines killed and 75 wounded.

Several nights later we were really bogged down in the jungle. My machine gun platoon was on the extreme right flank of the battalion. It was raining hard; the jungle was thick and wet. Just at dusk we got word that an enemy force of undetermined strength had moved in on a small hill directly behind our frontline troops. Just behind our troops was a small gully that ran the entire length of our battalion line. The enemy had moved into position to fire into the backs of our troops as soon as the sun came up. The order was simple. They had to be wiped out before daylight, and that meant moving into a position to attack and doing it in pitch-black jungle.

The reserve rifle company had been called in and had deployed up that gully. However, they had not started their attack and time was running out. The night wore on and those riflemen were still huddled in that gully because it was pitch dark and extremely difficult to move around, let alone mount an attack. I don't know what time it was, but I knew it was getting real late when I received orders to move my machine gun platoon to the extreme left flank of the battalion and secure the high ground behind the company's left flank.

Each step was a nightmare. We struggled with the heavy machine guns, ammunition boxes, as many hand grenades as we could carry, and all of our other weapons. Every movement was made in pitch black, the kind of black night that only a jungle can produce. Our point gunner finally made contact with the riflemen in the gully. I managed to link up with their commander and he told me it was suicide to attack that hill at night and I agreed, but we had orders.

When we found out that they had refused to go up that hill with nearly three times as many men as we had, we almost had a war of our own. Big Stoop Gaston had been seriously wounded at Guadalcanal, and others who had been wounded and since returned to my platoon threatened to start shooting up that whole company. I managed to get some control of my men and quietly assembled the platoon. We decided that the best and only way to do the job was to use all the guns abreast by using a three-man load on each gun. One man behind each gun as the gunner, lifting the trail leg with his left hand with his right hand on the trigger. Another man to carry the left tripod leg and one to carry the right tripod leg. A box of 250 rounds was placed on each gun. I lined them up abreast together with the squad leaders and their Tommy guns all in close formation. I felt that this would give us a solid wall of fire going up the hill.

We started up, lumbering to stay abreast as the first dim shafts of sunlight brought us vision. We made it all the way to the crest, then all hell broke loose. Every one of the weapons was blazing away as we walked head-on into the Japs. A Thompson submachine gun cut loose with a full clip just over my right ear. It was Herbie Lawrence, riddling a Japanese sniper in a tree just above us; the Jap fell on top of me, nearly knocking me down. I kept firing. A Jap with a weapon in one hand and a bottle of sake in the other stood up and opened fire. Wilson B. Faust, the wonderful Christian Marine who had sat by me when I was flat on my back with malaria in Guadalcanal and prayed out loud as the bomb cleared our heads, was struck. Faust fired every round of the 250 bullets in his machine gun, then fell dead. Gaston quickly cut down the Jap who had killed Faust. Our machine guns fired until nothing was alive, not even mosquitoes lived through that hailstorm. That battle was over when the last round was fired from the belts of ammunition in every one of those machine guns.

We finished the job in New Guinea and New Britain. On the twenty-eighth of April, 1944, the army's 40th Infantry Division arrived in New Britain to relieve the 1st Marine Division. We left the island knowing that we had accomplished the mission that General MacArthur had assigned to us. The airfields in western New Britain were in American hands. The door to the Philippine Islands was ajar.

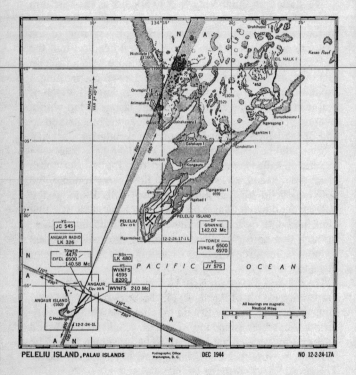

PELELIU ISLAND, PALAU ISLANDS   Hydrographic Office   DEC 1944   NO 12-2-24-17A
                                 Washington, D. C.

3

CPL. MELVIN CRUTHERS

April 11, 1944
To my wife—Mrs. Margaret Ann Cruthers

Darling,

First off I'll say that I love you even though this story has nothing to do with my personal feelings but is to acquaint you with the life your husband has led in the last months. Telling you straight from the shoulder, things that would never get past a censor. This is only for your own personal knowledge so don't show this to anyone if you don't want me court-martialed. The bearer of this letter is a very good friend of mine, a corporal who has been my squad leader ever since I joined the 5th Marines. He's from Pennsylvania, my home state, and his name is Corporal Perry Harman.

A lot has happened since the day I left you October 31, 1943 until December 25, 1943. And a lot more has happened from then until now. Up until Christmas my life was a series of moving around loading and unloading ships at all hours in all kinds of weather. On Christmas day we were squared away aboard ship and heading for my first blitz. It was the second blitz for some of the other fellows.

We left Milne Bay on a Liberty Ship, "Augustus Thomas," and our Christmas dinner consisted of cold canned turkey, hard candy, fresh bread, cabbage, potatoes (dehydrated) and gravy. We arrived at Oro Bay the next

125

day and spent two days at Oro Bay getting rearranged and
boarded an APD named the "Crosby." The morning of the
29th we landed on Cape Gloucester. We were greeted by
a dark and dense jungle that our bombers had blown to
hell. Occasionally you could hear the report of a rifle
from the fighting on the line. We spent the first day walking or maybe I should say running up to the front lines.

I was very sick on the first day. I almost crapped out on
the boys. I had heat exhaustion. We slept the first night in
a field of kunai grass up on a hill and it rained all night.
Cape Gloucester has one of the largest rainfalls in the
world as we soon found out. For over a month, the full 31
days, I was wet.

The next day, the 30th, I saw my first action. It was
called the battle of Johnson's Ridge, named in honor of
Lt. Johnson who was killed there. We just came out of
a patch of woods and bullets began whistling over our
heads. Our outfit was made up of a lot of green replacements like me, who had never seen action and about all
we did was get in the way of the older men.

The first action is sort of the most important action in a
fellow's life, for it wakes you up to the fact that you are
through playing war and are now fighting for more than
just patriotic reasons. You discover that you are fighting
for your life and the lives of the fellows around you. I'm
afraid I was not much use there because all I seemed to
do was to hug the ground, keeping out of the way of
whizzing bullets and looking with my mouth agape at the
things happening around me. I was talking with one fellow and all of a sudden, right before my eyes the fellow
had a bunch of gushing red holes in him from a Jap hand
grenade. They start helping, dragging and carrying dead
and wounded off of the line. Wounded young men who
smile and smoke a cigarette nervously and jokingly tell us
they feel sorry for us because we have to stay here and
fight while they are being evacuated. All of a sudden there
was this bloodcurdling scream, "Banzai!"

The Japs were making a bayonet charge which was

soon repelled. Things began to quiet down after that. The battle of Johnson's Ridge was over for us and it was over for Kermit Sheaffer, from Cleveland. We went all the way from boot camp together. He was killed. We had eight wounded and five killed. When we took over the Jap positions we counted 160 dead and never knew how many of them were wounded.

We then took over the second airstrip and set up a defense line. We stayed there until January 7, 1944. Anytime you're on line it is a time of waiting, working and standing nerve-wracking guard at night. There's more bugs, animals and birds around here than you could shake a stick at. We sleep in water and mud. A half dozen times a night you wake up to find a lizard or scorpion or snake or landcrab in your sack. (Bed.) Bugs on you all the time. Right then and there you have to decide who stays and who goes. Sometimes the critters win—temporarily. You have to find some means of winning your sack back. Believe me, a scorpion or snake does not make a very comfortable bed partner. Mosquitoes bother us continually with malaria. A new menace called the Typhus Bug took its toll.

January 7th we moved to our second positions above the airstrip. The most memorable thing that happened while there was a combat patrol under Captain Bacon. We went way up to the foot of the volcano. The trail was littered with Japanese dead. If you have not smelled a rotting body you can't imagine what it's like. It's the most sickening odor that I have ever run afoul of. It was on this patrol that I first actually stared into a dead Jap's face. It happened so suddenly that it gave me quite a shock. He was on the floor of a hut and a radio-man jerked the blanket off his face and he was staring straight at me. These Marines will do anything for souvenirs. When they shoot a Jap they practically have him frisked before he hits the ground. Japs are dirty animals and heathens. They very seldom bury their own dead. We were lucky on this patrol for we ran into no enemy opposition.

The 7th Marines had been fighting long and hard on Hill 660. Also known as Walt's Ridge. They were dropping back to our positions and we were to go and take their places. Gosh, you've never seen a more dirty, rugged, nervous and tired bunch of Marines in your life. They had been through hell and it showed. They mumbled, groaned and carried on something awful in their sleep. They even shot some of our own men that very night. I was glad when we moved out the next day.

We moved up on the other side of 660 and were lucky enough to get the beach defense. Then things were quiet for me until January 23rd. About our only hardship was the chow situation which had been pretty critical all the time and was to be critical for quite awhile longer.

January 23, 1944: On this day they decide to send a patrol over to Natoma Point and Dog Company Headquarters sends out a volunteer group of Bazooka men. So true to the Marines they came to the First Platoon and told me and a couple of others that we had just volunteered to be ammunition carriers for the Bazookas. Knowing that argument would avail me nothing, I decided to go. There was seven of us—Riley, Hunt, Rennick, Demery, Schmidt and Mitchell, (hey wait) and Cruthers. We were all under the idea that it would only be a one day patrol so we didn't even take a poncho or extra food. Well as soon as we hit the point all hell broke loose. We followed two General Sherman Tanks up the beach as they cleared a path for us with those big 75's. We were not supposed to be at the front like that but we were. I'd run and hit the deck more often than I did throughout my entire training in the Corps. Bullets were whining everywhere. We finally took over the point and then a Japanese Nambu machine gun and a 77mm gun started pot shooting at us from around the bay. I looked up at a big tree and a 77 shell hit it and threw shrapnel at three places around me. Somehow it started three fires. I was lying in a small bomb crater with a bunch of Bazooka ammunition, machine gun bullets were whizzing over my head but the fires were making it so hot for me I had to clear out. So I did. The battle subsided, then we made our selves busy carrying the wounded and the dead to the boats and placing them in neat rows. A good sight for civilian slackers to see. Riley and I carried a couple of them and boy was he mad.

We stayed on the point for a while with HQ and let the rest of the boys chase the Japs around the bay. The Japs opened up at us again with the 77 and we headed double time for holes again but they gave us the word that the Bazookas were wanted up forward to try and knock out the 77, so I ran to the front lines only to find out we were not needed. We ditched the bazookas immediately. We dug in for the night within spitting distance of the Japs using our hands, helmets and anything that would dig a foxhole. It was a long jittery night.

At dawn we were told that we had become attached to the 3rd Platoon as ammunition carriers for the machine guns to fill in for the casualties. Right off we commenced to push forward and we went about 100 or so yards and all hell broke loose again. The Jap machine guns, 77mm and now a 37mm gun. They were firing at us point blank. No more than fifty yards. They kept us pinned down for two hours. For 15 minutes they threw everything at us. They shot a 37mm canister at us. I was way in front of most of the fellows. Maybe that is the only reason I am here now. About ten feet to the left of me the shells were bursting and shrapnel was hitting all around me. I heard a couple of the fellows holler that they were hit behind me but I was in no position to offer aid. I was thinking of you, Margie, during the worst of it and I think that was all that kept me from losing my head. I thought to myself, "Oh boy! If Margie could see me now!" And started to chuckle out loud. Silly wasn't it? The Japs took a heavy toll on us that day and the Machine Guns I was with were credited with twenty Japs.

When we finally took over I found out that Riley was killed and Hunt was badly wounded. Five were left out of the seven. Every Marine was hit by shrapnel but some of us were not really hurt. I was hit several times but the shrapnel was spent and all it did was sting like the dickens. For the short time it lasted it was supposed to be one of the worst battles on the island. This one day patrol lasted twelve days. During these days we were shelled by a Jap sub, Jap mortars, snipers, strafed by our own planes, and bombed by Jap dive bombers. When we got back to Hill 660 we were a bunch of tired, hungry, worn out, shaggy, unclothed men.

After a couple of weeks we made landings all along the coastline on our way to Talasea. We capture and kill Japs on every beach head. The prisoners are starved sick and tired so we had no troubles with them. It took two weeks to get to Talasea. 90mm mortars took a toll on our Marines that day. Our mission now complete, we are taking it easy. The war is over for us as far as New Britain is concerned. Food was scarce and it had me worried but now we have food. Soon we will be leaving here for a liberty port. All the old men will be relieved. There will be vacancies open for rating and I expect to try hard to make at least Corporal. I've got many more tales to tell you, Margie, but they shall keep 'til I see you again. Maybe now you'll understand why I have not been able to write.

Your loving husband,
Pvt. Melvin F. Cruthers

P.S. The liberty port ended up being another island. That's another long story.

During the Depression my parents divorced and my mom raised four kids by running restaurants and truck stops. It was during Prohibition and my uncle was a bootlegger. I watched alcoholics steal the meager wages from their own families just for booze while allowing their kids to go hungry. I swore I'd never drink or smoke and I never have in my life. At sixteen my mother informed me that at the end of the current school year I would have to strike out on my own. I picked up subjects that would give me the additional credits to graduate from high school in my junior year. I graduated on June 4, 1941, and hitchhiked to Cleveland the next day. I owned a small handbag and had $1.50.

I was drafted on April 13, 1943. My cousin had been a Marine in WWI, and he was a very impressive man. I wanted to be a Marine. My roommate Lee Roarabaugh and I were drafted and called down to the Federal Building for our induction on the same day. We decided that we both wanted to join the United States Marine Corps. We were sorted out alphabetically and I didn't see him again until the end of the day. The army medics said that I was too small to be a Marine and should stay in the army. I was insistent so they sent me for a navy physical. The navy insisted that I stay in the navy because of my size and weight. I wanted to be a Marine and they finally forwarded me to the Marine Corps exam. They told me that I should go back to the army or navy. I insisted and finally was told that Marine inductees would be shipping out that evening at 7 P.M. at the rail terminal. When I finally saw Lee again, he had been told that he was too short for the Marines and ended up in the navy.

Boot camp was a very enlightening experience. I was the smallest man in my platoon and called the "feather merchant." The tallest man is called "high pockets." To relieve stress our DI would run us down to the beach and we would box. I boxed with a fellow named Ralph Perul from Cleveland. At the end of three rounds, Ralph looked like he had been severely wounded, covered with my blood. Another great buddy was Stephen Dosenczuk. We had a couple of very tough but good drill instructors. One was at Pearl Harbor when it was attacked. He and his wife lost their child in the bombing. He was one very bitter Marine. He was so filled with anger that the Corps refused him combat duty and made him a DI. He made sure we were tough enough to kill Japs.

I was supposed to go to radar training but the school was filled, so they sent me to radio school for twelve weeks. My bride to be, Margaret Smolenski, left Cleveland to be with me. Before she arrived, the base commander got orders to ship a number of Marines out of various schools and send them to combat training. I had a 90 percent record but it didn't matter, I was on my way to Camp Elliot. I was in a panic due to Margie arriving with no one to greet her and no place to live. My buddy Smith and me went AWOL to meet her and find a boardinghouse for her to stay in. We got away and back to Camp Elliot without being busted.

We had options for several areas of training, and since Smith decided on heavy machine guns, I did, too. They tried to discourage me because of my size, but I insisted that I could handle the weapon. I became an expert with heavy guns and in spite of my size managed to keep up. The heavy machine gun weighed forty-eight pounds and the tripod weighed fifty-two pounds.

When Margie left her job in Cleveland, her coworkers made her a wedding cake topped with a Marine doll and bride on top. It was a beautiful cake and the dolls were perfect, and she protected that thing all the way across the country like it was gold. My destination was pretty obvious and time to get married was running out. With much difficulty we got a license, which Margie had to pay for, and I got the Camp Elliot chaplain to marry us. Most of my buddies managed to get liberty and were there. That was August 5, 1943. A few weeks later I went aboard the USS *Mormachawk,* heading into combat. After we loaded aboard the ship and stowed our gear, we didn't pull out right away. Somebody said we were waiting for some special troops to board. When those special troops finally showed up, we discovered they were prisoners from the brig, and MPs marched them aboard still in their prison garb.

When we left San Diego the entire coast of California was blacked out. Lighting a cigarette at night could get you into serious trouble. The *Mormachawk* was a small freighter not made as a troop carrier, but it was pressed into service out of necessity. When we were ten miles out to sea, the prisoners were outfitted with uniforms and weapons. The first thing they had to do was clean and prepare their weapons for use.

They were mostly prisoners for minor infractions and a pretty good bunch of fellows that proved themselves later in combat. The *Mormachawk* was small and bounced over the huge ocean waves like a raft. The troops got seasick and it was awful. Half thought they were dying and the other half were afraid they weren't. It did not affect me or my appetite at all and I enjoyed the whole trip.

It took over a month to get to New Caledonia. That little ship zigzagged across the Pacific Ocean for that entire month. Each day we would stand in line for breakfast and then march to the back of this huge line of Marines that circled the entire ship to now get in line for lunch, then back in line for supper. It would take that many hours to reach the chow. We arrived in New Caledonia after dark and were shocked to see the whole coast lit up like Times Square. This was a war zone! We docked at Noumea and quickly found ourselves at Camp San Louis up in the mountains. There we joined the 1st Marine Division, Company D. I was privileged to join the finest bunch of Marines anyone would ever associate with.

New Caledonia was mountainous and beautiful. The training was hard and serious. It was all about living or dying. Our letters home were censored and by the time they reached our families they would be all cut up. You couldn't write anything that might reveal your location. But you could buy a fanfold postcard in Noumea to send home. No one explained that one to me.

One day a group of "volunteers" was trucked down to Noumea port to unload a ship of mortar ammunition. As the truck entered the city, I noticed this beautiful home with a lovely wall surrounding it. A line of servicemen stretched from the front door of the home to the gate in the wall and up the block. You would have thought it was the opening of a new Hollywood movie. It turned out to be a whorehouse, and the boys were standing in line for their special service. Scuttlebutt said that inside they claimed to have "Mary," the original "Bim Bam thank you Ma'am" girl.

Me and the other volunteers worked for thirty-six hours

straight unloading the ship into transport trucks. Somehow we were forgotten and no one bothered to relieve us. No food or drink either. One of the boys found a case of wine during the unloading and, being Marines, we naturally assumed it was our duty to make sure it wasn't poison or some sort of booby trap by the Japs. So we proceeded to get royally drunk. We were halfway through the case of wine when some observant jarhead discovered that we were getting plowed on special service wine for the Jewish chaplains. We stopped drinking immediately.

Dog Company was split up and its platoons were transferred to A, B, and C companies. My machine gun platoon became part of A 1/5. That is A Company, 1st Battalion, 5th Marine Regiment. It was the proudest regiment in the Marine Corps, filled with legendary Marines. We wore the French Fourragère, won by the regiment at Belleau Wood in France. Though these men were the finest warriors America had, there was a limit to how much any man could take. A few of the men were way past that time when they were supposed to be rotated back. Some had been fighting since Guadalcanal and were mentally worn out. They had been passed over for rotation and were ordered to stay with the regiment due to necessity. Some of these Marines were very bitter about it. Platoon Sergeant Antecki and his very best friend, company runner Private Ackerman, were two who should have been sent home. They both had a very defeatist attitude about surviving more combat.

We were loaded aboard ship and brought to Milne Bay, New Guinea, for more training. I was assigned to guard duty at a stockade. I was dutifully informed that after one shout to halt, I was to open fire. I was also informed that if a prisoner escaped on my shift, I would be given the honor of serving his sentence.

Soon we were aboard ship and transferred to Oro Bay in New Guinea. The army was camped out in tents by the beach where we were waiting to board ships for our assault on Cape Gloucester. This army boy was talking to his buddies, just blabbering away about something, then all of a sudden he stopped in midsentence. Just silent, like he had a stroke or something. I stared along with his buddies standing there waiting for him to finish his sentence, and when he didn't we all followed his bulging eyes to this cot next to him. There was the biggest snake I ever saw in my life, coiled up and staring back at him. His buddies grabbed up anything they could and clubbed and hacked the snake to death. When they stretched that thing out next to the tent it was fourteen feet long.

I was excited and nervous, as we were getting ready to disembark. We were ordered to leave everything in our seabags. Combat gear only. After that I stood waiting in line to board the APD *Crosby.* An APD is an old WWI destroyer that used to be a four-stacker, but in order to transport Marines, the navy removed two of the stacks to provide a place for Marines. They were usually lightly armed with three-inch guns and a couple of 37mm antiaircraft guns. They would drop Higgins landing craft over the side, and the Marines would go down nets to the Higgins boats, then hit the beach on those. We called them All Purpose Destroyers. There was a Red Cross tent set up right where we were boarding. Coffee and a doughnut for a dime. We were on our way into combat and nobody had a dime on them. I went over and asked for a cup of coffee. "That will be a dime," this lady replied.

"We don't have any money on us, ma'am. We're heading into combat."

"No dime, no coffee or doughnut, Marine."

They would not give a single Marine a cup of coffee or a doughnut if you couldn't pay, even though the ingredients came from our stores. We boarded the ship with a bad taste in our mouth for the Red Cross.

Cape Gloucester was a horrible place. I came down with heat prostration the first day. My buddies and salt tabs saved me. We force marched up to relieve Marines fighting on Johnson's Ridge. It was frantic and chaotic. I was very suddenly awakened to what war is. A young Marine was just above me on this ridge. I looked up at him and suddenly his eye was gone. It was just gone that quickly and replaced with a deep red hole. He fell dead beside me. I opened fire with the machine gun and kept firing until it was so hot that it continued to cook off rounds without my pulling the trigger. Our belts of ammo were 175 rounds. The only way I could stop the gun from continuing to fire was to twist the belt where the bullets entered the weapon. The bullets jammed the feed against the housing. It stopped the firing but it created a real problem getting that last bullet out of the chamber. I don't know just how long that battle went on because time means nothing during a battle; when it stops it might be nighttime and you have no idea when it turned dark. Marine gunners trained hard and we learned the nomenclature of every single piece on that machine gun. We didn't get out of machine gun school until we could tear a machine gun completely down and put it back together blindfolded. I quickly discovered just why that training was so important in the pitch-black nights on Cape Gloucester. We won the battle of Johnson's Ridge, though I was very little help.

We went on a patrol up into the mountains after that battle. The jungle was dense and scary enough without people trying to kill you, but that added to it. Though I had seen my first dead Marines, I really had not seen a dead Jap yet. Our patrol followed this small mountain trail, moving along carefully one step at a time. Finally we came upon a crude native hut. I moved up to the hut behind another Marine. The path was steep and I was about eye level with the floor of the hut. The Marine in front of me saw something on the floor of the hut through the open door and aimed his weapon at it. It was a mat of some kind covering something, so we prepared to shoot whatever was under it. He reached down, glancing at me, then ripped the cover off and flung it. The wide open brown eyes of a dead Jap were staring straight at me. I jumped a foot! It was a real jolt and it took a second or two for me to get my breath. The rest of the patrol was quiet and it was good to get back to the lines.

Later we moved to the base of a volcano that would rumble, shake, and act up every night around midnight like it had an alarm clock. If it erupted we were dead and knew it, there was no place to run. Mosquitoes came out at night in clouds so thick I couldn't see through them, and they bred malaria. These red ants swarmed over the men, and you had to burn them in the tail end when they bit into you because if you tried to pull one off, the tail would break away and the head of the ant stayed in your skin. Lizards were all over. They grew from five or six inches to five or six feet. We shot the big ones with M-1 rifles. Land crabs were everywhere, some the size of dinner plates. They had one big claw and they could really hurt you. I woke up with a scorpion looking at me on more than one occasion.

The birds were incredibly noisy and they would give away your position to the Japs. The fruit bats had a four-to-five-foot wingspan, and when they took off or landed at night it would scare the bejabbers out of you. The huge trees were another constant danger that normally I would have given no thought to. Many were two hundred feet tall. The soil was always wet, especially during the monsoon season. During storms these monster trees would fall without warning, landing with earth-shaking impact. We lost fifty Marines killed by falling trees. It is demoralizing to see your buddies killed in combat, but for me it hurt even more to see them die so needlessly in such accidents. Given the choice, every one of those fifty Marines would have chosen to die in combat. One night twenty-eight of us were trying to stay dry under a big tarp. Rainwater started rushing in over our boots and somebody suggested a move to a higher spot. All of us shuffled together over to the higher ground just a few feet away. The moment we reached the higher piece of mud, one of the giant trees came crashing through the jungle brush like a meteor hitting the earth. It crushed the exact spot where we had all been standing.

Practically all of us were plagued with jungle rot, fungus, typhus, ringworm, malaria, dysentery, and continual insect bites. When some of the men took off their shoes, the soles of their feet would come off with their socks. They couldn't get their boots back on. They had to wrap their feet with rags just to make it back for treatment. We took Atabrine for malaria. Salt tabs and Halogen tablets in your drinking water were a must.

The natives were amazing. They hated the Japs and loved us. Many Marines owed their lives to these rugged natives. They taught us how to survive in the jungle. There was this vine you could cut off at a joint and get a canteen cup full of cool, fresh water. And if you wanted more you just cut it off at the next joint in the vine. Sometimes we would run into a lime tree, or grapefruit, bananas, coconuts, papayas, and other edibles if you didn't mind fighting off the red ants to get to them. We used native guides sometimes. They showed us how to easily remove the hulls of the coconuts. Our machetes didn't do a very good job. A fallen coconut that was beginning to root in the ground produced a very tasty heart of palm in the new stems.

We didn't get mail all that often and when we did it was a big deal. One day I received a package that had been mostly destroyed in shipping. I got a wristwatch that was in pieces. One of the items was a Bull Durham bag full of colorful glass marbles from my mother. I could not believe that my mom would send her full-grown, married, and in-combat Marine Corps son a bag of kid's marbles. The guys got a good laugh out of it, but those colorful marbles turned out to be one of the best gifts we ever got. The natives would do anything for one of those marbles. My squad got a lot of mileage out of those little gems.

We got word to board trucks for a move up from guarding the airfield to relieve the men on Hill 660. Along the way we passed an army truck going the opposite way. On the back of the truck was my uncle, Ralph Figard. I hollered but he didn't hear me. I didn't even know he was in the service until that moment.

My lieutenant volunteered me, Ryan, a sergeant, and a couple of others to go along with B Company. We were to be a bazooka squad. I had never fired a bazooka and wasn't sure how it worked, but I could carry the ammo. We were told to leave everything behind. We were going to secure Natoma

Point and be back by noon. Ryan asked me what he thought he should take along, his pipe or the photo of his girlfriend. Since we would be right back he decided on his pipe. The first day on the point Ryan was killed. The second day the sergeant was killed. We dumped the bazooka and joined Company B's machine gun squad. We chased and killed Japs for sixteen days without any of our personal gear. Lack of food was a serious problem. Piper Cubs would attempt air drops of rations. The rations landed in the swamp and within moments sank out of sight. We shared everything we had between us, trying to keep the weakest man strong enough to go on.

By the time we got back, I was the only man still able to function. The rest had some pretty severe ailments. I was practically pulling guard duty by myself. I also had to go after our supplies and mail by myself since the others were unable. I told the fellows that I wanted to try and find my army uncle back at the airfield. They covered for me and I hiked back, hitching rides when I could, to the airfield where the army engineers were stationed. I found him just in time for chow. He introduced me to his buddies in the mess tent as the Marine nephew and they treated me like royalty. They moved me to the head of the line and piled up the food. It had been so long since I had eaten any significant amount of food that I couldn't make a dent in it. They understood, and when I left they took a pillowcase and filled it to the brim with food, candy, and cigarettes. Cigarettes like Lucky Strikes, Chesterfields, and Camels, brands the frontline boys never got to see. When I got back I was the most popular guy on Cape Gloucester.

I was soon returned to my own company and platoon. Jap planes would bomb and strafe us pretty regularly. I'd watch them come in and drop their bombs way off target, half the time they blew up the water out in the bay, then they would take off like scared jackrabbits before our boys would shoot 'em down. Word came down that we were moving out. We started making beach landings from small landing craft. Our goal was a place called Talasea about 125 miles from Cape

Gloucester. We would load up in the evening and travel all night, then make a beachhead in the morning and secure the area. It took a lot of beachheads before we reached Talasea. Finally we arrived at Talasea and got hit by heavy mortar fire, but we moved in on the area and began to secure it.

Talasea was a pretty nice place. There were hot springs, geysers, and our landing area had a nice home and a chapel. After a few days we started setting up home. I built myself a shelter that was off the ground to keep me dry and hired a native boy to help me out with this or that. I paid my number one boy with ration cigarettes and cookies. One day I decided to check out a trail. I was walking along when this cannibal stepped out beside me. He was big and ugly with a human bone stuck through his nose. A native policeman wearing a red cap and carrying a rifle stepped up behind him. The policeman was escorting him somewhere and with some effort explained that the big, ugly, black cannibal no longer ate people. It gave me the creeps to think I could have been this guy's breakfast.

Scuttlebutt had it that we were going to be sent to Australia for R&R. As rumors go this one went. We were sent to the Russell Islands and a little hunk of plantation mud called Pavuvu. From the ship, in the moonlight, it was a beautiful island. That was where the beauty ended. We were greeted by huge ugly toads. It was better than Japs, but the island had not been set up to handle troops yet so it became our job, setting up tents, digging drainage ditches, and cleaning up a coconut grove covered with years of rancid, rotting coconuts. The island was completely inhabited by rats, land crabs, and toads. I don't know if the Japanese or MacArthur devised this place for the Marines, but it was clear that they both hated us, and the feeling was mutual.

Besides the lousy conditions, we had lousy food. Riflemen don't make good cooks. We actually protested the bad food one day by staging a sit-in. The CO was not impressed, but we did get our point across. The food did improve but not the commander's attitude. We were called out twenty-four hours a day to pick up rotting, stinking coconuts. We loaded them onto trucks and unloaded them onto a pile at least two stories high and as big as a city block.

One day on Pavuvu, one of our gourmet cooks was making soup. He picked up the wrong can and dumped white gas into the soup. He could have poisoned the whole regiment! When the gas hit the soup it exploded and burned down the whole mess hall. Instead of helping to put out the fire, we all fell out into the company street cheering, yelling, clapping, and whistling. The CO was not impressed.

One day our little planes, the Piper Cubs, flew in with Bob Hope and his entire troop. It was incredible. He had Les Brown and his Band of Renown, Jerry Colonna, Francis Langford, Patti Thomas, and Hedda Hopper. It made a lifelong memory.

Soon after that wonderful event I was gratefully volunteered to pick up supplies from the island of Banika. It was an island supply base with a hospital and a Red Cross station. Once again going to the Red Cross netted me nothing. I had no money because we hadn't received any pay. The Red Cross had no sympathy toward anyone without nickels or dimes. I actually saw cigarettes and beer with notes on the boxes saying that they had been donated by General Motors for the boys in the service and that they were not to be sold. The Red Cross sold them. They had nude pictures of the ladies that worked on the island. Regular photos of the girls working there, not movie stars or anything. They sold them for five dollars per print. I was ticked off at the Red Cross. This was the last straw for me. Most of the men were pretty sour about the Red Cross.

By the time we got Pavuvu near livable, we were readied for combat once again. We loaded onto DUKWs and made a practice landing. The DUKW is a tracked vehicle that traveled on land and water. It would hold my machine gun team of eight men plus a couple of extras. After a few days of practice landings, we were loaded aboard ships and taken to Guadalcanal, where we were assembled for transportation to our next combat assignment. While on the Canal my platoon sergeant challenged the platoon sergeant from another company to a contest of who had the best machine gunner. After getting permission from the brass, the machine gun squads from the two companies set up a range in the jungle and each gunner got to compete against each other. There were three gunners from each company, and quite a few men from the division came to watch and cheer. The contest was judged on how fast a gunner could prepare his own heavy machine gun, lock and load, and zero in on the target at about one hundred yards. The winner was decided by the best, tightest pattern of bullets on the target. I managed to beat them all and won a fifty-dollar bet for our sergeant. He insisted that I take half, and I stuck that twenty-five bucks in my pack.

Within a few days we were loading our gear aboard LSTs and we knew we were about to make a beach landing somewhere. Running through water up to your waist under fire is a scary proposition, but if we didn't want that job we had no business joining the Marines in the first place and we knew it. Somehow in the midst of the organized chaos of preparation we discovered that our machine guns were missing for the whole company. I was in total panic. This went over like a lead balloon, and me and a few other gunners got the chore of touring Tulagi Harbor in rough seas, going from ship to ship searching for the missing machine guns. We finally found them aboard the wrong LST and with great difficulty got the precious weapons back to our ship just as we got under way.

Once we were at sea, we got the word to form up on deck. Our CO let us know that our goal was the island of Peleliu in the Palau Island chain. None of us had ever heard of the place. General Rupertus had evidently estimated that it would be a seventy-two-hour battle. He was about seventy-two days off in his estimate. We were very curious about the place. It was just a small coral island with a good airfield that took up a major portion of the island. As we sat on deck getting the details of the landing, I don't think anyone considered the notion that we were about to become part of Marine Corps lore or that the little coral island would forever be known to many as Bloody Peleliu.

The saltwater was hard on our weapons. We spent a lot of

time fieldstripping the machine gun and oiling it along with every other weapon we carried. We had to carry everything onto the beach—guns, water cans with hoses, tripods, ammunition, and all of our personal equipment. I knew that we wouldn't be in the first wave, machine gunners were usually not in the first wave but right behind the first guys. We had so much to carry that we made easy targets. We also immediately drew sniper fire. Machine gunners were always among the primary targets the enemy tried to knock out. I knew that but you couldn't dwell on it.

Our platoon leaders went over the usual orders, of course. The Marines never stop training, even when you can already do it in your sleep, and our sergeants were not shy about repeating themselves. "When you hit the beach you will not stop! You will not stop to help the wounded or dying. Corpsmen and other Marines will come behind us for that duty! Is that clear?"

"Aye, aye, sir!"

Each day the same, each day checking and rechecking equipment and always searching the sea for some dot of land that might be Peleliu. Then on the fifteenth of September we saw it. From that moment the training was over. You couldn't help but look around at the faces of your buddies and wonder who would make it and who wouldn't. I nervously checked everything again and again. All of a sudden some officer or sergeant was yelling, "Saddle up! Move it, Marines!"

It was my turn. I couldn't look for too long as we headed toward the island. If you stuck your head up out of that Higgins boat it might be your last move, but every Marine had to peek. The island was a smoky inferno from the pounding our ships and planes had given it. It seemed like every Jap on that piece of coral should have been dead. They were not very dead, or if they were, their ghosts had plenty of ammunition left. Mortar rounds exploded with big splashes that drenched us with saltwater. I could see two or three DUKWs burning from direct hits and I knew there were a lot of dead Marines in those things. I climbed out of our Higgins boat and tried to keep my machine gun and nose above water.

Mortars, machine guns, and everything the Japs had hit that beach all around us as we came out of the water with wet and heavy loads.

I hit the beach with Rufus Sherrard and six or seven other men in our machine gun squad. Rufus Sherrard was a string bean boy from Texas and one of my very closest buddies. Our orders were to get that machine gun into a position to defend the front line. Trying to run through water and then sand with all that gear and all those bullets and all that fear was the hardest sprint I had ever attempted. You could see the sand kicking up from near misses and hear the whining bullets when they were close to your ear. We ran past a lot of dead and wounded Marines and the firing was intense. I jumped over dead buddies and pressed on, just praying that none of those rounds had my name on it. Later I found out that two of the dead men I ran past were Platoon Sergeant Antecki and company runner Private Ackerman, both killed on the beach. They both had hopeless attitudes about making it through another battle. I ached inside. It was chilling and Sergeant Antecki's words haunted me. "You can avoid death only so many times, Mel."

It was about three hundred yards from the beach to the edge of the airfield. It felt like three thousand yards when Rufus and I spotted a bomb crater at the edge of the airfield, and that was our front line. We set the gun up inside that bomb crater, and scared or not we moved like the well-oiled machine gun team that we were. The men in the squad spread out to protect the flanks of the gun and I opened fire on Jap muzzle flashes across the airfield. There were wrecked Jap planes scattered around the airfield from the working over our boys had given them from the naval and air bombardment. Some of the wrecked planes had been shot down by our pilots in dogfights above. I spotted this dead Jap pilot near us, just a few yards from our crater. He had bailed out and his chute didn't open. He landed on that hard coral airfield and all that was left was a compressed circle of uniform and body about eighteen inches in circumference. He had just turned into a bloody pancake, bones, head, feet, arms, all tamped into that coral as if a big steel press had stamped him into a flat circle.

Time in combat can never be calculated like normal time. Hours can be like seconds and seconds can be like hours. A day under continuous fire can seem like a week and you just lose track of what day or week it is. The Japs were putting up a stiff defense. We had been in that crater for some time and that airfield was one hot zone. The air was filled with lead. The whining of near-misses sent chills down my spine if I let myself pause to think about it. Tracers laced the air from every direction. I thought I saw something sort of big moving, kicking up coral dust. I peeked over the edge of our crater enough to see clearly. My eyes bugged out and my heart started to double-time. I gaped with mouth open as Jap tanks came across the airfield right in front of us.

"Tanks!" I yelled and my heart started pounding faster than the .30-cal. Then I spotted more of them coming along the side of the airfield. I figured that some of our Sherman tanks had made it ashore by then, but they weren't here yet, so it was just Marine versus tank until our own tanks got ashore. Our bazooka men started to let 'em fly. I heard a hit, then a second explosion and knew we were cutting them down. Marines started firing rifle grenades from all over. They must have got a couple hits, but there was so much lead flying I couldn't tell for sure.

"Hey, did you see that?" somebody yelled.

"What?"

"Stufflebean just ran out and dropped a grenade in the hatch of a Jap tank!"

I didn't know the guy and I didn't see it. We were lying in coral dust inside that crater, firing at any target that showed up. Machine guns tend to draw attention, and with that .30-cal blazing out hundreds of rounds per minute, sometimes you don't hear anything else. In spite of that I suddenly heard and felt this terrible noise behind me and Rufus Sherrard, my A-gunner. I ceased fire and looked behind us. The business end of a Jap tank sat rumbling on the edge of our bomb crater. The earth vibrated beneath me as the 37mm turret gun loomed over us. The main gun couldn't fire on us because we were too close and under it. Then I saw the barrel end of the front machine gun begin to lower. It leveled in on us, ready to fire down into the crater. I grabbed Rufus and screamed at him, "Get back under the tank!"

We scrambled over to the other side of the crater and under the front of the tank just as that machine gun opened up with a long burst of fire. Our bodies had left imprints in the coral dust on the inside bank of that crater and the dust impressions of our bodies were riddled with holes. We'd have been shot to pieces. The tank backed up and started to swing around to our side of the crater. I stood up behind my machine gun with my .45-caliber pistol out. The tank swung around, moving past our position. I spotted something move on the back of the tank. A camouflaged Jap rolled over on the back of the tank; he had a Nambu machine gun. I guess he was about ten feet away. I raised my arm and shot him in the back of the head behind the ear with the first round I fired. Another Jap lying beside the one I had just killed rose up to open fire with another Nambu machine gun. I started shooting him as fast as I could pull the trigger, but by then I think the whole 1st Marine Division opened up on him and just blew him to pieces. They were both real dead, but neither Jap rolled off the tank because they were tied to it. That tank was immediately hit by everything. Bazookas and rifle grenades. Flaming metal flew in all directions. The Jap tank stopped and the hulk that was left of it sat burning white and orange. I could feel the heat like a furnace stoked too hot.

I don't know how long the battle had been going when our tanks showed up, but when they did we were sure happy to see them. Within moments of their arrival the Marines fighting for that airfield were entertained by a fantastic tank battle right in front and all around us. The Jap tanks came out to challenge our Shermans in the center of the airfield. The Japanese tanks didn't have a prayer. One of our Shermans opened up with his big 75mm gun and the first hit blew the entire turret of a Jap tank right off. The Marines cheered like

Sixteen-year-old Ted Eleston is the third in line with a pack-horse carrying a .30-caliber heavy water–cooled machine gun.

From left to right: machine gunner Werner Heuman, unknown Marine, and Ted Eleston. Far right is Michael "Moe" Angelo, standing with the water-cooled .30-caliber machine gun. December 1940, Cuba.

Fifth Marines hit the beach. Guadalcanal.

From left to right: General Vandegrift, Colonel Edson, Lieutenant Paige, and Sergeant Basilone at the ceremony in which all four received the Congressional Medal of Honor for their actions on Guadalcanal.

Lt. Mitchell Paige receives the Medal of Honor on May 21, 1943, in Australia.

Mitchell Paige meets movie star Gary Cooper in New Guinea in 1943.

Captured airfield at Pelelui, the site of a tank battle.

The day after a tank battle, witnessed by Melvin Cruthers on Peleliu airfield.

Caliber-.30 air-cooled machine gun in action. Peleliu. Note coral terrain.

Seriously wounded machine gunner PFC Win Scott was placed in a row of dead Marines like this.

Seventh Marines rest after fighting in the Chosin Reservoir.

Marines march in subzero temperatures near the Chosin Reservoir.

First Marine Division counterfires with .30 calibers. Note the many empty ammo cans.

Marines face the Chinese along the 38th Parallel in Korea. The dug-in Marines are armed with a .50-caliber machine gun.

Looking for targets and sniping with a .50-caliber MG on Hill 229 (Bunker Hill).

Dan Bogan with a rifleman on the right flank of his machine gun. Bunker Hill, 1952.

Col. H. D. Adams, CO 1st Marine Regiment, presenting the Silver Star to Cpl. D. J. Bogan in Korea. January 13, 1953.

A Marine machine gunner lies exhausted but well armed in Korea.

An M60 machine gun team in the 5th Marine Regiment in Vietnam.

After a night assault in Nong Son, barely visible dead Viet Cong are scattered on the road. July 5, 1967.

A "mule" on top of Nong Son on the morning after the battle.

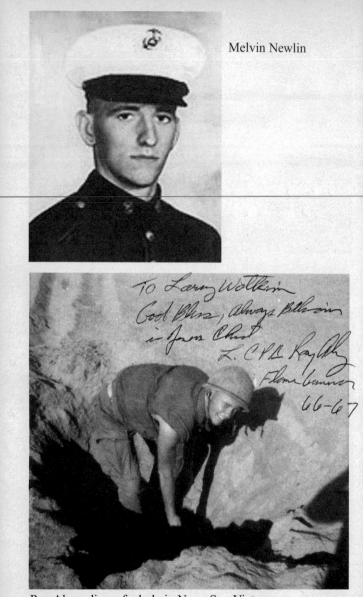

Melvin Newlin

To Larry Wilkin
God Bless, Always Believe
in Jesus Christ
L. CPL Ray Alvey
Flame Gunner
66-67

Ray Alvey digs a foxhole in Nong Son, Vietnam.

On the morning before the attack, Marines tested flamethrowers by burning off brush atop Nong Son. Had they continued, they would have revealed weapons that the VC had prepositioned there. Note orange barrel of defoliant (Agent Orange).

A dead VC sapper in a trench atop Nong Son on July 4, 1967.

A Marine machine gunner clears a jam during Operation Harvest Moon in Vietnam.

Some of the dead Marines from Operation Kingfisher with their mourning comrades.

Johnnie Solis E-2/2 helps a wounded Marine in Operation Kingfisher.

L.Cpl. Jack T. Hartzel before a patrol.

"Body damage assessment"

we were at a football game each time a Jap tank went up in flames. I watched as a Sherman blew the turret off another enemy tank. A moment later Japs scrambled out of the burning hulk and I mowed 'em down with the .30, along with every Marine near us. My A-gunner gripped my arm and pointed at this Jap tank charging straight toward us and our line of Marines. A Sherman tank pulled right in front of our line and right in front of my position and faced him. The Jap was blasting away at our tank and those 37mm shells were just bouncing off it chiming like a dollar hammer hitting a church bell. Our tank did not fire for what felt like an eternity. I was fascinated and starting to worry as the enemy tank got closer and closer. The Jap tank was within fifty feet and I started having some serious doubts, but then, *bam!* One 75mm shell blew that Japanese tank to pieces. It exploded, burning pieces of steel rained down all around us, and we cheered like mad. I couldn't believe what a show we were watching. The Jap tanks burned all night long. Every so often the fires would touch off an explosion that sent shrapnel and pieces of burning metal whizzing by. The fires gave us light to see any possible assaults coming across the airfield.

Daylight finally came, but no rest came with the light, only snipers. The next day and every day we were continually harassed by Japanese snipers. Machine gunners had to worry about snipers constantly. I hated them and I took it personal since I was one of their favorite targets. This one sniper was effective from the base of the Umurbrogol Mountain on the other side of the airstrip. Nobody could spot him because the Arisaka rounds used smokeless powder, and he would only fire one or two shots, quite accurately, and then hold off for another twenty or thirty minutes. Finally he fired and I just happened to be looking in that direction. A puff of coral dust floated up right in front of a small dark slit in this hill on the other side of the airfield.

"Hey, Sarge!" I called out. "I saw a puff of coral dust from the sniper!"

"Turn your gun on it!" he shouted and crawled over to our crater.

I moved the gun and sighted in on that dark slit. We just waited for him to make another move. He fired again and the sergeant pulled the trigger of my machine gun. The gun was sighted in perfectly and a stream of tracers disappeared into that dark slit. We never heard from that sniper again. The wreckage of a Japanese plane was near enough to get to, so I crawled out to it and tore a piece of the aluminum fuselage off of it and brought it back to the crater. I pulled out my penknife and used it to fashion out a watchband that wouldn't rot off in the tropical climate.

We lost so many men on the first day that by the second day on Peleliu, personnel were being shifted all along the line. Rufus was put in charge of his own machine-gun squad. I was made a squad leader of our gun and my assistant gunner was Jim Bowen. Jim was a real handsome guy who was built strong. Jim and me would put on wrestling matches for the guys back on Pavuvu just to entertain the troops, and he was a great friend.

Pretty soon word came down the line that we were going to attack across the airfield, and there was more than one lump in more than one throat. We loaded up the heavy .30, tripod, water jacket, and ammo, and took off at a dead run. Machine gun bullets were raking everything around us and the sound of lead singing by my ears was terrifying. We made it to the middle of the airfield and dived into another bomb crater along with about a dozen other Marines. In front of us, between our position and a heavily fortified hill, lying just at the edge of the airfield, was our CO, Captain Dusenbury. He looked to be badly wounded but not dead. The Japs could have killed him but they preferred to wound a man and wait for the other Marines to come after him, thereby getting more targets.

"Jim, we have to go after him," I said.

"Mel, you're the better gunner. You should stay behind the gun and cover me. I'll go get him."

It was true that I was probably the best gunner and so I agreed. I tried to raise the machine gun to a firing position, then we were raked by enemy machine gun fire. I tried again and they nearly took my head off. Each time I tried to raise up to fire, the enemy machine guns blasted us and all we could do was stay down. Then we heard that rumble and this time it was one of our Shermans rolling up. He moved up between us and the enemy ridge. Jim jumped up and ran out behind the tank. He grabbed the field phone on the back of the tank and communicated with the driver. Jim maneuvered the tank around the captain so Jim was able to grab him and drag him back into our crater. We all respected Capt. Julian A. Dusenbury, he was a fine company commander and a fine man. He was hit in the legs and immobilized but able to communicate. We made him comfortable, then prepared to move out again, leaving him in the care of others.

I threw the gun over my shoulder with the water jacket resting on my neck. Jim picked up the tripod while the ammo carriers in the squad readied for the run. We jumped out of the crater and dashed for the opposite side of the field. Bullets hit everywhere. It was an all-out battle for every inch and the Japs were throwing everything they had at us. I knew bullets were hitting real close to me with each step. When we finally reached the other side of the airfield and dived for cover, I immediately started setting up the gun. I opened fire and nothing happened. I checked the ammo and it was fine. No ruptured cartridge, no jam. Then I saw a bullet hole in the water jacket. The gun was inoperable. That water jacket had rested right on my neck, and in all the excitement and chaos I never even noticed that I was hit.

We set up our positions and stayed there a few days. There were minor skirmishes along our lines at night as the Japs would infiltrate where they could. They never hit us, but you had to be ready every second. Where our position was situated, there was a cavity in the coral with a stream of water running through it. We tested it and it was good water. It was heaven sent. For the whole time we were in that spot we didn't have to drink out of the fifty-five-gallon drums of water they brought ashore. This water was a lot better. We got some replacements from the Pioneer Battalion. It meant another ammo carrier and someone else to stand guard. This kid we got was scared to death. He would just bury his head in his foxhole and cry, so I ended up having to stand his watch and mine.

One morning we got the word that our area was cleared out. It was September 27. Somebody yelled to get saddled up to move out, we were going to secure the island of Ngesebus. Ngesebus was attached to Peleliu by a narrow causeway. We started getting our gear together and ready for the move. I sat thinking about what I had lived through already. The casualties were just horrific, and though the Japs were being killed to the last man, the cost for the 1st Marine Division was terrible. Scuttlebutt said that the 5th Marine Regiment alone had taken more than a thousand casualties. I checked and rechecked the machine gun and equipment, then sat awaiting the word to rush forward. Waiting was sometimes worse than attacking. It gives a man time to think and that's not always good.

I sat staring out at some of the most rugged terrain imaginable. Jagged and ugly beyond comparison. Fragmented stumps that were once trees and coral landscape that did not look like part of the earth. Ten million places for a sniper or machine gun or 75mm cannon to hide. Not just camouflage but nearly invisible to the point that you could walk right up on an enemy gun within spitting distance and not see it. The chances of coming out unscathed seemed very remote at best. I started to think of home and Margie and my job after the war. I could not help but think about getting hit, how it would happen and where. Being blind would be tough. I'd hate to lose my sight, I thought. If I couldn't see, I wouldn't be able to go back to my job as a tool grinder. I thought about losing my arms and discounted that for the same reason; it'd be pretty hard to be a tool grinder without any arms. I glanced at my legs and decided that if I lost some part of my body I'd prefer that it be my leg since I sit down on my job anyway.

"Saddle up! Move out!" somebody shouted, and I got up with the machine gun over my shoulder. The rest of the squad jumped up, too. There was a rugged, dusty road of coral leading to the Causeway that went over to the small adjoining island of Ngesebus. It was 10 A.M. and the Japs controlled the Causeway. It was our job to take it. We were getting close to the Causeway itself when all hell broke loose. Blue-white tracer rounds from enemy machine guns filled the air. Marines dived for any cover they could find. The blast from a heavy gun fired on us at almost point-blank. I dived for a bank along the side of the road. Suddenly the blur of an incoming object came at my head so fast that I could only tuck my chin down in time for it to smash against my helmet. It bounced hard off of my steel pot, steel striking steel, jarring my senses for a moment. I grabbed my helmet by instinct, checking to see if I was wounded and thanking God to be alive. The round object bounced off of my helmet and into the embankment, then rolled around until it stopped by my boots. I stared down at it. It was the helmet of a young Marine. The face of a young man stared at me from inside that helmet. His chin strap was still on. Vomit rose up in my throat but I swallowed it down.

There was no time to stare. Incoming fire slapped the hard coral rock and dirt like popcorn popping. Then another blast from a heavy weapon. It sounded like the Jap equivalent of our 37mm antitank gun. Jim set up the tripod and I leaned to my left to yell instructions to my squad. It was the oddest sensation—as I tried to put weight on my right leg to turn, my foot fell asleep. I tried to move but it was asleep. I looked back and my right leg was gone well above the knee. There was lots of blood and scattered parts but it was blown completely off. I removed my belt and tied it around what was left of my leg for a tourniquet. The men in my squad shouted for a corpsman and finally got one. He did what he could. They carried me to the rear and got me into the back of a jeep with three other casualties. I was sitting up and con-

scious enough to watch the corpsman driving like a madman. I could see bullets bouncing off the hood of the jeep
while others made holes in the hood. The corpsman tried to
drive at full speed with his head down. I felt my head go
down and everything went black.

I opened my eyes and saw that I was in the aid station with
a bunch of wounded, and there was a Catholic chaplain over
me performing last rites. I looked up at him. "You're wasting
your time, Chaplain. I'm going home." It went black again
and then I was bouncing up and down for some reason. I
opened my eyes and this time I was in a boat. There was a big
ship beside us. It was the hospital ship, USS *Relief.* Moments
of lucidity were rare after that. I would hear conversations
fading in and out and I knew I was in a bed with bars on the
side. I heard them saying that I was out of it and trying to get
out of bed to walk, so they had to put up bars. I don't remember trying to get up.

After a while I was conscious enough to want to write
home. One of my buddies from my platoon, Gilbert Brown,
was aboard ship for awhile. They said I was in shock and I
guess I was. I couldn't control my hands and arms. I wanted
to write Margie to explain what had happened. I wanted to
tell her I was on my way home. I asked Gil to write the letter
for me since I couldn't control my hands and arms. I dictated
a letter that he wrote and mailed for me.

Meanwhile back in the States, Margie had not heard from
me in quite a while. She was worried and started talking
to her roommate, a lady named Mrs. Fletcher. Margie told
her how we met and told of the great party her fellow em-
ployees had thrown for her before she left Cleveland. She
told Mrs. Fletcher about the wonderful cake they had given
her with the little bride and Marine on top, and Mrs. Fletcher
smiled and said how wonderful that was. Margie asked her if
she would like to see them, she had saved them from our
wedding cake. Mrs. Fletcher said yes and Margie set about
unwrapping the treasured items. When she unwrapped the
Marine doll, its right leg was broken off above the knee.
Twenty-four hours later Margie got the letter telling her that

I had lost my right leg above the knee and was on my way home. I still have those dolls. Margie died in 1987. But the Lord gave me a new wife named Wavell O. Spencer. Life has been very good to me, and a disability is a detriment only if you allow it to be.

KOREA 1950

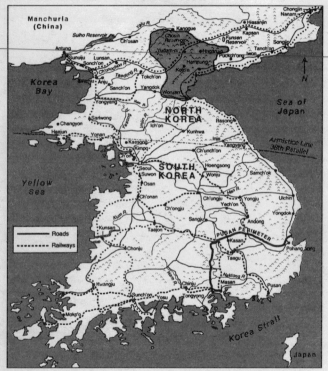

MSR TO CHOSIN RESERVOIR

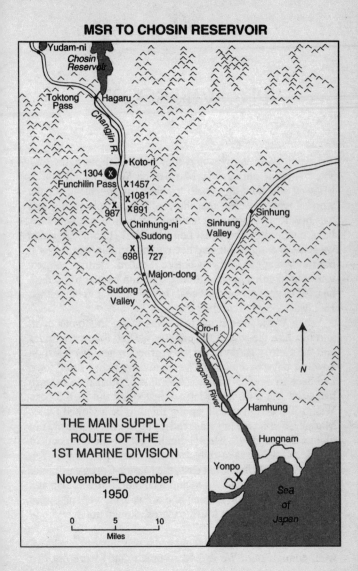

Yudam-ni
Chosin Reservoir
Toktong Pass
Hagaru
Changjin R.
Koto-ri
1304 ⓧ
Funchilin Pass X1457
X1081
X 891
X 987
Chinhung-ni
Sudong
X 698   X 727
Majon-dong
Sudong Valley
Sinhung Valley
Sinhung
Oro-ri
Songchon River
Hamhung
Hungnam
Yonpo
Sea of Japan
N

THE MAIN SUPPLY
ROUTE OF THE
1ST MARINE DIVISION

November–December
1950

0   5   10
Miles

4

PFC WIN SCOTT

I went to the movies and they showed these newsreels. They showed our prewar Marines on Wake Island and at Midway and how they were training and preparing for the worst. I walked out of that theater blinking because the sun was bright, and there was my dad. "Win! Son you won't believe this, but the Japs just bombed Pearl Harbor!" My dad was pale and angry. He had been in the army in World War I, but never made it overseas before it ended. He immediately went out to enlist again and they told him he was too old, so he tried to get into the Seabees. He couldn't get in that either. He always deeply regretted that.

When World War II started I was living in Connecticut, and just like the rest of the country we had the metal drives and the victory gardens and we yearned to hear the latest on how our boys were doing. The postmaster in our small town had been in the 5th Marines. A couple of other men in town had been Marines, and Marines just stood out as the best. Well, I had already made up my mind to be a United States Marine, so at fourteen I was ready. The Marine Corps did not oblige. It was 1948 when I finally got in. In Connecticut the Corps would take only two applicants per month. You couldn't just get in all that easy, the Marine Corps was pretty darn picky about who got in and who didn't. It was also at a time when President Truman and a few army generals were trying to dismantle the Marine Corps, though not everybody was aware of that.

I did my time at Parris Island and it was thirteen weeks of, well, enough said. We drilled so much that I wore out two pairs of boots. Finished Camp Lejeune and got my orders, FMF, Fleet Marine Force, and I was on my way to China by way of the Southern Pacific Railroad. It was 1949 and America got hit by a terrible storm. I looked out the window in Winslow, Arizona, and there was snow all around the palm trees. Finally got to San Francisco, boarded the USS *Breckenridge* to relieve the Marines that had been in China for so long. Somewhere in midocean our orders for China got changed because the communists had taken the country and we were no longer welcome. That news changed my destination to the lovely island of Guam. There was nothing on Guam except Japanese soldiers who didn't believe the war was over yet.

The place was a battleground and it looked it. There was a group of civilians, sort of like Seabees, called the Brown Pacific Maxim Company. It was their job to clean the place up, to remove old mines, bombs, or weapons to make the place available for use as a military base again. The 1st Marine Provisional Brigade landed on Guam after a long stint in China. These guys were mostly from the 1st Battalion, 9th Marines. These were "old China hands," the saltiest old Marines I'd ever seen in my life. I was a brand-new boot, and throwing me in with these guys was like feeding a Christian to the lions. They had big mustaches and tall Russian boots. They wore these sewn-in Russian or Chinese cuff links that were not Marine issue or at least nothing I'd ever seen before. Their dungarees were white from repeated washing and they had Chinese buttons embroidered on their blouses. They were salty and mean as snakes. It took about an hour or two with these guys before I was in a fight and I learned a lot right away. They made me a machine gunner and that was it, brother. They taught me that machine gun. They were not happy being on Guam after so long in China, and they griped about it incessantly until finally 1/9 got sent back to the States.

I got transferred to the 5th Marine Regiment. Well, I knew all about the 5th Marines, every Marine knew what kind of legends had fought with the 5th Marines. From the second I joined the regiment we did nothing but train in the field. Taking that machine gun apart day and night. Just one field exercise after another, and these Marines were trained and ready, brother. For a rest we made beach landings off of the USS *Pickaway*. These grunts were ready for battle at any moment. We trained so hard it made you think there was a war coming, but there was no war. It was nothing special, it was just the price you paid to call yourself a Marine. These men were professionals, the very best at their job, and their job was war even when there was no war.

The only thing you could do when off duty was hike the nine miles to the main base. I had a couple of buddies there, guarding Japanese admirals who were now POWs. They had National Bohemian beer from Baltimore, with the cone tops, this old 3.2 beer left over aboard ships after the war. Made you sick as a dog and, of course, being Marines, we drank it. There were caves all over Guam and we'd explore them when we could, but you had to take a rifle with you because there were still Japs on the island. My bunk mate was a guy named Mike Yearsage from Chicago. He was a specimen. He played football back in Chicago. We played football on Guam. Our field was made up of crushed coral. We played tackle and it was reminiscent of the old NFL. Guys just got tore to pieces on that coral. Mike was a star on that coral field.

Just about the time Guam was fit for living, a typhoon hit the island. They put us underground in an ammunition locker. We rode it out for three days, but the island was wrecked. Most of the outfit was being shipped back to the States, but I put in for overseas duty and got it. I got shipped to Japan and became part of what eventually was known as the 1st Marine Brigade. There were ninety-nine Marines at the base I got sent to, Yokosuku. It had been a Japanese naval officers' barracks and was relatively unscathed by the war. It was a beautiful barracks with wood floors. I went to sleep that first night with no warning of how things got started around there each morning. At 0400 hours, a fourteen-piece Marine band marched down the center of that beautiful barracks playing "Stars and Stripes Forever." It's bad enough waking up to a bugle, but a fourteen-piece band will shake even the drunkest Marine into combat condition. That was our awakening for each and every day.

I jumped to attention and next thing I knew we were hitting the drill field. We trained with M-1 rifles and I mean trained. We drilled as well as the commandant's own. I was a guide arm, and our outfit could flip those M-1 rifles around the way a majorette flips a little baton. These were outstanding Marines, I mean squared away. This was during a time when the country as a whole had dropped its guard again. A time of peace and prosperity, and a lot of liberals were crying for the military to be downsized and President Truman was succeeding in his effort to disband the Corps. Many of our military units were not combat-ready. They had become as soft as the leaders guiding our country. But, by God Almighty, the United States Marines sure weren't getting soft. By 0630 hours we secured from drill work and moved on to physical training just as the navy boys were waking up and wandering out of their barracks, yawning and stretching and shuffling toward chow with their shirts not even tucked in. They would watch us and shake their heads in disbelief at how hard and how long we trained.

When the 7th Fleet came in, the Marines from the ships would come ashore and drill, leading to some severe competition. The Fleet Marines are supposed to be some of the sharpest drill teams in the world. We blew their socks off in every single drill. I served with some of the most squared away Marines in the Corps. Out of those 99 outstanding Marines stationed at the Japanese naval barracks in Yokosuku 66 would be killed or wounded or missing in action in the coming months. Without their sacrifices and many others like them, we would have lost the Korean War. They stopped the North Korean army and gave 'em their first defeat of the war. That was in and around Pusan just before they were about to finish us and the South Koreans off.

Well, we started hearing scuttlebutt that we would be staying in Yokosuku to guard that area. The first group of Marines that got sent to Korea were guys they took out of the brig. Then another group of our guys got orders for Korea.

My buddy and old bunk mate Mike Yearsage was in that group. Then word came back that Mike Yearsage from Chicago was the fifth Marine killed in Korea. That hit home. I didn't find out until much later that Mike's squad had been killed and he was wounded and captured. The Koreans tortured him all night trying to find out where the rest of the company was and he wouldn't talk. When Mike's body was escorted home, Mike's dad got the Marine in charge of the burial detail drunk. After the Marine was drunk, he told Mike's dad how Mike had been tortured to death. I always wanted to deck that idiot for telling Mike's folks about that.

A few days after Mike was killed, I found myself on board a ship heading for Inchon, Korea. I got attached to C 1/5, that's Charlie Company, 1st Battalion, 5th Marine Regiment, 1st Marine Division. When the brigade was put together for the Inchon landing, it was made up of Able and Baker Companies. When Charlie Company was added, we were over our normal strength so some of our men were transferred to A 1/5. We had a really fine Marine in C 1/5 named 2d Lt. Bardemela "Baldy" Lopez. He was a graduate of the Naval Academy and just an outstanding Marine. A lot of the men really loved that guy, and when he got transferred over to Able Company we felt the loss. Baldy hit the beach with A 1/5 and charged over the seawall at Inchon. A grenade landed right in the middle of a bunch of his men at that seawall. Baldy pulled it into his stomach to save his men. He was the first Marine to win the Medal of Honor in Korea.

I missed the Inchon landing and got thrown in as a replacement when the Marines were already inland. I was with a rifle squad. We were getting ready to cross the Han River, and crossing rivers is nervous business. At one point a machine gun squad had set up on a small rise to give cover fire on Hill 105. Corporal Holbrook came running up yelling at this lieutenant, "Lieutenant! That machine gun squad is set up in the wrong place! They're too exposed to enemy fire!"

"They're staying put, Holbrook."

The whistle of an incoming artillery round grew shrill as it neared. The impact zone was a direct hit on that machine gun emplacement. In that instant, nine U.S. Marine machine gunners were killed, and I was immediately ordered back in machine guns.

Corporal Holbrook walked amidst the blood and carnage of what had been an entire machine gun squad moments earlier, then sprinted up to that lieutenant and yelled into his face, "You just got my whole machine gun squad killed!" Corporal Holbrook had been a corporal on Guadalcanal in 1942 and he was still a corporal and it was 1950 and another war. He was one outstanding machine gunner, but couldn't stay out of trouble. I was glad this old salt was now my corporal, but I was no fool about the joys of being a machine gunner. They made me an ammo humper. Our TO or table of organization called for four ammo humpers in a machine gun squad. We carried two boxes of ammo each and there were 250 rounds per box. I had an M-2 carbine and I hated that thing. It had a banana clip and I taped two clips together for a quick reload. It had a fast cyclic rate of fire but it just felt like a peashooter to me. It was made by General Motors Inland Division, stamped right on the thing like it was something to be proud of.

I was sitting and waiting for the word and praying to Jesus about the future or lack of it when I heard someone yell, "Hey, Scotty! Come up here!" I looked to see who was calling, and it was this buddy of mine from the Yokosuku guard detachment waving at me from about thirty yards up the hill. There was one huge shell crater nearby, but it was a good distance from my buddy. When I reached him he just pointed. I looked and there were three dead North Korean soldiers without a drop of blood on any of them. They'd been killed by sheer concussion from a round fired by the USS *Missouri*'s 16-inch guns. One of the dead Koreans was an officer, and he was sitting up looking perfectly natural. Natural enough to startle the crap out of me for a moment until I realized he was dead. He had died with his right hand held out in a fist and some Marine had placed a toothbrush in his mouth.

Word came a few minutes later and my heart was in my throat. We moved down to the Han River and boarded amtracs. It felt like it took a long time, but I was already discovering that time in a combat zone can't be judged by a clock. Twenty seconds can feel like an hour. We disembarked the amtracs on the outskirts of Seoul and fought our way to the Imperial Palace. The combat was hit-or-miss. One day the fighting would be vicious and the next day the enemy would just fade away. There were pockets of North Koreans putting up tough fights and our job was to isolate them one at a time and kill 'em. Seoul was a different kind of fighting. Some of our NCOs had been officers in World War II and were now back to being sergeants and corporals. One reason for that was all of the cutbacks in military spending. Men who wanted to stay in the Corps had to take a cut in pay and rank. I'd hear 'em talking and griping, and many of them agreed that only on Okinawa had they seen the kind of fighting we were seeing now. We were finding out that Seoul was a big city. A lot of the time our unit was on the outskirts of Seoul. The enemy had turned everything into a bunker. They barricaded the streets with Russian tanks. Nearly all the fighting was house-to-house and street-to-street. It was platoon, squad, and fire team–level fighting. We moved up on a battered house. Guns got set up and we laid down as much fire as we could in an effort to draw fire from the enemy. Once we did, four Marines would move out. Two on each side of the street. I'd open fire through the windows or doors of a house across the street to keep any gook's head down while two Marines moved into position to toss grenades inside. As soon as the grenades went off, the Marines rushed in blazing. Then they'd give a signal and it was our turn. The Marines who had just rushed the first house now opened fire on our objective.

They poured lead into the house directly across from them. Me and another Marine rushed the house and threw in grenades, then hit the dirt and prepared to charge through the door after the blasts. Each time it was frightening and your adrenaline shot through you until everything tingled. The house was smoky when you entered and you shot anything that moved, then quickly trained your weapons on the next house across the street. We leapfrogged right down the entire street like that. There were snipers everywhere and we had to deal with them one at a time. We leapfrogged from house to house and building to building one block at a time until we killed or captured every North Korean in Seoul, and we did almost all of it with nothing but grenades, pistols, and shot-guns. Of course, our .30-caliber machine guns put out some serious fire. There was no front and no rear in this battle and I didn't like that, you just couldn't let your guard down for a second. Our unit wasn't even in the middle of the city, but it was still scary.

You couldn't tell who was the enemy and who was a civil-ian. Civilians were all over the place trying to get out of the city or just out of the middle of firefights. We got word to make a move to another street and I started checking my grenades and ammo when suddenly this mob of civilians appeared, running right at us, some screaming, all trying to get away from a battle going on in their neighborhood a block over. There were hundreds of them, so many that they blocked our movement down the street. No one shot them but they were lucky, there was no way of telling if they were really civilians at first. We moved them and moved on.

The city was filthy. There was junk everywhere. Dirty farm animals were running wild, and you never knew if that movement was an animal or a North Korean or some poor civilian caught in the middle of this hell. The enemy had T-34 Russian tanks and artillery set up here and there to put up blocking actions. We called up one of our M-4 Shermans and thanked God when that monster rumbled down the street and opened up with that cannon. I thanked God for our tanks more than once in Seoul. If there were no tanks around, we were using the same tactics Marines had always used, get close enough to kill 'em and then kill 'em. We ran into a bar-ricade made out of trolley cars and enemy machine guns. We killed them with the usual fire team tactics and moved on.

I had never seen the way people had to live under the rule of communism before, and when there was a lull in the fight-ing I'd find myself looking around like some dumb tourist.

Big pictures of Stalin hung on buildings, like he was God.
Propaganda was on every telephone pole or anyplace the
commies could stick it. Somebody yelled, "Saddle up and
move out!" My squad moved toward the telephone exchange
building for the city of Seoul. It was a fairly modern-looking
structure. Outside the building was a parking lot, and right
there in the middle of all this killing was a long, neat row of
cars, all parked in a perfect line. One of our bazooka teams
moved near us and got set up. I watched and wondered what
the plan was, then *boom!* They shot a round that went right
through each of these neatly lined up autos. It was the weird-
est thing to witness, and I knew that I would remember seeing that bazooka round going through those cars for the rest
of my life if I had the rest of my life.

We pulled out when Seoul was secure and got the word
that we were going into North Korea. I found myself on
board the USS *Bayfield,* an old World War II attack personnel auxiliary ship. They yanked the whole 1st Marine Division out and put us on ships of every kind. Some of our units
were even on old Japanese landing craft. Others were aboard
Coast Guard ships and anything that would float. It was
awful, but better than walking to North Korea. Everybody
expected a beach landing like Inchon, only bloodier. I
climbed down into the pit of that old ship with the rest of the
company and knew this was going to be one bad trip. We
were stacked five men deep in the hold and still had to find
room for all of our gear. If you coughed you hit the guy
above you. We were almost situated when some bonehead
tripped off an accidental discharge with his Browning automatic rifle. There was nothing you could do but cringe as that
bullet ricocheted all around the inside of that ship's hold. By
a sheer miracle no one was hit. Something like that tended to
bring out the worst side of old Marine Corps salts, and I was
real glad I wasn't the bonehead with that BAR.

We were on the *Bayfield* for two weeks. What we thought
was going to be a typical Marine beach landing under fire
turned out to be anything but that. It took a long time for the
harbor at Wonsan to be cleared of mines. The ships would

just go back and forth as the minesweepers tried to do their job, and pretty soon the Marines called it "Operation Yo-Yo." These mines were bad news, though. They were real trouble. Every few days we'd hear this big explosion and one of our minesweepers would be gone. They were Russian mines that wouldn't go off when the first ship passed but would count two, three, or four going past before exploding. We called them counter-mines. By the time we came ashore the North Koreans were long gone, and the U.S. military that had come by the land route was already there enjoying a Bob Hope show. Man, did we hate that. The whole 1st Marine Division was ticked off and embarrassed.

As soon as I hit the beach I ended up running into this buddy of mine that I'd known since grammar school, Joe Shehan. He knew we were landing and he found me on the beach. Joe was in the 103d Naval Seabees as an electrician's mate. We had a good little reunion and of course the inevitable ribbing and then the serious question, "Why in the world would you join the Marines, man? Are you crazy?" It was just starting to get sort of cold and we hadn't been issued any cold weather gear. Joe knew that the Marines were heading north to find and kill the North Korean army and he knew how cold it was going to be real soon. He gave me what became my most prized possession in the months to come. A navy "watch cap." It fit under my steel pot and came down over my ears.

Chesty Puller's 1st Marine Regiment boarded gondola cars for a train ride north to Kojo. The 7th Marine Regiment and the 5th Marine Regiment boarded two-and-a-half-ton trucks for a forty-three-mile trek from Hungnam to Chinhung-ni through relatively level country, but it began to get hilly just north of Majon-dong. From Chinhung-ni to Koto-ri the road became a treacherous oxcart path of dirt and gravel until it turned to mud and ice no more than twelve feet wide. We did finally get our first issue of cold weather gear, and it included these things they called "shoe packs." They had a rubber bottom and leather top with a felt liner inside. They were fine if you just sat around. Whoever invented the "shoe pack" had never been in the United States Marine Corps. We didn't do a lot of sitting around. I found out right away that after a long march, your feet would sweat inside these things; they didn't breathe at all, so then the sweat turned to ice and your feet would freeze. Frostbite casualties started becoming serious as we moved north. We kept heading north up this winding, narrow road that passed through little villages once in a while. We moved through Oro-ri and on up to Majon-dong, the elevation going up and temperature going down with each step.

Every mile of that road became more treacherous than the last. In most places the road was too narrow for trucks and tanks, but with each unbelievable challenge came a solution and we pushed on. Our engineers had to shore up ancient bridges to hold the weight of our tanks. Some of these bridges passed over deep ravines. I don't know if the road had a name, but for the 1st Marine Division it was the MSR, or main supply route.

The MSR rose like a snake of ice for three thousand feet. Rugged rock cliffs on one side of the narrow road, and deep, dread-inducing chasms on the other. In some places a truck could slide off the edge and probably never be seen again. At other places the ridges alongside the road would rise a thousand feet above us. I looked up and sure felt vulnerable, but we kept pushing on under MacArthur's orders to link up with his 8th Army Group. Our orders were simple and about as Marine as possible: find and kill the rest of the North Korean army. The North Koreans had melted away. We'd hear scuttlebutt every once in a while about Marines making contact with a batch of them, and each time the enemy took a beating, but for the most part what was left of that army was dead and gone. There was also some persistent scuttlebutt about the Chinese entering the war, but it seemed that no one thought they really would. At one point an advance patrol from the 7th Marines had made contact with Chinese troops and actually captured a few of them, but the brass downplayed it. The best scuttlebutt was that we'd be home by Christmas, that the North Koreans were beat.

Machine gunners and mortar men had to carry pretty

heavy loads along with all the cold weather gear, so sometimes we'd get rides for a ways on tanks or trucks. When we
stopped, we went out on patrols in search of the North Koreans. There was no real rest, but as gunners we tried to take
turns on who went with each patrol. We stopped in this village and these North Korean police came to us with information on where some communist troops were hiding. They
said they could show us a shortcut to attack them. I don't
know why, but somebody trusted these Koreans, and this
other machine gun squad got the job of going with that patrol. The corporal from that gun squad came running over to
us hugging this scrawny little brown and white chicken.

"Hey, would you guys watch out for our chicken while we
go out on this patrol?"

"Absolutely," I said, taking the chicken from him.

He headed off and the second that patrol was around a
bend, I twisted that chicken's neck and the men started pluck-
ing. I took off my helmet, pulled out the liner, and somebody
threw in some water and we started a fire. Somebody had
rice and somebody opened up a can of C rations and we
threw it all together in my helmet. We sat there like a bunch
of wolves just smelling real food cooking. I started basting
the chicken with the chin strap on my helmet and the chin
strap caught on fire. I panicked for a second but finally put it
out by dipping it inside the helmet. When it was cooked we
scarfed that food down and you never saw happier Marines.
That was the best meal any of us had eaten since we landed
at Inchon. We started singing and laughing. I felt great.

It was two or three days later before that patrol got back.
They had been led into an ambush and a couple of our guys
had been killed. It held up the entire 1st Battalion. When they
finally got back, that other machine gun section came looking for their chicken.

"I'm real sorry, corporal. That chicken got away the day
after you guys left on patrol."

"What? You let it get away?"

I nodded sadly. He walked away cursing but he believed

me. Thank God he was too tired to notice all the feathers
lying around 'cuz it was too cold to fight.

The last serious contact we'd heard about was Chesty
Puller's 1st Marine Regiment being in a shootout with about
1,200 North Koreans on Halloween. The Marines lost 23 KIA
and killed over 200 North Koreans. Everything else I heard
about was pretty much small-unit stuff. It was November 2,
and that was the only thing I was sure about. The other thing
I knew for sure was that the coldest wind I'd ever felt in my
life was stinging my skin like hot grease. It was blowing in
from Manchuria and the sweat on my face turned into ice.

We stopped, patrols went out, and positions were set up
along the ridges. Word filtered back that the 7th Marines had
hit something big up ahead at a place called Sudong-ni. No
one knew at that moment just how big it was, but by the next
day the word was out that the 7th had run into the 234th Chinese Regiment. That was the first action in Korea for the 7th
Marine Regiment and they did a good job. Knocked out five
Chinese tanks and decimated an entire Chinese regiment.
That 234th Chinese Regiment took so many casualties that it
never saw action again.

Well, we knew now that it was no longer just scuttlebutt.
The Chinese were out there in some strength. After that
slaughter, what was left of the Chinese pulled back and the
1st Marine Division kept moving forward. Everyone from
MacArthur to Truman hoped it wasn't a sign of things to
come. No one knew that ten Chinese divisions had crossed
the Yalu River, hiding in caves and forests during the day, moving only at night. They had been given one specific order,
wipe out the 1st Marine Division. They believed that if they
could knock off America's best, the war would end quickly.
There are twelve thousand men in a Chinese division. How
ten divisions could cross the Yalu River and move that far
without being seen by our spotter planes is remarkable.

We kept moving. Through Sudong-ni, Chinhung-ni, Fun-
chillin Pass, and up to Koto-ri. Koto-ri was seventy miles inland, so we had no naval gunfire for support, and a lot of the
old salts didn't like that one bit. Every so often we would

pass these hydroelectric plants. The Japanese had taken over Korea in 1910 and had enslaved the Korean people for the next thirty-five years. The Koreans hated the Japanese, and for good reason, but the Japs had made some improvements to this primitive land. One of the things they had done was to build dams and hydroelectric plants. The Changjin River came down through this huge man-made reservoir named the Chosin Reservoir. Changjin Valley ran up alongside of the reservoir. Along the road at the northwestern edge of the Chosin was the village of Yudam-ni. A few short miles from the northern edge of the Chosin Reservoir was the Yalu River and China.

The division set up its HQ on a small plateau at Koto-ri. I had this buddy there when we finally got a few replacements. We hadn't gotten any since the battle of Seoul. My buddy saw these three combat officers report in to HQ and all three got assigned to supply. One was Lt. Hal Williamson and the others were captains. Well, they were not happy. Hal was so mad, he came out slapping the tent flap so hard that he decked a guy coming into the tent. He looked down in total terror at a very familiar face, one he had served under on Guam. A face that was now second in command of the 1st Marine Division, General Craig.

"Oh, God! I'm sorry, General! I didn't see you!"

"I guess you didn't, Lieutenant!" General Craig barked, then recognized the young lieutenant helping him up. "Hal?"

"Yes, sir."

"What are you doing here, I thought you were still on Guam. What's wrong?"

"I'm sorry, sir. I was just upset about my orders. I'm a combat officer, sir. They just put me in supply and two captains just got the same treatment in there right now!"

The general looked angry for a moment, then said, "Come with me, we'll talk to General Smith about this. We can't have combat officers sitting around in supply at a time like this."

Just like that we got a new captain for Charlie Company. His name was Captain Jones. The other captain went to Fox 2/7 and ended up winning the Medal of Honor. Our captain was twenty-nine years old and we were sure glad to see him. He was an old man and already had won the Navy Cross. He would win a second Navy Cross with us in a few weeks. All three of those officers were just outstanding combat men, and that tent flap incident probably saved a lot of Marines and killed a lot of Chinese.

We moved out again, up to a place called Hagaru. General Smith, commanding general of the 1st Marine Division, decided to stop there and make Hagaru the division headquarters. The terrain was frozen but relatively flat. He also decided that the Marines were going no farther without some way of being resupplied. He ordered our engineers to work on chiseling out an airstrip in the ice. Again, no one knew what a brilliant move that would end up being. That leveled piece of ice would end up saving the lives of thousands of Marines. We had the best combat officers in the world, but I believe there was a senior officer named Jesus Christ who made a couple of those decisions for us. In James 1:5 the Bible says that if any man lacks wisdom, let him ask of God and it will be given to him. But in Exodus the Word of God says that some men have been endowed with the spirit of wisdom. Maybe it was just God keeping His promise to protect a nation that honors God. Besides the obvious, incredible bravery, whatever other reasons, we had some outstanding officers and NCOs who made decisions that kept the 1st Marine Division from being annihilated.

We pushed on up through Toktong Pass and all the way to Yudam-ni on the north edge of the Chosin Reservoir. The road became more treacherous with each step. Walking on it was difficult and getting vehicles up it was nearly impossible. We started doing patrols every day, some big, some small. It was getting brutally cold, the most bitter cold in over one hundred years. Officers were telling the sergeants to make sure the men changed socks. We each had two pairs of socks, and you had to keep your feet dry or they'd freeze, but even changing socks was becoming more and more difficult.

My urine would turn to ice before it hit the ground, so just relieving yourself was misery.

We were up on ridges watching the engineers trying to grade that airstrip. They even worked at night using lights, and all the while being shot at by snipers from surrounding hills and mountains. We had shelter halves that two Marines could put together to make a little tent, but trying to get a tent peg in the ground was hopeless in most places. Some gunners just crawled inside their sleeping bags and tried not to freeze to death in their sleep. I tried to eat but even the ham and limas came out like a popsicle, and the most food you could get off it was by licking at its edges until some frozen particles came loose. An artillery battery set up on a ridge near us. Bob Johnson was in that artillery battery. Bob had served with the 4th Marines in China and was a buddy of mine and a real good guy.

It was so cold you just didn't want to expose any flesh, but the Marine Corps ain't no democracy and I didn't get any vote. Word came down to start getting ready to go out on patrol. I peeked out of my sleeping bag, down at the road near the village of Hagaru, and I saw this big fire going. Some of the villagers had piled up logs and managed to get a good-sized fire going to try to warm up. I felt sorry for those people. I just couldn't figure out how they could survive in temperatures this severe. I saw a couple of Marines drifting down that way from the artillery position and I knew they were going to try to get some blood flowing again beside that fire. After a bit, they shuffled away back toward their positions, and one of them was Bob Johnson. I saw Bob and this other fellow, a PFC, later, and mentioned how I envied them by that fire.

"Scotty, you ain't going to believe what happened down there."

"It's unbelievable!" the other Marine said. "We were stomping our feet by these other fellows trying to get some feeling back and Bob starts talking to these guys down there."

"Yeah. About what?"

Bob shrugged. "I just said, oh my God this is the coldest I've ever been in my life."

"Yeah. So?"

"And he says, me, too. Then he says, I think it's supposed to get better tomorrow."

"Yeah, so?" I asked, still waiting for some sort of punch line.

"Then I say that I sure hope so because I can't even get my food unfrozen enough to eat. Well, then he agreed and we exchanged pleasantries, and after we've warmed up a little I finally say to the guy that we have to be getting back to our position. Then he says, yes, us, too. Then I say, we'll be seein' you later and I sort of nodded good-bye and headed back to our position."

"Then what?" I asked.

The PFC's eyes bulged with new information. "So I say, hey, Bob. What language was that you were speaking down there to those guys? And Bob says calmly, oh, that was Chinese Mandarin. Then Bob and me look at each other like we just saw ghosts and we both look back down at the fire. Oh my God, Bob! Those were Chinese troops! You were just shootin' the breeze with the enemy!"

"It was unbelievable, Scotty. I guess we were all too cold to think."

I stared at Bob and the PFC and laughed but a part of me wasn't all that amused, and we all wondered aloud just how many Chinese were out in those snowcapped mountains.

Charlie 1/5 got the word to take a hike back up the east side of the reservoir and look for the enemy. The Changjin Valley ran up alongside the reservoir, and we kept going and going. We ended up following this big trail that went back about ten miles. At one point the word filtered back to hold up and each of the two hundred Marines in the column was thankful to hear it, especially the men packing the heavy machine guns and mortars. Our point men had come across fighting positions dug out of the frozen earth, and they were freshly dug. I could just feel that something was about to happen.

Word came down the line to saddle up and move out. I

don't know how far we went but the next time the word came back to halt, I lifted my head up enough to notice that we were deep into this big, wide, frozen valley with snowcapped ridges that formed a horseshoe surrounding us on three sides. My eyes were so cold I couldn't focus for a few moments. I rubbed and blinked away the frost from my eyelashes. Slowly my vision broke through the freezing blur and I was able to make out the dark forms of men in the snowcapped ridges around us. Then, like someone had kicked me in the stomach, I suddenly realized just how many mustard brown, cotton-padded uniforms were positioned in the white ridges above us. There were thousands of Chinese troops looking down on us from the encircling ridgeline. Marine helmets started turning, and the word came back down the column, "Everybody turn around and move slowly back."

We started marching back the way we had come. We didn't run or panic or do anything fast. We just walked right back out of there and no one fired a single shot. When we got back, our CO reported that there was no longer any doubt that the Chinese were there and in great strength. First Battalion stayed on the east side of the reservoir for the next four or five days before we got the word to saddle up. It was November 27 when trucks started arriving to pick up the battalion and take us back down to Hagaru, through Toktong Pass and up to Yudam-ni. From there the Marines were to push one hundred miles across impossible terrain to link up with MacArthur's 8th Army Group.

Able and Baker Companies began loading onto deuce-and-a-halves. 1/5 was to join up with the rest of the 5th Marine Regiment and the 7th Marines at Yudam-ni just as army units started arriving and taking up positions. We were waving at them and yelling and watching in wonder as the army rolled in with all this great equipment. They had everything. It was a mechanized outfit with quad-fifties and 20mm cannons, heavy artillery, but the breaker for us was when they started setting up a full field kitchen. We couldn't believe our eyes. What we didn't know at the time was that they were coming in all scattered, piecemeal, a unit at a time, real hodgepodge. The 31st, the 59th Field Artillery, the 32d. They were part of the army's 7th Regiment and were moving down from the north. For whatever reasons they ignored the advice of our officers to take up the same defensive positions that we had been in. There, communications between units was unorganized and they were too spread out.

Charlie Company got to watch the army moving in while Able and Baker boarded trucks and headed out. Typically, the Marines didn't have enough trucks, so our trucks would have to bring Able and Baker on that long, dangerous trek along that narrow sheet of ice they laughingly called a road, up through Toktong Pass, down to Yudam-ni and then come back again for C Company. By the time the trucks got back for us it was starting to get late in the day, and by the time we reached Toktong Pass it was dark. I was in the back of one of the canvas-covered deuce-and-a-halves when I saw the truck behind us turn on its lights. Pretty soon all the trucks had their lights on as we came down into the valley of Yudam-ni, where the tiny village, about twelve huts, sat beneath the western ridges of the Chosin Reservoir. I saw bright flashes off to our right in the white mountains but I couldn't hear anything.

At that same moment those poor army guys on the eastern side of the Chosin Reservoir were being overrun by the Chinese 89th Division. Out of the 3,000 soldiers who had replaced us, three weeks later there were only 600 left to form muster. We pulled into this field and my buddy, Zarback, or Ziggy as we called him, and I put up our shelter halves to try to block some of the freezing wind. We still didn't know what was going on, but I knew that it was the coldest night of my life. We were told it was 20 degrees below zero, but the hard, biting wind was killing me more than the temperature. The company set up in a perimeter in this field. I kept watching the flashes up in the mountains but there was no word on what was happening.

It was pitch black other than for those occasional flashes up in the mountains. With the suddenness of a scream, the lights went on everywhere. Flares coming down on parachutes, bugles, explosions, incendiaries, whistles, and everybody shouting. Thousands of Chinese had attacked the 7th and the rest of the 5th Marine Regiment up on the ridges. Many enemy troops were swarming down the slopes and had broken through our lines around Yudam-ni. Green tracers went by my shelter half, so much fire that if I lifted my hand it would have been shot away. It was utter chaos at first, then our officers and NCOs started forming us up. "Saddle up and head over to the 3d Battalion, 5th HQ!"

Ziggy and I grabbed up the gun and ammo and personal weapons and took off in that direction. I had my M-2 carbine slung across my back so I could carry the gun over my shoulder. Tents had been set up for the 3d Battalion, 5th Marines Headquarters. Ziggy and I ran right into one of those big tents to try and get our bearings. It was black outside with lots of shouting, total chaos. I looked up and saw the stars through hundreds of bullet holes in the top of that tent. I grabbed Ziggy. "Let's get the hell out of here!" We ran out of the tent and into more confusion, with enemy troops running around visible only for moments in the light of flares or explosions. I knew they had overrun the perimeter. We couldn't tell friend from foe.

Then somebody shouted out real loud, "Charlie Company! Form up here!"

I don't know who screamed the orders but by the grace of God, somehow we formed up and we were moving up Hill 1282. Word came down the line we were to reinforce Easy Company, 2d Battalion, 7th Marine Regiment. They had been hit by huge numbers of Chinese and were being overrun. The situation was critical. We had to get up that 1282 feet of ice, and we had to be there now.

I couldn't see anything clearly. We started the climb up 1282, and somebody ahead screamed back at me, "Machine guns! Keep up!" The faster I tried to climb with all that weight, the more I slipped back down the slope. Suddenly a man slid past me, then two more. They were wounded. Then more wounded were sliding down the trail with corpsmen trying to help. They were men from 7th Marines, and it was

frighteningly clear that things were really bad up on top.
Flares gave off an eerie flickering light, and my night vision
came and went with bright flashes throughout the ridges and
valley. Easy Company, 2d Battalion was made up of about
60 percent reservists. They had been badly hit. Many had
been caught in their sleeping bags, dragged down the slopes
by the Chinese, and bayoneted to death or shot on the spot. The
ones still alive were putting up a vicious fight. We couldn't see,
men were slipping and sliding back down the slope, wounded
were coming down constantly, it was chaos. The CO, Captain
Jones, finally called us to a halt until we could see what we
were doing.

The lead elements of the column made it to just beneath
the crest of Hill 1282 around 0430 and came under heavy fire
from about one hundred yards above. A sergeant named
Murphy from E 2/7's 3d Platoon showed up and filled Captain Jones in on what had happened. E 2/7's main position
had been overrun and he was forming up survivors to make
a stand. It appeared that all of E 2/7's officers were down and
casualties were terrible. Easy Company had lost 120 killed
and wounded but had not given up the fight. Over to the left
of the crest was a platoon from A 1/5 holding on to a spur of
the hill.

A few minutes later I saw John Yancey. Yancey was a living legend, a World War II Raider and one of the toughest old
Marines ever. He was one of the few officers left in Easy 2/7,
and they were bringing him down. As all the wounds were to
his face, at first I couldn't even tell that it was him as they
carried him down the slope. He had caught two or three .45
slugs in the face, his face was a mask of blood and white
bone, but he wasn't whimpering and was still tough, though
I didn't think he would live. One eye was busted out of the
socket, his jaw broken with a .45 slug, and he was bleeding
from a wound near his nose.

The lead elements of the column were under intense fire
from machine guns and grenades being thrown down from
the summit of the hill, where at least fifty Chinese were positioned to hold out while they waited for reinforcements.

Captain Jones positioned two of his platoons along a line beneath the crest and called in 81s or 60mm mortars from the A 1/5 mortar section below. I saw the first shafts of sunlight, not really light but no longer totally dark. Captain Jones personally led the two Marine platoons ahead in a frontal attack, running uphill into the Chinese machine guns. The Marines charged up that snowy hill through a hail of machine gun fire and overran the Chinese, finishing them off in hand-to-hand combat.

We all rushed forward up to the top. "Get down!" a voice shouted from somewhere in the snow-covered ridge ahead of us. "The Chinese are making another frontal attack!"

My heart skipped a couple of beats, but between the fear, adrenaline and cold I was thankful it didn't just stop beating altogether right then and there. I reacted as every other machine gunner did. We ran forward, the snow and ice crunching under our boondockers, running like men with a hundred pounds of cement in their feet, jumping over or stepping on top of the dead. We dived into what had been Easy 2/7 positions. Dead Marines and dead Chinese were lying everywhere. Ziggy threw down the eighteen-pound tripod and popped out the legs. I put in the pintle in the top of the tripod to lock the gun in place and pulled back the bolt. The first ammo carrier opened a can of .30-caliber ammunition and loaded the gun while the squad leader, Corporal Holbrook, pointed out our field of fire. I started firing at the oncoming Chinese as Ziggy and Chick Sorenson opened fire with their carbines. Somebody opened another can of ammo and within seconds the gun was blazing and Chinese were dropping everywhere. The assault was beaten back and I just stared ahead numb and waiting.

Wounded and dead lay in dark clumps in the white snow, you could see the bodies when a flare popped open above or a shell burst sent out a flash of light. Our machine gun squad had to spread out to fill in the line. Daybreak was bringing more vision every second and the visions were horrific. Grenades were all over the place. Ziggy took over the gun and I crawled into a small hollow that someone had tried to carve out of the ice, but it was no real cover. The ground was frozen harder than concrete. We opened ammo boxes for the gun and prepared for another assault. Bugles resounded throughout the mountains, Chinese troops blew whistles and screamed. In the dim light of flares I could see enemy troops swarming over, then down snow-covered hillsides farther away. It was a paralyzing sight. I aimed my M-2 carbine at a Chinese soldier and pulled the trigger. Nothing. It was frozen and I didn't even have a .45 pistol. It was all one big chaotic event. Absolute insanity.

There was a dip in the landscape beyond our position, and we had no clear field of fire at the oncoming Reds until they charged up out of it and straight at us. I saw a wooden box nearby and crawled over to it. It was a box of grenades. I slid it across the snow, back to my position, and up beside me. In the dim light of flares I read the date clearly printed on the wooden box. These were 1917 World War I–issue fragmentation grenades. I broke it open and it was filled with these old, yellow-colored grenades. A moment's fear gripped me; were they too old to work in this extreme cold? There was no time to do anything but pull the pins and pray to God that the ancient grenades would still explode.

I pulled a pin and threw and before it exploded I had already pulled the pin on a second. I couldn't see the enemy, but the explosion brought a scream and I pulled the pin on a third and threw again. I kept throwing grenades until it felt like everything had to be dead. I stopped. My arm and shoulder ached, sore from throwing grenades. Bugles and whistles signaled that more Chinese were coming. "Get the gun in position to fire!" Someone screamed the order.

We tried to get the gun into a position to fire down into the defilade to our front, but there was no cover for the machine gun as we moved it into a firing position. I crawled out in front of the gun and grabbed a dead Chinese soldier by his mustard-colored uniform and dragged him up in front of the gun. I crawled back out and grabbed another body while one of the other Marines did the same thing. Enemy fire was sucked into the snow, thudding against the frozen earth all around us. Our gun position was open and vulnerable. There was only one way to build a bunker for the gun. Dead bodies froze into blocks of human ice very quickly. I grabbed the feet and Ziggy lifted the head of one and we piled him on top of another one, then we dragged two more up and piled them just like sandbags.

Another assault rushed at us and bullets thudded into the human bunkers. Men were wounded by bone splinters as bullets tore away pieces of our human sandbags. The Chinese threw grenades up at our positions and explosions rocked the entire defensive line of Marines, but our return fire was murderous. Most of their grenades were concussion grenades that knocked a lot of men out temporarily but didn't kill too many. They also had German potato-masher fragmentation grenades, which were more deadly, but sometimes there was no way to know what you just got hit with until the onslaught was over and you felt for holes. I kept throwing grenades as the gun opened up. I knew that every time that .30-caliber started firing, we would become a focal point for the onrushing Chinese. I threw grenades as fast as I could pull the pins and heave.

I don't know how long that assault lasted, time was impossible to calculate, it felt like days but it could have been minutes. Finally the firing stopped and we sat stunned and shaking from fear and the cold. The Chinese were dead. I think nearly every single gook in that assault was killed. Flares floated down on tiny parachutes. The barrel of the .30 had turned yellow and green from the type of gunpowder in all those Chinese concussion grenades. Not until that moment did I realize how many grenades must have landed around us. The smell of cordite was suffocating. I wondered if I would ever hear the same again, the ringing in my ears from the blasts was bothering my concentration.

"Drag back the wounded!" A voice shouted out something the men were already doing during the lull. Marines from below were bringing up more ammo and grenades. We tried to resupply each position and drag wounded and dead back to corpsmen. A lot of the shallow holes had been chiseled out

by the Chinese who overran Easy Company 2/7. Those foxholes had many dead and wounded Marines in them now. I
found the Easy Company runner in a hole with his commanding officer dying in his arms. It was a heartbreaking scene
but there was no time to mourn. The runner was wounded,
too, but looked like he would live. A corpsman showed up
to help.

Corpsmen ran around tirelessly trying to save the wounded.
It was nearly impossible to find the wounds on each man in
the dark through all the layers of clothes we wore, and re-
moving those clothes with frozen hands was no easier. The
only blessing about the extreme temperature was that it froze
the blood right away, which kept a lot of the men from bleeding to death. It also froze the morphine curettes, and the only
way to stop them from freezing solid was for the corpsmen
to keep them in their mouths. Each corpsman could hold
about four in his mouth. When he reached a wounded Marine he would take one out of his mouth and stick the
wounded man with a shot of morphine, try to find the wound,
bandage it, get him to the rear if possible, and move on to the
next wounded Marine.

Suddenly there was another charge and it was frenzy. I
shot some and missed some as they leaped over our position.
Marines behind us and on our flanks must have killed most
of them. I couldn't turn the .30 around, there were too many
still coming so I fired until no one was alive in front of us.
Morning came and I breathed a sigh of relief. It wasn't really
light yet, but the horizon was visible now and I knew that if
we could just hang on another hour or two we could make it.
If we could hang on until daylight our air cover would be
overhead. Everyone knew it but no one could speak it. The
exhaustion was overwhelming. We had to hang on til daylight, I knew that was our only chance.

The horizon got lighter and lighter, bringing hope with it.
Then it was daylight. Chinese lay frozen in grotesque positions where they fell. I heard cymbals and whistles echoing
through the icy mountains. I was behind the machine gun as
another wave of Chinese charged over slopes beyond us.

Soon they would be in the defilade to our direct front, then up and on top of us, trying to take the summit of 1282. Controlling the peaks above the Chosin was crucial. Marine riflemen had moved into flanking positions and were pouring it on. I fired the .30 into the charging Chinese. I could see the hits as pieces of their cotton-padded uniforms would explode, sort of like when you shoot a bird and the feathers fly everywhere. I kept firing, trying to keep the bursts as short as possible to keep from burning out the barrel, but it reached a point when I had to keep firing or let them overrun me. Ziggy or Chick threw snow on the barrel to keep it cool. I fired until there were no more targets. The snow was splattered red with human remains. Wounded cried in pain for a while, but their cries faded as they froze to death.

During the lull we moved around our position trying to clean up the area. I crawled out in front to move piles of dead Chinese out of our firing lanes and the squad got more ammo ready. Others tried to build bunkers out of the dead or find weapons that still worked. I was checking ammo belts and rechecking the machine gun when I saw this big Marine crawling through the snow near us. He was crawling on his elbows and knees while cradling an M-1 Garand in his arms. I watched the guy struggling, he was a wire-layer and he had this big roll of heavy com-wire on his back. The guy was actually sweating, his face was drenched with sweat and it was at least twenty below zero. That communication wire was heavy. He saw our machine gun and stopped.

"Hey! Any of you gunners got a pistol you wanna trade for this M-1?"

Every machine gun squad leader and first gunner carry a .45, but no one was going to give up a .45-caliber pistol on Hill 1282. I yelled back at the guy, "I don't have a pistol but I've got an M-2 carbine that don't work!"

"I'll take it!"

I looked at the guy like he was nuts, then I jumped on that deal! I grabbed up that useless M-2 and ran it over to the guy. His name was Vernon Kilde, a big Norwegian. I know he had a heavy load, and laying communication wire from Yudam-ni to the top of 1282 had to be one awful job, but there were dead Chinese lying everywhere and the danger was a little more than obvious. He took it anyway. I went back to our human machine gun bunker hugging that M-1 like my favorite gal. Soon after that I started really worrying about the guy.

Suddenly another wave of mustard-colored uniforms appeared and the cracks of M-1 rifles and our machine guns cut them down. As one line of Chinese dropped, grenadiers, troops carrying only grenades, would pick up their dead comrade's burp gun and continue the charge. These burp guns had been designed by the Finns in 1940 to fight the Russians. They were made for close-in combat and not real powerful, but they fired 71- or 72-round drums. They put out so many rounds-per-second that when a Marine was hit by a burp gun, he usually caught more than one bullet. Some Marines were hit three or four times and still fought. The weapon got its name from the *burrrrrp* sound it made firing full-automatic. Hundreds of slugs sang past our ears and even more thudded into the human bunker that protected the machine gun. They came running, throwing concussion grenades and potato mashers. Their grenades didn't have the killing radius or amount of shrapnel that our grenades had, but the blast put every man in momentary shock. Their strategy was to get close enough to fire point-blank with the burp guns.

Somebody broke open another box of machine gun ammo. I opened up again, along with every able-bodied Marine in Charlie Company. The rush was beaten back, our fire was accurate and deadly. Only five or six Chinese troops were able to retreat out of what appeared to be an entire platoon.

The day was wearing on. We knew we couldn't keep this up. Our casualties were mounting and there seemed to be an endless supply of Chinese ready to die in front of our machine guns. Bugles sounded, then whistles as Chinese commanders signaled their troops for another charge. A Chinese platoon appeared in the snow and blood. Marines rained grenades down on the Chinese as riflemen started picking them off. I opened up with the .30 and worried that the barrel would melt. We carried spare parts and spare barrels, but right now I knew no one would have time to unscrew that barrel without burning the flesh off his hands, then find another barrel, screw it in, measure the head-space, and open fire again.

They charged throwing grenades and firing burp guns, and we shot them as they ran right up to us. Some ran right past us and I could smell the garlic even through the cordite. Those men with .45s had them drawn and shot down Chinese at point-blank range. The knockdown power of the .45 was tremendous.

It got quiet again. The smell of garlic was heavy in the air. You could always smell the garlic on the Chinese and North Koreans, and it was thick in my nostrils. I couldn't see them but we knew from the smell that they were close. We pulled the pins on a couple of grenades and tossed them out in front of us. The explosions brought a groan. Then I heard firing behind us and to our flanks as Marines killed off those CCF troops that had broken through. The fight never stopped. Marines on both sides and somewhere to the rear were fighting for their lives. Then the shooting slowed. A single shot would ring out every so often as a Marine would finish off one of the gooks that had made it through our line.

Men stared wild-eyed with shell shock and waited for the next charge. Somebody yelled out a strange order or maybe it was just a Marine Corps suggestion. "Open your C rats and take out the cigarettes and sugar! Don't leave anything good for them!"

I couldn't see and didn't care who had shouted, but everyone understood and started opening their C-ration packages and laying their sugar and cigarettes around the edges of their fighting holes. The men started eating everything they could so the gooks wouldn't get any of our food when they overran us. The strangest emotion seemed to take control of me. It seemed to come over every Marine on the hill. I knew now that we were not giving up that hill and that we would hold it or die. There was no doubt in any of our minds and therefore only one conclusion, and any second thoughts or confusion were absolutely removed. Hold or die. The fact that there was no doubt in our Marine Corps minds about what had to be done seemed to give every man around me a strange sense of serenity. I prayed to the Lord Jesus and felt calm, almost curious, about the outcome.

Chinese troops rushed at us again, running and stumbling over piles of their own dead. I opened fire again. Soon I had to cease fire as all of my rounds were hitting piles of dead enemy soldiers. I crawled out along with Ziggy and Chick and I don't know who else. We started dragging and shoving the piles of dead away to clear a field of fire for the gun. Bullets from Chinese troops on the other side of the defilade were hitting all around us as they spotted what we were trying to do, but they kept missing. Finally we shoved enough dead away to open up a firing lane again. They came at us again and the .30 barked until it jammed for good. The barrel finally melted and the gun went silent. I grabbed up that M-1 and Ziggy started pulling bullets out of the machine gun belts and loading them into M-1 clips. Thank God the M-1 fired the same round.

We took turns firing that M-1 until the barrel was smoking. I lost count of how many clips of eight rounds we went through. That M-1 was no .30-cal, but it saved our lives and held the position as it knocked Chinese down with one powerful .306 round at 2,700 feet per second. The M-1 was 9 ½ pounds, 10 when loaded, gas operated, and absolutely dead accurate at 600 to 700 yards. Every Marine trained with it constantly, and there wasn't a man in the division who couldn't hit a C-ration can at 700 yards with that weapon. It ejected the clip out the top and before it hit the snow, Ziggy had another one ready or I had one for him. Every twelve-man Marine squad had three BARs, Browning automatic weapons, to support the rest of the squad carrying M-1s. When you threw in the machine gun squad, that was some awesome firepower. A lot of Chinese were discovering that. Marines were crawling out and rolling piles of dead away to clear firing lanes. Pushing dead soldiers aside so I could kill more was something I could have never imagined.

I wasn't sure we could hold out much longer. We had no barrel for the gun and Charlie Company was taking more and more casualties. It looked like hand-to-hand combat was only a matter of time, and I was trying to steady myself for that moment. The roar of a dark blue Marine Corsair ripped past so low that his wingtip was beneath our position. He strafed the enemy troops with devastating .50-caliber machine gun fire. He swept up and around as another Corsair repeated the strafing run. Hot shell casings from the Marine fighters landed all over us, bouncing off some of our helmets. They came in again, this time firing rockets. I thought I heard myself cheer but I was so cold it may have just been my mind cheering. It broke the back of the sixth enemy charge. The white slopes were littered red with the carnage. The 1st Battalion of the 235th Chinese Communist Regiment was basically dead. Over four hundred Chinese lay dead on 1282.

The day wore on, and it became quiet except for the occasional sniper round, and no one paid any attention to those. I got up and walked around the hill just to get some blood back in my legs. Marines were walking around all over trying to do the same. Pretty soon the order was passed from one leatherneck to another, "When you come off the hill, carry your dead with you." I didn't know what the plan was other than we were leaving the hill. I looked around for a dead Marine to carry but I couldn't find one, so I lugged the .30-caliber machine gun over my right shoulder with the M-1 slung across my back. Word came, and the men headed down that frozen rock called 1282.

I had one last look around, it was like a second glimpse at a nightmare. I turned and headed off down the slope and found myself pretty much alone. From a distance I heard a rumble sort of echo through those miserable mountains of ice. Then I didn't hear anything. It happened quick. *Baaam!* An artillery shell landed down the slope in front of me. Yudam-ni was farther down in the valley in front of me and I could see people down there, moving away from incoming artillery. I had heard incoming artillery and it's nothing I looked forward to, but I wasn't getting all upset about it, just sludging on. *Baaam!* Another round hit closer to me. They were walking a barrage toward our guys going down 1282. I looked ahead and saw a ridge. "If I can make it to that ridge, I got it made," I mumbled to myself. That was the last thing I remembered before the pain.

I don't know how long it took me to wake up. I forced my eyes open first and I was facedown in frozen brush. My ears were ringing something awful and I could not think clearly. I had no idea where I was. I remembered pretty quick that I was in a war. My back felt wet and that wet was spreading around and it was warm, so I knew it was blood. The cobwebs cleared enough for me to think and what I thought was not good. I was sure that my back was blown wide open. I started taking inventory. I looked for my right hand and was happy to find it attached, then the left. I had a mitten on and there was a shrapnel hole in it. The mitten was filling with blood but I didn't care, it was my back I was worried about. I couldn't tell how bad my back was, was I bleeding to death or what? Fear really gripped me, and I guessed that I was about to go into shock or maybe I already was in shock. I had never felt this scared in my whole life. I'm dying, I thought to myself. I'm lying here just dying all alone. There's nobody to help and I'm going to just lie here and die in this stinking place called Korea. I suddenly hated the idea of dying all alone. I got angry about it and yelled, "Corpsman!" No one answered. I raged up the energy to yell again, "Corpsman!" I was dying. I tried again, "Corpsman! Corpsman up! Corpsman!" I don't know how many times I screamed out or how loud it really was.

Suddenly I heard footsteps breaking through snow and ice coming toward me. I heard a voice. "Hey, buddy, I ain't a corpsman, but can I help you?"

"Go get a corpsman!"

I heard him running away. Artillery started blasting the reverse side of the slope that I was on. They blasted the hill above me. Ice and rocks thumped everywhere. When debris hit my back I felt it. I heard footsteps running toward me again.

"Doc!" I yelled.

I don't think he answered.

"Give me a shot!" I said.

I glanced up. He carried the morphine in his mouth so it wouldn't freeze and he had to remove his mitten. He started cutting away my clothes around my right shoulder and then stuck me in the right shoulder with the morphine.

"That M-1 across your back just saved your life, Marine."

I don't know if the corpsman moved me himself or if another Marine was helping, but I felt myself being rolled onto a poncho and somebody was dragging me down the hill and it sure wasn't no sleigh ride. Everything went gray.

I opened my eyes and I was lying on my stomach on a stretcher inside a big tent. It was like waking up in heaven, I could feel warmth. I looked around and couldn't believe my eyes, they even had a stove in that tent. A few minutes later, wounded started being carried into the tent and lots of these Marines were in real bad shape. A couple of corpsmen picked up my stretcher and carried me outside to make room for more seriously wounded. They placed me on the ground and the sun was shining bright as can be, but it was freezing. They went back into the tent and I just stayed there, happy I was still alive. That happy thought evaporated with the sound of a big C-119 cargo plane flying past pretty low. I twisted to look up and saw him about five hundred feet up and right over me. I could see guys shoving cargo out the back of the big plane, huge crates of supplies. They were on chutes but when they hit the ground, everything shook. They were shoving cargo right out on top of me. Another one flew by and more crates of cargo slammed to the earth close enough to shake me. I just kept telling Jesus that it wouldn't be right for me to make it this far and get crushed by cargo. I was worried.

Scuttlebutt got around, even to the wounded. We became aware of the situation. The 1st Marine Division was surrounded and cut off by ten Chinese divisions, although at that point they no longer had ten complete divisions. We had bloodied their noses real good and the gooks suffered terrible casualties. The MSR had been cut by the Chinese. That seventy miles of steep, twisting ice and gravel was the only way out of there, and we were going to have to fight our way every step of that seventy miles. It was around this time that President Truman and I guess a lot of others had unofficially and behind closed doors written off the 1st Marine Division. Many didn't think it was possible to come out of there against such odds and in such weather. It was also at this time that the commanding general of the 1st Marine Division sent a response up the chain of command that said, "Since the Marines were totally surrounded, they would do the only thing Marines were trained to do. They would attack the enemy." A junior officer got a little testy with some reporter who said something about the Marines retreating. His response was, "Retreat hell! There's Chinese in every direction! We're just attacking in a different direction!" And he was right. We attacked down that seventy miles of gravel and ice until the Chinese were minus some of those ten divisions they had sent against the 1st Marine Division.

I was placed on a trailer that was pulled by a jeep. That jeep had four stretchers in the back of it and two more on the trailer. It was slow going, and the convoy had to stop often as Marines up ahead shot their way through roadblocks and ambushes while Marines above swept the ridges clean in one tough battle after another. Guys walking alongside the road would help me as we went along. A chaplain came by regularly to check on me. When one of the wounded died, they would sometimes strap the body across the front of one of the trucks or jeeps just like you did a deer in hunting season.

It was very cold, it seemed like it would never be warm again. I could tell I was drifting in and out of consciousness. I opened my eyes once and knew I had been out. I found myself staring off into a valley once just as a flight of Corsairs swooped down with loads of napalm. Just seeing the fire made me think warm and I knew a bunch of Chinese were thinking real warm right over there. Corsairs came in again firing rockets. It sure felt good seeing those guys on duty.

The jeep stopped. I could hear firefights going on in the surrounding hills and ridges along each side of the road.

At night they threw a tarp over us. The next morning, when they removed the tarp, the ground was white with fresh snow. Each day changed. One would be gray and overcast and the next it might be real sunny. Even in the sun it wasn't warm but it made you feel warmer mentally. I could hear a guy on the jeep groaning. He just kept whimpering and groaning. The guy never shut up. I tried to talk to him at first but then I gave up.

Debris littered both sides of the road. Trucks and jeeps that had either been hit or broke were set on fire. There was crap everywhere that Marines were just dumping as loads got too heavy. We stopped and started, stopped and started over and over, and each time it hurt some of the badly wounded. The road was narrow and rough. I saw bodies strapped on the barrels of artillery, on the sides of trucks, or across the hoods. Bodies were tied to any available space. They were all stiff. Boots sticking out of ponchos. Sometimes I'd see bare feet sticking out of a bag. We ran out of body bags or ponchos and sometimes I'd see the whole corpse strapped to a vehicle. You could tell the color of their hair, even the hair would freeze stiff. The second day out of Yudam-ni the guy on the trailer next to me died.

I lost track of time. I was in and out constantly. We were near Hagaru-ri. Somebody came around and unloaded the litters. I wasn't sure if I was dreaming, I wasn't fully conscious. I felt myself being lifted up out of the litter or at least I thought I was being lifted. I forced my eyes open and found myself in a sandpit by the side of the road with a bunch of corpses. All dead Marines. They were all frozen solid. Some of the dead were in horrible positions, legs and arms sticking out, broken in grotesque angles. I couldn't hear a thing. Then it hit me like a bayonet! They think I'm dead! They were leaving me with the dead to be taken out last.

"I'm not dead!" I started screaming. "I'm not dead! Hey! Somebody! I'm not dead!"

"Take it easy, Mac," a voice said calmly.

I took a breath and calmed down. I was so thirsty I couldn't stand it. Finally a Marine came by and offered me a drink of juice. "You want the can?"

"Yeah!"

He gave me this big quart can of pineapple juice. He held me up 'cuz I was on my stomach. He helped twist me around and my back didn't seem to hurt right then. I gulped that juice down and it ran all over me. I drank until I couldn't get any more in me.

Somebody said it was December 5. They had placed a lot of the litter patients in a row near the airstrip, it was actually more of an ice-strip than an airstrip. I knew I was close to the runway because I kept hearing airplane engines. The harsh cracks of M-1s and .30-caliber machine guns came from somewhere nearby, it was a serious firefight. Off to one side of us a flight of Corsairs was bombing the crap out of somebody. I lifted my head enough to watch the action. I saw Marguerite Higgins walking around all the wounded guys. She'd stop and kneel down to interview them. She was one of the most famous war correspondents we had in Korea. I was still on my stomach and didn't look presentable for any woman to see. Sure enough I saw her coming toward me. She knelt down and said she wanted to talk to me. I told her to go to hell.

I was exhausted. I had not eaten any food in seven days. Somebody gave me a couple of shots of morphine during that seven days but no food. I was going in and out. I found myself on a stretcher on a DC-3. When it got warm inside, the smell of the filthy, wounded Marines made some people sick. We landed in Osaka, Japan, and they put us in an army hospital. There were not enough beds so they put men in the hallways, and we smelled really bad. I heard some army nurses screaming and managed to see what had happened. A grenade had rolled out of one of the men's pockets and down the hall. "Get those dirty Marines out of here before somebody gets killed!" We loved it.

They finally took us to Yokosuku Naval Hospital. I got the steel out of my back and the chief of staff presented me with my Purple Heart.

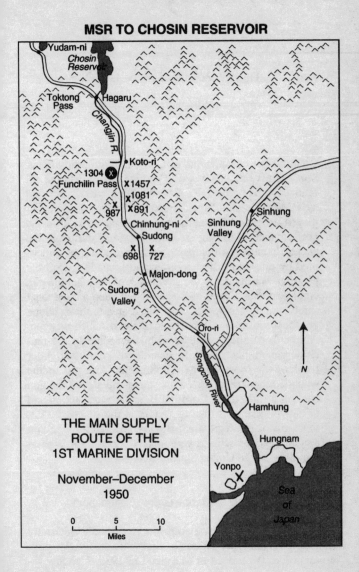

MSR TO CHOSIN RESERVOIR

Yudam-ni
Chosin Reservoir
Toktong Pass
Hagaru
Changjin R.
Koto-ri
1304 X
Funchilin Pass
X 1457
X 1081
X 891
X 987
Chinhung-ni
Sudong
X 698
X 727
Majon-dong
Sinhung Valley
Sinhung
Sudong Valley
Oro-ri
Songchon River
Hamhung
Hungnam
Yonpo
Sea of Japan

N

THE MAIN SUPPLY
ROUTE OF THE
1ST MARINE DIVISION

November–December
1950

0   5   10
Miles

5

CPL. DAN BOGAN

Silver Star

Citation: For conspicuous gallantry and intrepidity in action against the enemy while serving with a Marine infantry company in KOREA on 23 August 1952. Serving as a Machine Gun Squad Leader, Corporal Bogan displayed exceptional courage and professional skill in the performance of his duties. Under cover of darkness, the enemy launched a company strength assault, accompanied by intense artillery, mortar and grenade fire on the position. When enemy fire struck one of the machine gun emplacements, Corporal Bogan disregarded his personal safety and moved across an exposed area to the machine gun position in an effort to repair the disabled weapon. Although painfully wounded while en-route to the machine gun emplacement, he dauntlessly continued. After reaching the position, he administered first aid to the wounded men, reorganized his squad and placed the gun back in to operation. Corporal Bogan's quick action and initiative were contributing factors in the successful defense of the strategic area, Bunker Hill, and his gallant and courageous actions were in keeping with the highest traditions of the United States Naval Service.

E. A. Pollock
Major General, U.S. Marine Corps, Commanding

I grew up in rural New Hampshire. Never saw electricity til I started school. My father got a job with the GAO, a government job. We moved to Maryland in 1939. I vividly remember the day World War II broke out, car horns blowing, people yelling to each other to turn on their radios and screaming, "We've been attacked!" I was eleven years old and it was exciting and scary. I remember how proud me and all the adults were when we heard how the Marine detachment on Wake Island kept holding out against impossible odds. When they beat back the Jap landing and sank those ships with so few Marines, I was ready to join up. Then came news about Guadalcanal and what a job the Marines did against all odds again.

We had blackout practices, civilian spotters on the roofs of our buildings, and air-raid wardens. Then those little banners with the gold stars started showing up in the windows of neighbors, signaling that someone in their family had been killed in action. We had metal drives and you could get into the movie houses for free if you brought in scrap iron for the war effort. I bent up some of my mom's pans so I could see the movie about Marine machine gunner Al Schmidt. He was a hero on Guadalcanal with his water-cooled .30-caliber machine gun. When Marines found him the gun was out of action, his crew killed. He was wounded and blind and holding a .45 pistol. They thought he was going to commit suicide, then he squared them away. "Show me where they are so I can keep shooting!" If somebody had told me then that in seven or eight years I'd be heading into combat with the exact same machine gun that the great Al Schmidt had used, I wouldn't have believed it.

All of my family had been in the navy and air force. I remember that all of the WWII vets that I met had never actually been in combat. I wanted to see action. There was one outfit where there would be no doubt about seeing action. So I enlisted in the Marines. My dad was pretty upset about it, but he got over it and was proud of me.

Once I got out of Parris Island, I knew I was not the same person. There's no way to explain how the Corps makes men out of boys, you've got to live it. It's not just training, you can train a bunch of men until they're tough, they might be in super shape, might be able to swim underwater for a long

time or do one-arm push-ups all day, but that doesn't make
them Marines. At Camp Lejeune, I was assigned to machine
gun platoon. The first class was on the nomenclature of the
Browning Model 1917A1, the water-cooled .30-caliber heavy
machine gun. Our instructor was a WWII vet, Corporal Hor-
vac, a reserve Marine pulled back into active service because
of Korea. When he started pulling the parts off that gun, I
thought he'd never stop.

It was called the heavy gun and for good reason. Full of
water it weighed 32 pounds and the tripod weighed 51 pounds.
In front of the water jacket where the muzzle of the barrel
came through was a gland-nut. The back end of the gland-nut
had a groove called a cannular groove. A strip of asbestos
soaked in oil was wrapped in this groove as a seal against
water leakage, then the gland-nut screwed into the water
jacket that the barrel projected through. A small can of these
asbestos strips soaked in oil were carried in the spare parts
kit by one of the ammo carriers.

We practiced day and night on this nomenclature. Finally
we could change barrels blindfolded in seconds. Then the
classes on functioning began. This involved firing on the one-
thousand-inch range, the targets being one-inch squares in
various patterns to teach traversing. We learned about beaten
zones, the area of bullet-striking, indirect fire, range cards,
and all pertinent phases of machine gun operation. We were
taught that certain targets are not machine gun targets, like a
lone enemy soldier. I was to never give away the gun position
frivolously. Once a machine gun opens up, the life expectancy of the gunner is measured in minutes at best, but it
wasn't just your life you were risking. The whole platoon of
Marines depended on that machine gun and on you being
alive to operate it.

A squad consisted of a squad leader, first gunner, second
gunner, and five ammo carriers, one of whom also carried a
spare parts kit for the gun and steam-condensing device. The
first gunner carried the tripod. When we set up he dropped
the tripod, leveled it, and got into position behind it. The second gunner placed the gun on the tripod by placing the pin-

tle through the opening on the tripod, tripping the pintle latch, and opening a can of ammo, then feeding a belt of ammo into the gun. He would also hook the steam-condensing device to the water jacket on the gun and place the other end in a water can. This device was merely a length of rubber hose that would divert any steam from the heated gun back to the water to condense. The first gunner latches the traversing mechanism to the gun to prevent "free" gun, pulls the bolt back twice, then the gun is ready to fire. All this has to be done in about twenty seconds while people are trying to kill you. The ammo carriers spread out on either side of the gun with their M-2 carbines to protect the flanks of the gun, leaving ammo near the second gunner. Often, in case of blind spots in the terrain, a BAR, Browning automatic rifle, man was placed to cover any blind spot.

On January 28, 1952, I arrived at Camp Pendleton for advanced infantry training. We learned that parts of Camp Pendleton were still working ranches. The Corps decided it was time for us to spend a week in the mountains at the Pickle Meadows area, located near Bishop, California. It was on the 38th parallel, and we were being prepared to fight in Korean winter conditions and altitude. We were designated the eighteenth replacement draft, but we were not drafted, we had joined the United States Marine Corps. We ended up experiencing the late winter of '51, all of '52, and most of '53 in Korea, so getting used to all the cold weather clothing, boots, and equipment proved crucial.

The Corps is famous for genuine characters, characters that Hollywood couldn't dream up. The old salts or even some of the new Marines were unlike any other people on earth. We had a character in our outfit named Cowboy. Cowboy was from Colorado, and if you were getting ready to walk into hell that guy could make you laugh. He said things with a straight face and you wondered if he believed them himself. He didn't look like a cowboy, five-foot-four and thick with muscle, one of those no-neck guys. We were out in the field and the wind was blowing fierce. The worst we had ever experienced. Cowboy tugged on his ear and said, "I remember a storm back in Colorado where the wind blew so hard they had to put blankets over their horses' asses to keep the wind from blowing the bits out of their mouths." He said it slow and serious as if it were the gospel truth.

The base camp was at 6,000 feet elevation and we climbed as high as 9,000 feet. We pitched camp on about eighteen feet of snow. It was packed so we didn't sink. We paired off, snapped shelter halves together to make tents, and tried to not freeze to death. It got to be minus 34 degrees at night, so we had to keep our C rations and canteens in our sleeping bags, to keep them from freezing. The Corps provided "aggressors" who would ski into camp, fire off blanks, and ski away. We had to get into our cold weather gear, Mickey Mouse insulated boots, etc., grab our web gear, and pursue them.

We looked like a bunch of monkeys playing football as we stumbled around half asleep, each of us in the other guy's way, and every move we made seemed to make the situation worse. It was as much fun as a cold-water enema. So there we stood, the followers of those Guadalcanal and Iwo Jima heroes, freezing in the dark night, boots on the wrong feet, trying to find a way to take a leak through four layers of disarrayed winter gear, everyone mad enough to kill with their bare hands. We never once saw the "aggressors," but we could hear their laughter in the cold midnight air.

Through the misery, we were learning how to survive and work as an effective fighting unit in the worst of conditions. We were soon able to deliver effective firepower under any conditions. Now we were ready to tackle another chore. Korea. After a weekend in Tijuana, we loaded our packs and boarded trucks for the trip to San Diego, where we boarded the MSTS ship, *General Gordon*. It was a typical, cramped Marine Corps cruise with endless chow lines, and it seemed to last forever.

We made a brief stop in Kobe, Japan. It was my twenty-first birthday and I was sitting in this outstanding Kobe bar with Sergeant "Zig." Zig was an old salt. He talked rough because he was rough. Zig was a Marine and to those that know, that's the only description needed. He had a chestful of campaign ribbons earned killing Japs, and he still had no love for the Japanese. He'd seen his share of atrocities by the Japanese, as had many of the "old salts." The bartender was American and he paused to look at Zig and his campaign ribbons.

"Hey, Mac. Were you on Iwo Jima?"

"Yeah," Zig said.

"I was a machine gunner on that beach," the bartender chimed in gruffly.

Zig slapped me on the back. "The kid here is a gunner and it's his twenty-first birthday!"

That old machine gunner looked at me and threw down his bar towel. The drinks were free and they kept coming. God only knows how or when or why, but we ended up somewhere in Kobe and some Japanese kid came up to Zig and me. The kid was holding this card. The card said that his grandfather had been killed in the war and he'd appreciate some money for his family.

"Get the 'ell out of here. For all I know I killed him!"

That was Sergeant Zig. The old salts were hard men. They'd tell you straight up that a Marine has only one true purpose and that is to kill any enemy of America, if you don't like that job, then get out of their Marine Corps. After several hours ashore, we boarded ship and were off for Korea. I was on a ship going to war as a Marine. There's excitement and then there's fear-driven excitement. I was excited and I was scared. Not as scared of any enemy as I was of letting other Marines down.

We anchored off the coast of Korea and my first view of the place was in the dim, predawn light when sea and sky meet in the same leaden color. The background was high, snowcapped mountains and it appeared to be a dark and sinister place. The air was biting cold as we went down the nets to the ducks, or amphibious six-by-sixes (DUKWs), for the two-mile ride to shore. We were all busy with our thoughts and there was no talk. It's not that Marines are not talkers, they are, but I learned something the old salts already knew:

professionals knew when to chat and when to think. We landed on the east coast and were trucked up to Camp Tripoli, where I joined D Company, 2d Battalion, 1st Marines. Somehow I got assigned straight into a rifle company with a heavy machine gun. Normally I would have been thrown into a weapons company. You learn some things real quick in the Corps, one of those things is to not question, just obey orders.

At last we came face-to-face with Marines who had been through the hell of combat, and how green we looked to them was evident in their eyes. They were glad to see us but obviously withholding judgment until we proved ourselves as Marines in combat. They didn't give us much attention since they had just come off the line and had important matters to tend to. The beer ration was due. The beer truck finally arrived and the men enthusiastically pitched in to get it unloaded. I was busy lending a hand but not too busy to notice a North Korean soldier approaching with his hands over his head, waving a surrender leaflet. He came toward us, and the salts looked at the surrender leaflet. One surly looking sergeant glanced at the leaflet, then flipped a thumb at the North Korean with a gesture that said I'd just shoot you if I could spare the time. "Go over to Easy Company to surrender, we're busy, pal." The gook wandered off searching for someone he could surrender to, and I knew that he must have been thinking that all he had ever heard about the U.S. Marines was true. They were crazy.

I settled into a tent and met some of the guys I would be serving with. PFC Fribisher was from New York, a laid-back guy who took each event in stride. He was a little taller than my stocky five-foot-eight build, thin and talkative. Nothing could stop the chatter, he had opinions about everything. A real nice guy and a big help in getting me familiar with routines. The outfit had just come off Operation Killer and they had plenty of stories. PFC Hagara ended up being one of my ammo carriers. He had made a checkerboard out of cardboard on the troopship and no one could beat him. He gambled on everything. He was a smaller-built man, about my size, from Chicago. He said that every time they caught him gambling back at Lejeune they took his winnings and gave it to the Iwo Jima monument fund. He sort of thought of that monument as partially his own.

Within a week we loaded onto trucks and drove all night over to the other side of the country. It was cold. We rode on top of all that gear in the truck. Every so often the convoy stopped so we could get some circulation back in our legs and take a leak. We finally stopped at some barren hill and that was our position for a few days until we went to another hill. We caught some incoming fire but nothing serious, still it showed me that this was no drill. We quickly discovered that the Korean War had settled into a form of trench warfare almost like World War I. Hundreds of thousands of Chinese were facing Allied troops in somewhat of a standoff. Our tanks were in fixed positions and used mainly as artillery.

We arrived at the reserve area to regroup before going up on the line. The next morning I met Gunnery Sergeant Schooley, the platoon sergeant that my machine gun squad was assigned to. I began as the second gunner on my first hill, Hill 101. I was awakened late that night for my first watch in a combat zone. The night was bright with stars. We were on the crest of a long ridge with a deep valley between our line and another ridge. It was real quiet but I had questions that had to be answered so I said to the guy I was relieving, "Which way do I watch? Where are the Chinese supposed to be?"

He pointed to the hill on the other side of the valley. "Watch that." He disappeared. I sat staring into that cold night thinking how peaceful it was and what a strange introduction to the Korean War.

The next morning we were standing and talking about nothing important when PFC Fribisher hollered, "Incoming!" Everyone dived for cover. I landed in a hole full of empty C-ration cans as mortar rounds started exploding all around us. I was amazed that Fribisher had heard them coming or knew they were coming toward us. In a very short time I acquired the skill of hearing a "one away" and knowing about where it was headed. I don't know how it happens, but every combat veteran developed that skill.

A few nights later I sat huddled behind some sandbags and the .30-caliber machine gun, just staring, eyes straining with the fear that I might miss seeing that one enemy soldier before he saw me. Or would it be the first Chinese soldier in a wave of a thousand, how fast could I knock them down, would it be fast enough? Suddenly I saw a light, and I knew that couldn't be possible. I rubbed my eyes and leaned forward as if that would make a difference. It was a light! At the base of the enemy hill, a man was walking back and forth carrying a lantern. I knew even before the word came down that he was attempting to draw our fire so they would know our positions for a mortar attack. We had a term for this sort of job in the Corps, a real ——it detail! I sat watching that poor gook and thanking God I never ticked anyone off bad enough to get a job like that. We could have killed him easily but this was our first example of the lengths the communists would go to just to locate our machine guns. If I opened up on a single soldier the gooks wouldn't have time to kill me, some old salt would beat 'em to it.

Statistics so far in Korea had proved that once you opened up with the machine gun, your life expectancy was counted in minutes or less. Hearing stats like that made us gunners patient. Our guns would have lots of targets before this war was over; a noise in the wire, a single gook, these were targets for the riflemen to deal with or we could throw a grenade, but never, ever fire the machine gun.

Gunnery Sergeant Schooley was a short-timer in Korea and in the Marine Corps. He had nineteen years in the Corps. He was a good leader and I could talk to him and he was open to suggestions. He was about six feet tall and heavy, but he wasn't fat. He carried a Smith & Wesson .38-caliber revolver, the Combat Masterpiece model. It had a heavy frame much like the modern magnums. I also had bought one of these in California before boarding ship. Many Marines had personal weapons because they were easier to carry in the trenches than the Garands or carbines. Scuttlebutt said that the Chinese were grabbing guys in their sleeping bags on outposts and carrying them off. So as a precaution, many of us took our pistols into the sleeping bags with us. We had a common saying about that heavy .38-caliber revolver. If one of us "bought it," then their buddy would have a matched pair of pistols.

One day I went from gunner to squad leader, then eventually section leader for guns. I hardly ever had my TO strength of sixteen men. The rifle squads were always requesting a machine gun to go out on endless patrols or outpost duty. With such a shortage of trained machine gunners, I ended up sharing in every duty, depending on the situation, to give the guys a little break.

We were back on the main line of resistance, the MLR, when this truck came rumbling up from the rear. We were getting ready to go out on a patrol, and this young lieutenant and a couple of his men came around handing out something called a "flak jacket." No one had ever seen these things before and we were to be a test case. They wanted us to wear them out on this patrol and then report on what we thought of them. The men put them on with the usual gripes and questions, but no one thought that much about it. For machine gunners it was just more weight to hump up some mud-covered hill.

We moved to Hill 191, called Gibraltar. It was about two thousand meters in front of the MLR. I had an A4 air-cooled .30-caliber machine gun and my squad plus a rifle squad with us. Our job was to set up on this ridge and give covering fire for a patrol up on Gibraltar. Down below the ridge were rice paddies and relatively flat land. The patrol was led by Joe Galvin, a full-blooded Navajo from Arizona. Joe was a great guy and a good friend, rugged and tough, all Marine. I watched Joe's patrol come toward us from our left, but higher up. We could see the men clearly. I had my squad lying prone on either side of the gun under these little pine trees. Suddenly green tracers streaked through the air, a Chinese machine gun firing on Joe's patrol. I followed the green tracers until I saw the enemy muzzle flash, then laid on the trigger until my tracers were on target. Fire on the patrol ceased, then the Chinese machine gun redirected its fire toward us. I was used to seeing tracers going out, but seeing tracer rounds coming right at me sent chills down my spine. Bullets sang just over our heads, snapping off the tops of the small pine trees we were under. I got a good bead on the muzzle flash and sent two short bursts of about twenty rounds each into the enemy position. My red tracers seemed to hit right on the mark.

We sat there waiting for more incoming fire, but that was it. I knew in my heart that I'd just killed a Chinese gun team. "We must have struck home," one of the guys said. Suddenly a green flare went up, which translates "haul butt" 'cause here come mortar rounds. We jumped up and ran down a drainage ditch alongside a rice paddy, and as crooked as that stinking ditch was, those mortar rounds followed just behind our every step. I ran as fast as I could move, but trying to run with a heavy machine gun and all the gear was like running underwater. I felt like I was moving in slow motion. I could see the bunkers and trenches of the MLR ahead and thought we'd made it, then *bam!* A round dropped right between me and the guy about ten yards behind me. In an instant I was skidding on my face from the blast. When I knew I was still alive, I glanced back. The Marine behind me had been blown backward on his butt. We looked at each other, then both got to our feet feeling our legs and arms, checking for missing limbs or blood. I guess we had the necessary parts 'cuz we took off as fast as we could run. Eventually we made it back to the MLR.

As soon as we returned from that patrol, some officer showed up wanting to know what we thought of the new "flak jackets." I looked mine over, feeling it with my hands until something sharp cut me. I found a quarter-size piece of shrapnel embedded in the shoulder of the jacket. I gave the officer a hearty approval rating for the new jacket. They had just a few of them, so we got to wear one only when we went out on patrol. Later on everyone was issued a flak jacket.

Soon after that our lieutenant called my squad and Joe Galvin's squad to his bunker.

"You men are volunteering to go out and get us a Chinese prisoner. You'll move into enemy territory and set up an ambush. Guns will cover but don't open fire until the prisoner has been clobbered." The lieutenant looked at big Joe. "Corporal Galvin, you'll take out the last man in an enemy patrol if you can. Let the patrol pass, then Corporal Galvin will take out the last man. At that point I want guns to open up, then beat it back to the MLR with that gook. Now don't kill him, Corporal, just knock him out, we need him."

"Aye, aye, sir."

Cpl. Joe Galvin had arms as big as my legs. He was the obvious choice for the volunteer work the lieutenant had in mind. Joe filled this old sock full of sand to knock the guy out with and off we went into the freezing night. There was always some part of a plan that somebody never figured on. Nobody figured on this kind of cold. It was freezing. We sat in ambush for several hours before a Chinese patrol came by.

I had my own job to do and couldn't see what Joe was doing, but he must have done it right. Somebody yelled and I opened fire on that patrol of gooks. I sent out enough lead to kill the whole patrol, and the ones who weren't hit scattered. We were in enemy territory, and the only thing that mattered now was throwing out so much lead that no gook in range wanted to lift his head until we could make a run for the MLR. Then that one part of the plan no one had thought of had to be dealt with. We'd been lying in ambush for so many hours in the cold that there was no blood and no feeling left in our legs. Men pushed to their feet like drunken mannequins trying to walk. Moving was sheer agony, running was out of the question. I think someone was firing at us, but the fear and adrenaline rushing through my ears as we made our way back kept me from noticing it. We made it back to the wire, then climbed up and over the trench line, tired and frozen. Joe Galvin dumped his new Chinese friend in front of the CP like a farmer drops a bale of hay. The intelligence guys took over, and I never knew if the risk was worth all of our lives or not. But then again, the Marine Corps is not a democracy, and if you want a vote on orders you better join another outfit.

As weeks turned into months I found myself on hill after hill, each had a name. I was on Hill 101, 181, 191 or Gibraltar, Hill 157 known as Vegas, then Checker Board, Yukon-Congo, Bunker Hill, Hill 229, Yellow on the MLR behind Bunker Hill, Reno-Carson, and finally Inchon. These hills were generally along the 38th parallel, and that line was known as the MLR, main line of resistance. The war was dragging on with politicians making decisions that military men should have been making. They were sending me machine gunners who didn't know much about guns. I was now one of the "old salts."

On many occasions when we had a night patrol out, we'd get word from the CP to open up with covering fire. I couldn't trust the new gunners with this job. It required a knowledge of range cards, indirect fire, and various other details about the machine guns that the new guys just didn't know and had had no time to learn. It seemed that no matter what my title was, squad leader, section leader, I was always the guy pulling the trigger behind the gun. We seemed to get a new lieutenant every month, then he would be reassigned to another part of the line or back to the rear. After shifting around all the time, the Marines got to know where the hot spots were and where it was relatively safe.

One night we were on the line in a place that just didn't see that much action, and that was just fine with us. This green lieutenant came up and ordered one of my guns to go out on a patrol with a rifle squad led by him. They were my guys, but I didn't go out this night. When they came back, I heard every detail in triplicate from the new lieutenant. Apparently on the way up the hill, one of my ammo carriers tripped and his ammo box came open. The lieutenant was there and saw that the box was empty. The lieutenant chewed him out and demanded to know why there was no ammo for the gun. The ammo carrier replied, "Why the crud should I, there's no guts in the gun!" The gunners had decided to lighten the water jacket and back plate. The barrel and a few rather important parts were all removed. The gun was an empty shell. I made sure every gunner got the word. That lieutenant couldn't wait to get transferred.

At some point I ended up at a place called Outpost Yellow. It was at the end of a little ridge that ran out about 250 yards from the main line of resistance. We had to go out to that position before daylight and come back after dark. Gooks looked down on this little peninsula into no-man's-land from higher positions. If you tried to make that trip during daylight, gook snipers opened up on you coming and going. I'd hear the rifles crack and you could feel the close calls down into your soul. This was the one place we would put a half belt of ammo in the gun, take a deep breath, then open fire like in a John Wayne movie, spraying lead and praying that the snipers ducked long enough to miss their shot. Each time I had to go out on the end of that ridge, I felt like I was on an island and the water around that island was made up of Chinese.

One morning before daylight I made the run along the ridge out to my hole. The night crew had been hit out there, and when I dived into my hole, I landed in the blood-soaked lap of the biggest gook I ever saw. I started fighting for my life, my heart stopped beating, I was sure of it, then at some point during that fight I discovered that this giant gook wasn't fighting back. He was cold dead. It took a minute for me to settle. I never felt so happy to be with a dead guy in my life. I sat on him until I had enough control to check him over. He had a nice burp gun. I tagged the burp gun with my name, rank and serial number and brought it back the next day when I made the sprint to safety.

When I got back, I turned it in to be claimed if I ever made it home. The Chinese burp gun fired about 1,000 rounds per minute. Some had drums and some had clips. I think our fastest-firing weapon was the M-2 carbine at about 750 rounds per minute. Every time I heard one of those burp guns fire, I knew how it got its name, and when a Marine was hit by one he was almost always hit by more than one round. They didn't have the knockdown power that our weapons had, but when I heard that sound I knew the Chinese were right on top of me. I couldn't help but think about it and wonder how many rounds I might be able to take and still live.

The next day I started the perilous journey out to Outpost Yellow again. Each hour seemed to take a year in Outpost Yellow. We made our way out and took up positions. A few hours passed with some shelling, as always. The sun was coming up. I heard something moving my way, gritted my teeth, and aimed. A young Marine crawled toward me, holding his right ear, bleeding. He crawled into the hole beside me and looked at me incredulously. "Bogey!" He called me by my nickname, but I wasn't sure who he was. "You know that giant rifle the gooks use to shoot at spotter planes?" His expression was not a look of pain but astonishment.

"Yeah," I said, staring at the blood pouring through his fingers that were pressed against his ear. I knew exactly what he was talking about. I didn't know what it was called, but we had all seen the Chinese using this giant rifle that was seven to eight feet long, and they would take single shots at our light planes that spotted for our artillery.

"Well, I watched this little gook trying to manage the biggest rifle I ever saw and I couldn't believe the little bastard was able to fire it!"

"And?"

"He was able to fire it! I saw him aiming it but I was so fascinated, I forgot to duck! He put a hole right through my ear lobe!" I started laughing but he didn't.

A few days later I was in the same fighting hole. I heard the faraway whistles getting closer and hunkered down. Chinese artillery and mortars started tearing the earth apart all around me. I dug my fingernails into the dirt and tried to crawl under my helmet. Chinese troops would attack behind that barrage. There were only two machine guns out there at a time and two men to a gun plus a rifle squad. Machine gunners carried a paintbrush to clean off dirt from incoming mortars and artillery. I started brushing the dirt off of the gun after a close hit covered us. Someone shouted "Bogey!" from the other side of the crest. I recognized Sergeant Burleson's voice, the squad leader.

"Bogey! Throw a grenade! Get me out of here! Gooks all around me!"

I yanked a grenade off my cartridge belt, pulled the pin, and tried to judge where his voice had come from on the other side of the ridge. There was no time to guess twice, I tossed the grenade about where I heard his voice. It went off and he came flying over the crest of the hill and dived into my fighting hole. He was bleeding from both legs and looking like a man who was thrilled to be alive. We pulled a pin on another grenade and tossed it over the crest.

"Burleson! You okay?"

"Bogey! I was trying to get up the nerve to jump and run, gooks all around me, and your grenade landed at my feet. You got me in both legs, it's my third Purple Heart and I'm going home! Thanks, pal!" He grabbed another grenade and joyfully tossed it over the ridge, then did it again like a man celebrating. Daybreak came and the Chinese pulled back. They left some dead behind, in their mustard-colored uniforms.

We were pulled off the line for a while, then sent right back to Outpost Yellow. First night out a brutal firefight erupted to our right as the Chinese hit the company next to us in strength. When the firing stopped, it became dead still. That strange silence seemed to always follow a firefight. Then all of a sudden this angry Marine yells out at the top of his lungs and it felt as though every person in Korea heard it. "Come on back and fight, you sons-of-bitches!" I got goose bumps the size of apples. I never felt more proud of being a Marine. I would have reenlisted right there, right then on the spot, just to be in the same Corps with that fella.

Time in a combat zone is not like time anywhere else. An hour can feel like a day and a day can feel like a week. On Outpost Yellow a day felt like a month. No matter how much training we had in the States, nothing prepares you completely. You quickly start to pick up habits and little tips that might mean life or death. We carried our ponchos folded over the back of our cartridge belts, not because we thought it might rain, but because it was our body bag. I could never get used to seeing the poncho-covered body of a dead Marine on a stretcher, only the boondockers and canvas leggings visible as he was carried to the rear, his work done.

Incoming mortar and artillery rounds threw dirt over everything. I spent each day wiping the gun clean and digging my hole deeper. On Outpost Yellow we learned to dig with bayonets, quietly. The Chinese were close. Throwing close. If they heard entrenching tools, the grenades would start flying. They had a type of grenade with a bamboo handle and a rag inside. They pulled the rag out and it acted like a tail on a kite and it would keep the grenade going straight. Those suckers looked as big as a GI can coming in!

As usual, we had only two A4 air-cooled .30-caliber machine guns out on the end of that ridge at a time, with two men to a gun plus a rifle squad. And as usual, any movement during the day drew immediate fire. It was still daylight. I had one of the A4 machine guns, and the second gunner was in a hole with me on the left flank of the ridge. Incoming fire was sporadic, but often enough and close enough to keep me busy with my paintbrush cleaning dirt off the gun. My partner stared at our left flank and I kept watch on our right. Chinese were just below the crest of the hill to our front and we heard them digging in. With each clear digging sound I got more and more uncomfortable. Like every gunner in the Corps, I wanted to remind somebody that I didn't have a bayonet on the end of that .30-cal.

Those miserable *thump, thump, thump* sounds began increasing, quickly. Incoming mortar fire came down like steel rain, covering the entire knoll we were on. My men on the other A4 machine gun were over toward the middle of the knoll but out of my sight from our hole. They were fairly new guys but I felt that they could handle the job. The truth was that I was praying to the Lord that they could handle the job. I had no choice in the matter, we were so below our TO strength. The riflemen wanted a machine gun to accompany them on everything but a piss-call, and me and my guys were getting worn out. I could hear the constant *thump* of round after round heading our way, and all I could do was keep my head down. Shrapnel sang past our ears like bees buzzing. Somehow through the reverberating explosions, I heard a familiar voice yelling "Bogey!"

I looked up over the edge of my hole and there was Gunnery Sergeant Schooley. I couldn't believe he had crawled up to our hole through that much incoming. Before I could speak, he yelled out, "Toss me a Willy Peter!" I started searching for a Willy Peter, a white phosphorous smoke grenade to give him. We used them to hide our movement when we had to remove wounded in the daylight. "I got some casualties over here! I've got to get 'em out!" Those were the last words that Gunnery Sergeant Schooley ever said. Shrapnel tore through his head and he died right there that very instant. I went numb with shock. I couldn't move at first. I just stared at the dark red blood coming out of his head. I admired him so much, he was what Marines were supposed to be, and it seemed impossible that this good and capable man could die so suddenly. I yelled, but the incoming blasts swallowed up any sound coming out of my mouth. I wanted to stop and cry right there, it just seemed proper, but I had no chance to stop. Tears came out of my eyes, but I shook myself out of it as incoming fire continued ripping our knoll apart. I pulled the pin on the Willy Peter and threw it to cover our corpsman as he dragged Gunnery Sergeant Schooley's body away. Then it got hot and heavy until I thought we would all be dead soon. So much fire that there was no time to dwell on the loss of such a good man. It seemed to hurt even deeper when a short-timer was killed. He would have been home with his family in a few weeks. No casualty ever left a bigger hole in the outfit as the loss of Gunnery Sergeant Schooley.

When that day ended, we got replaced on Outpost Yellow and returned to the MLR. PFC Singleton walked up to where I was slumped against the inside wall of a trench and sat down beside me. PFC Singleton was the Marine on the other A4. Singleton was a new replacement but proving to be a

good Marine. He was a draftee, and Marines did not like
having draftees in their Corps. The Marine Corps had never
done much drafting, and the old salts were very against it.
Some of the draftees became real Marines while others could
not measure up. Singleton was from Indiana, a tall, lanky
farm boy who hadn't quite filled out his frame yet and appeared awkward, but he wasn't. There was nothing awkward
about him. His eyes always had a twinkle in them like he was
remembering a good joke. In short, a real nice kid who was
becoming a Marine.

"Bogey, we were in our foxhole when a round hit and partially buried us, me and my second gunner. Then a gook crept
up and grabbed the machine gun and left another satchel
charge. I screamed for the second gunner to throw it out before it went off. I couldn't reach it!" He spoke as if he were
pleading for my understanding, it wasn't necessary but I understood the feeling. "I was buried up to my armpits from the
first blast! So instead of throwing it out, he poked it with his
carbine and it went off. It killed him." His voice changed,
dropping with his chin.

"What about the gun? What about the machine gun, Marine?"

"I managed to get to his carbine and I killed the gook after
the satchel charge went off. We got the machine gun back,"
Singleton said. He looked done in. We didn't spend much
time eulogizing when a man died. You just couldn't let yourself or you would not be able to perform your duty when the
time came, and the time kept coming.

I knew the kid who had been killed. He was another
draftee and was a good fella, but much too slow-witted for
combat. He should never have been with the Marines. The
draft may find you warm and breathing, but the simple fact is
that some people simply cannot adjust to the rigors, both
mental and physical, of combat with United States Marines.
It's not harsh and it's not bravado, it's just the truth. I had a
couple of men in my squad that just could not cut it as
Marines. They had been drafted and thrown in with professionals, and in this profession there was no time for sympa-

thy or a slow learning curve. One such man was a guy named Simpson.

Simpson had been drafted, from Chicago or Detroit, we were never sure. He was not a bad man, but he was no combat Marine. He had worked in a place that cast train wheels. A job where everything was either hot or heavy. He had a limited education. He told me he was sending his money home so his sister could stay in school. I admired that. Simpson was an ammo carrier for one of the guns and he was simply terrified of the "goops" as he would call them. Naturally every time he called the gooks "goops," it cracked us up. His terror made him absolutely ineffective when lives were on the line, but he tried. I felt sorry for him. For some reason he seemed to have great faith in me, so when I was on watch he'd put his sleeping bag in the trench near me. I don't know why he had so much faith in me keeping him alive, we were all scared. That's what all the training in the Corps was about. You had to stay effective despite your fears.

The rainy season started. The bunkers filled with a foot or more of water, for days after the rain stopped the roof of every bunker dripped incessantly. We threw our packs into the foot or so of water, then squatted on the pack and leaned back against the wet clay walls of our bunker or trench. Rivulets of muddy water ran down our backs and we tried to sleep that way. Wet and cold and filthy.

Simpson crawled into a hole that had a corrugated roof and sandbags. The rain kept coming down until the hole was completely filled and Simpson had his face pressed against the roof to breathe. He would not get out of that hole until he had to make a choice between drowning and risking getting hit.

We got word that we were going out on a patrol with a squad of riflemen. I took Simpson aside and tried my best to calm him down, but all he would do was repeat to himself, "Them goops. Them goops are everywhere. Them goops are gonna kill me sure." It was tiring but finally I got him calm enough to carry the ammo. We all feared this guy was going to get us killed. At night he'd thrash around in his sleeping bag fighting them goops in his sleep.

I stared out on watch at the black night. I turned at the sound of truck engines. I heard a lot of commotion down behind me. Trucks were moving into position down below us to fire their rocket launchers. I'd never been this close to those rocket launchers before and I was really interested. Scuttlebutt said they could launch 144 rockets in twelve seconds. I watched them prepare for firing and I noticed that they never shut the truck engines down. That was so they could get the crap out of there once the "rocket ripple" was over because it was a sure bet that the Chinese would throw everything they could back at that spot. I was a little slow in realizing that once they fired their rockets and raced away in their trucks, I'd still be here. They opened fire and I had never experienced anything like it. The noise and fire were unbelievable. The blasting and light was so intense I was mesmerized. As fast as it started it was over, and I watched in awe as those trucks hauled butt out of there.

As I stared at the trucks speeding away, I could sense the presence of someone beside me. I glanced left and recoiled at the sight of another human beside me who had seemingly come out of nowhere. It was Simpson. The whites of his eyes alone were big enough to give away our position and he was shaking like crazy. He was absolutely petrified. I grabbed him by his shoulders and made him look at me. "It's okay! Snap out of it! You're all right, Simpson. Do you hear me?" He nodded and picked up his sleeping bag to get back in it and discovered that it was completely zipped up! I stared at that in utter disbelief. You had to be more than just a little scared to get your whole body through the face hole of a sleeping bag that fast. I don't think people in a circus act could pull that off.

Being in charge of a crew of men was a wonderful out for me. I could forget about my own fear sometimes because I had to think only of the other men. It was a mind game and for me it worked. I was thankful I wasn't a lone rifleman. The Marines had a saying that seems like a cliché, but it sure ain't no cliché when you're in combat. "There are no atheists in foxholes." I bet every Marine in Korea could recite the Twenty-third Psalm by heart. Occasionally a chaplain would set up a little service on the hood of a jeep or anywhere handy, and if you were on your way out on a patrol, raid, or ambush, most of us joined in the service. I wondered how any man could handle it without faith in the Lord or prayer. I doubt many did.

At some points along the line we were so close to the Chinese that we could hurl insults as well as grenades at each other, and we did. Some gook would shout out "Truman eats ——it!" A Marine would reply with a compliment about the gook's mother or some other kindhearted sentiment. The worst crap our government ever came up with and dared to call food was C-ration ham and limas. One of my gunners opened up a can of ham and lima beans and the ham was a long string of fat tendons and little bits of ham all strung together. He said, "Hey look, I think I got the ovaries!" This night we found ourselves at one of those spots along the line where we were about thirty to forty feet away from the Chinese line. I got my C rations and sure enough I got ham and limas. That was it. I reared back and threw that can over to the Chinese. A few seconds later they threw it back! I knew then that they weren't totally stupid.

It was rare that we ever got a night's sleep between patrols, outpost duty, H&I firing, and just jumpy COs who were forever telling us 100 percent watch. Depending on where you got stuck along the MLR had a lot to do with how we interpreted what 100 percent watch meant. They brought up some corrugated sheets to put over us, then we lined these with sandbags or straw mats that the Koreans had. We had one cover built up pretty good and I knew it would take a direct hit from a 61mm mortar round, but if it got hit by two or three we'd be in trouble. The Chinese had this 76mm mountain howitzer, and when it sent a round your way, it screamed all the way in. Fortunately for us it often fired duds. One night we took three direct hits from a 76mm mountain gun. All three were duds. It fired on a flat trajectory so it hit the front wall of our bunker and shook the bloody crap out of us big time, but not one round exploded. We looked at each other and every man knew that was just God saying, I'm not taking you home yet. We had almost recovered mentally from that when the first of three mortar rounds hit. Each one was a direct hit on our bunker. I started wondering if some gunner had pasted a giant target on the outside of our bunker. The mortars were more serious because they came down on top of the bunker. We had two layers of sandbags, but after a hit I knew another hit in the same spot would come through, so we took turns running outside to fill in the new hole with whatever we could. The Chinese mortars didn't have delayed fuses and that's all that saved us.

Life inside those trenches and bunkers was miserable. You couldn't tell the Chinese from the giant rats, so you couldn't sleep. Those rats would run around up on the roof of our bunkers and drop dirt and rocks down. Night after night with no real sleep. One night my nerves were on edge. I heard rocks and pebbles rattling in the box of old C-ration cans. It was all I could take. It was a continuous racket and you couldn't take anything for granted because I knew it could just as easily be some gook with a bayonet coming in. I jumped up and barked, "Everybody outside for a minute! I'm going to get rid of the friggin' rats!" The men grumbled and cursed and crawled out half asleep. After we all stepped out, I pulled the pin on a grenade and tossed it inside our bunker. After the smoke cleared we all went back to sleep. No more rats that night.

It turned winter and they issued us those big insulated boots that we called "Mickey Mouse boots." We never hiked in them but carried them on a pack board until we got to an outpost or whatever. They made your feet sweat and then you'd get trench foot or frostbite. We had two pairs of socks, the ones on our feet and one pair tucked inside our clothes to dry out. I had to crush the fresh pair before putting them on. They were always stiff with ice. I had just put the freshly crushed pair on when we got word to move up to a hill.

We made it up to the hill to relieve another company.

There, I discovered a .50-caliber machine gun with a jammed cartridge in the chamber. I had read the .50 manual once or twice and was fairly familiar with the weapon. I held the bolt back halfway, which enables you to unscrew the barrel from the receiver. I poked a cleaning rod down the barrel and pounded out the jammed brass. You always count the clicks when you unscrew a machine gun barrel because this is the amount of head space the gun requires to shoot well. My fingers were frozen but I wanted that gun to work. Too few or too many clicks and the gun runs rough or not at all. This .50 had six clicks, which seemed strange since most .30s had fourteen to sixteen clicks. I fixed it so I could fire single rounds or auto. I couldn't wait to try it out. It was an excellent weapon and I grew real fond of my .50-caliber. It had a scope on it and I used it for sniping during the day. At night I'd use it for H&I, harassing and interdiction fire.

Each day I'd lie beside that .50 with binoculars, looking for targets. It had a maximum range of 3,400 yards, but sniping 1,800 yards or so was more than enough. I wanted targets up on their line, not some poor slob back in the rear on R&R. I had it on a tripod on the parapet of my hole with camouflage netting over it. One day I spotted a gook digging in his trench, he was in only about knee-deep and his back was toward me. Below him was about a twenty- to thirty-foot drop-off, much like in a gravel pit. I estimated him to be about 1,800 yards, so I cranked one off. I saw dirt kick up a yard or so below him through the scope. This was armor-piercing incendiary ammo and it explodes when it hits. I watched him jerk around when he heard the pop but then he just turned and went back to work. I brought the gun up a click and fired another round. Another Marine watching through binoculars gave a grimace and a groan. "That guy's hemorrhoids will never be a problem again."

"Whoever's behind him in the chow line can move up a step," I replied.

A few nights later I cleaned the pot burner they issued us for heat in the bunkers and my hands were completely black from soot. After that I climbed up to the .50 and pulled the tracers out of the ammo belt and started the nighttime H&I firing with API ammo. I was kneeling over the gun with my hand on the traversing mechanism as I fired, and suddenly the gun blew up. The flash blinded me and for a moment I thought my hand was blown off. I fell back against a trench and stared at my hand. Blood and soot and bone. "Corpsman!" I shouted. Our new corpsman sprinted up to me breathing hard. He looked at my bloody, soot-covered hand. Flesh was gone from a couple of my fingers, the bones were real white. He stared in a state of shock and I was the one bleeding everywhere! He got me down to the battalion aid station where they probed all the metal out of my hand, bandaged me up, and sent me right back up the hill to my position.

We figured afterward that a bent rim on a cartridge didn't allow the round to center in the tee slot. When the bolt started forward, the round struck the side of the breech instead of going into the chamber. Apparently the round exploded from front to back and as a result a lot of pieces of that round landed in my left hand. Fortunately the cover of the gun buckled but held so I didn't get all that steel in my face. We never did find the extractor. When I told the chief corpsman what had happened, he said, "No Purple Heart."

"What? Why not?"

"It wasn't enemy inflicted."

"Who do you think I was shooting at with that fifty? The friggin' rats?"

Being a Marine, griping was my Corps-given right, but being a Marine it did me no good. My wound didn't keep me from standing my watch. The only difference was that now I was one-handed and couldn't pull the pin on a grenade if I had to. One of the other Marines rigged a piece of plank with a nail half driven into it, then he leaned it near the bunker so I could hook the ring on the grenade if needed. Soon after that it was needed. The Chinese probed constantly and the only way to respond without giving away the gun position was by throwing grenades down in the wire when they tripped one of the cans we had set up or if they opened fire.

The nail worked but it was nerve-wracking and I wanted my left hand back, and if I had to have half my hand blown up I wanted that darn Purple Heart.

We were supposed to be up on the line thirty days, then back in reserve for a period of time. This naturally depended on the tactical situation. We had been up on the line for seventy days in the same clothes. We smelled awful but since every Marine stunk so bad, it didn't matter until some poor replacement showed up and nearly got sick just being near us. The 2d Battalion finally got pulled off the line and sent to Inchon. We sailed to an island in the Yellow Sea and embarked on a landing. It was unopposed but the weather made it awful hairy. Some of the landing craft had to beach themselves. Word came down that we were clearing certain islands in case any of our planes got hit and couldn't make it back.

Our left flank was right in sight of the peace talks at Panmunjom. They had four big barrage balloons marking out the neutral area. I sat in my fighting hole and watched a convoy of big new cars going in and out every day bringing the officers and diplomats to negotiate the end of the Korean War. Some officers showed up one day and made us all sign a paper stating that we wouldn't shoot into the neutral zone. Some of the guys way over on our left said the Chinese were forming up for attacks out of the neutral zone. When we asked what they did about it, the reply was not diplomatic. "Screw that paper you signed! Shoot 'em!"

I finally got an R&R in November, after nine months of being on the line. They flew us to an air base on Honshu. Man, it felt great to take a shower and change into some clean clothes. A train ride took us to Kyoto. It was 1952 and some of the Marines with me had just been killing the Japanese a few years earlier, but I never ran into any resentment from the Japanese. They were polite and friendly at all times. I met some wonderful people, who all happened to be women, so I proceeded to maintain the Marine Corps reputation in situations such as this to the best of my ability.

In December, I was sent back to Division HQ to attend

NCO leadership school as required once you reach the rank of sergeant. I got back on line near the end of December. I had so much fun on R&R that I lost fifteen pounds. I was standing watch and thinking about Japan when this loudspeaker over on the Chinese side started playing music. Then they said in English, "Good evening officers and men of the 1st Marine Division." They went on with some typical communist propaganda and most of the guys sat listening and slowly becoming annoyed by it. They started playing this Chinese music. That alone was enough to tick off Marines. I was on a .50-caliber machine gun and straining to see where that loudspeaker was coming from. I went down the line stopping at a couple of bunkers trying to get sound azimuths of where that sucker might be set up. I got a fix on it and crawled back to my .50 and cranked off a few rounds in the direction I thought it was coming from. The music stopped cold and we never heard another bleep out of that loudspeaker. The guys were very impressed with my accuracy and so was I.

We tied C-ration cans to the wire with little pebbles in them so they'd rattle when the Chinese bumped into them. At first rattle we would throw a grenade. We also had C-ration cans out on the wire at various locations with the open end facing us and a chunk of white cloth inside the can. If anything got between us and that can, if we couldn't see that cloth, we'd throw a grenade and look for blood or a body the next day.

I was called over to another company one day. They had a jammed .50-caliber machine gun and wanted me to fix it. After I fixed it, I heard the lieutenant whisper to the gunner, "Make him try it out." It sort of ticked me off that they didn't trust my work, so I looked through the scope and spotted a gook kid about a thousand meters away. He looked to be about fourteen years old, but he had a gun and he wasn't hunting pheasant. I lined up on him and fired, and he went down. When someone gets hit by a .50-caliber round, they don't just fall, they sort of explode. I leaned away from the scope and turned to the lieutenant. "It works good, sir." Then I got out of there as fast as I could, knowing the incoming rounds would be landing any moment.

We had been up on the line for some time when we got word to pull back to a reserve area for a rest. We got placed near a British outfit, it was the Leicester Regiment. Those guys drink gin like Marines drink beer. I found one of my machine gun squads gathered around a couple of jugs of gin. When I asked how they got it, one of them sheepishly confessed, "We traded one of our machine guns to the limeys, Sarge." I wasn't sure whether to put 'em up against the wall for a firing squad or cry. The rest of that day was spent tracking down that machine gun. I ended up having to trade away a good bit of our beer ration to keep peace with the United Nations.

It was night, we got the word to move up on Little Gibraltar, Hill 229. This was a hot spot and everyone knew it. My machine gun squad crawled up to the top of the hill along this narrow path. There weren't too many trees left on the hill, but there were some. Incoming fire was so intense that we feared lifting our heads even to make the next crawl forward up that path. Shrapnel whirred past my ears like bees searching for someone to sting. PFC J. Simpson was up ahead and whining constantly, "Goops gonna kill me up here for sure." The path followed the curvature of the slope we were crawling up, and the trajectory of the incoming artillery shells whistled just above our heads the entire way up. They were so close that if one of us stood up I was sure an arty shell would go right through him. It was slow going or no going as the squad had to just push their faces into the dirt at times and pray to God to live through the next moment. A shell hit a tree, causing an air-burst. Shrapnel hit everywhere and I thanked God there were few trees on Gibraltar. I pulled my face out of the dirt just as a grenade rolled into me from someone ahead. We moved forward again until the blasts were too severe to move and again I shoved my face in the dirt and tried to climb under my helmet. I looked up as another grenade rolled into me from someone up ahead losing it. I thought of Simpson. I hooked them on my cartridge belt and crawled forward again.

"Betty Grable!" some Marine forward shouted. That was our code for a corpsman. I knew we had wounded up ahead. "Betty Grable!" The shout rose over the explosions. Several more times the call "Betty Grable" came down the line. A corpsman was up and running. I sat there hoping heaven had a special place for corpsmen, I never saw one hesitate to run to the aid of a fallen Marine no matter how bad the fire was. I never found out who got hit, but we finally reached the top of the hill and got into a trench. The shelling never let up. We had an A4 air-cooled .30-caliber machine gun with us and a rifle squad along with the machine gun squad.

The shelling was nonstop and I found a bunker the gooks had built when they had the hill. I dropped down into this dark hole that was like climbing down into a manhole. Inside, it was roomy enough for my squad. I sat back against the wall of the bunker and a brilliant flash blinded all of us. An artillery shell made a direct hit on the entrance. It became pitch black. The entrance was sealed with dirt. Old Simpson started praying and repeating over and over, "Sergeant Bogan! What we gonna do? What we gonna do?" He was frantic. The hole was L-shaped, so no one was hit by shrapnel, but being buried alive sent a wave of phobia through all of us. Not a one of us would have chosen being buried alive over getting shot. I started poking around and digging like a dog. It seemed to take forever but finally some dirt fell in, and gradually we got enough dirt down so we could get out. That hole represented security for a while, but we were sure glad to see the stars above us after that, even if it meant less security in a trench.

As the sun brought first light over the steep purple mountains, the artillery and mortars continued with no letup. As daylight brought more vision, I could see some gooks off in the distance in a burial ground. We started shooting. One gook was behind a burial headstone and I kept trying to pick him off, but he kept behind that burial stone. I heard something overhead and I looked up. A flight of four gull-winged

dark blue Marine Corsairs roared by just above us, blasting
with those big .50-cals and dropping so much brass that it
sounded like a horse galloping past as the brass hit the
ground behind, beside, then ahead of our squad. I watched
happily as that burial stone and the gook behind it were oblit-
erated. The Corsairs made pass after pass, those guys were
good. They came in so low that falling brass from their .50s
bounced off Marine helmets, and it was hot.

We took an endless pounding from mortars and artillery,
pure insanity. Our radio was blown out, our lieutenant was
hit. Word came down that we were going back to the MLR.
It was late afternoon of a very long day, and I carried one end
of the stretcher the lieutenant was on all the way back to the
MLR. My gunners and riflemen covered our rear as we traveled back. Gibraltar was two thousand meters out from the
MLR. It was a grueling hike, my hands were blistered and
numb from the weight of the stretcher, and mortars followed
us the whole way. As we approached the MLR, Captain Car-
penter, the company commander, ran out beyond the line to
greet every one of us. His face said as much as his words, he
was absolutely surprised we were alive. "I can't believe it!
We haven't seen the top half of that hill all day from the
smoke and explosions! How did you men live through it?"

No one answered because no one knew.

Just before they loaded the lieutenant into the jeep ambulance, he called me over. He shook my hand and thanked me
for carrying him in. I never saw him again, he was a fine officer. None of my gunners were wounded, it was miraculous.

A few weeks later the new platoon sergeant came up to me
and told me they wanted to court-martial Simpson for dere-
liction of duty. Because I was his section leader, I had to ap-
prove it. All I could think about was Simpson's little sister
being able to stay in school with the money he was sending
home. Simpson was a good man but he could not function
under fire. In spite of that, I just couldn't say yes to a court-
martial. "I just can't go along with a court-martial, Sarge.
Give him a job in the rear someplace." I didn't know where
he went, but very soon after that Simpson left the front lines.

It wasn't too many days after Simpson left that D 2/1 moved up to take positions on Bunker Hill. I guess none of us had any real idea how bad Bunker Hill was, you hear scuttlebutt but you don't know until you take up positions where Marines have already died. I had sixteen machine guns on Bunker Hill, those we brought with us and guns from the last outfit we were replacing, which had taken heavy casualties and had had no gun teams for many of their guns.

We had some heavy water-cooled .30s and some lighter A4s. That water-cooled .30 was a pretty versatile weapon in trained hands. When we set up on the MLR, we would sand-bag the tripod in, level up the gun, then take readings from a traversing mechanism on prominent points of terrain. Then we would put a little stick in the ground under the barrel at each of these points that we had picked out. Later I made sure each gun would coordinate an FLP, or final line of protection, with the other guns to our flanks and agree to a setting on each gun so that the firing would interlock with another machine gun. FLP was defined as a steady band of fixed grazing fire so that, theoretically, there would be continuous bands of interlocking fire that no one could get through. This tactic could be used only on the main line of resistance, or MLR, from fixed positions. In other places, like Bunker Hill, we had to get the light .30s set up on the spot and work with what we had. We tried to place a BAR, Browning automatic rifle, to cover our blind spots that the .30 couldn't hit.

In fixed positions we would put these little "aiming stakes" in the ground under the barrel at the various targets we chose, then we would take the coordinates for traversing and elevations and mark them down. When a gunner got all this done, he had to make a range card. With that range card you could fire cover for a returning patrol at night. The CP would give you the location of the patrol coming in, and you could use your range card and open up with cover fire without killing your own Marines. We'd pull the tracer rounds out of the belts and still hit our targets, with a little less danger of giving away the gun position. Unfortunately, most of the replacements I was getting didn't have enough training in machine gunning, other than the basics, and much of this indirect fire and other knowledge was beyond them. By the time we hit Bunker Hill, I was satisfied if a new replacement could feed a belt of ammo and hit a target.

After dark we moved onto the forward slope and set up in foxholes previously dug. I had two men and myself. We set up in a very small, shallow hole. I tapped one of my men on the shoulder. "Pass the word. One will dig this hole deeper, one will man the gun, and one will sleep. Every hour or so we'll switch." When it was my turn to sleep, I went up the slope to another hole about thirty feet away to crash. I left my M-1 rifle with the gun, but I had my pistol.

I fell asleep and dropped into the most realistic dream I can ever remember having. I could hear my old man giving me the devil for not helping him rake the leaves. He shouted so loud that it startled me awake. I opened my eyes. It took me a moment or two to figure out that raking the friggin' leaves was not the problem. The earth was shaking around me as fire, explosions, dirt, and rocks rained down on me. I looked down about fifteen yards to where my gun was positioned and a round roared in with a near-direct hit. The explosion was horrific. It looked bad. I yelled out to my guys, "Watch out, I'm coming in!" I was half scared they were dead and half scared they'd kill me, thinking I was a gook coming in.

I jumped up and ran for the gun position, and it seemed like each step was followed by an explosion. My legs and arms were stinging from hot shrapnel. I dived into the hole. Both gunners were wounded, covered with dirt, the hole was half filled with dirt, and the machine gun was on its side, the web ammo belt burning. Explosions were ripping the hill apart all around us. I scooped dirt onto the ammo belt to put out the fire, pulled the gun upright, repositioned it, took aim at the onrushing shadows, and opened up. The machine gun was firing like a car missing a cylinder, and I knew that the head-space was probably screwed up from the explosion, but gooks were dropping dead in piles out in front. I laid on the trigger of the .30 with one hand while I felt through my cartridge belt for the first aid pack. I managed to get bandages from my jungle kit with my left hand. I flipped bandages to the dazed gunners. They tried to patch up their bleeding wounds. They had shrapnel holes all over them and were half out of it, disoriented from the explosion. I kept firing but the gun was running rough, not giving the clean bursts it usually produced. I thanked God it was still sending out any bullets at all. My fire was having an effect. The other guns were firing and our tracers looked like a picket fence, thousands of bullets.

My legs and right arm were stinging like somebody was putting out cigarettes in my flesh. I hadn't even noticed that I'd been hit until then, it was too chaotic to feel anything but fear. Continuous flashes from enemy and friendly muzzles broke the darkness into irregular patterns. Large, bright flashes from mortars silhouetted Chinese troops off to my right flank and gave me momentary targets. I swung the gun in that direction and laid out as much lead as I could. My wounded second gunner struggled into position and worked at feeding in another box of ammo. I couldn't tell just how bad either of the men were hit, and there was no time to ask.

Suddenly the Chinese broke through the right flank. I could see Chinese troops overrunning our positions through the white shell bursts. Just as suddenly, Marines charged forward in a barrage of muzzle flashes, killing Chinese as they charged until they swept the Chinese troops back down Bunker Hill. I kept firing as did every gun still in action. Explosions erupted all along the left flank as incoming mortars and artillery tore Bunker Hill to pieces. Horns and whistles signaled another enemy attack. A swarm of Chinese troops charged forward the moment the barrage lifted, sweeping through our left flank behind what sounded like hundreds of burp guns and grenades. Chinese commanders used bugles, whistles, and horns to direct their troops, and the noise from those stinking horns and whistles had me crazy mad.

We fired and kept firing. Once again I saw Marines rise and push the Chinese back. Some of the fighting was hand-to-hand and Marines were swinging everything from rifles to entrenching tools. I saw glimpses, like a movie missing pieces of the film, the view flickering in the light of sporadic explosions, some large and some grenade-sized, and all of it saturated with unending muzzle flashes that stole my night vision. The battle continued throughout the night. Every time I thought it was over, the Chinese would probe another point along our line. Some were probes in force and others were squad or platoon size. Incoming fire silhouetted some probes, and when those Chinese troops got caught in the light they were chopped to pieces. Every muscle in my body had tensed to a point of utter exhaustion, whether from fatigue or adrenaline or just fear made no difference, the drain and furor was all-consuming, devastating, physically and emotionally. A swarm of Chinese suddenly broke through the right flank, whistles and horns, grenades and burp guns. Again, Marines killed until they took it back. Incoming rounds covered us all with dirt, it was raining rocks and dirt. I feared the gun would jam from the dirt alone. My wounded gunners worked to keep the .30 firing, one feeding ammo while the other shot Chinese on our flanks. Every Marine was totally involved in stopping the attack, no one hollered, only hand signals, staying alive was every man's goal though many sacrificed that most precious gift to save a buddy or a position.

Silence. I don't know how or why but everything stopped except for the random shot here or there. How that happens with such apparent precision, turning to that eerie silence, I guess no Marine will ever know. I was drenched with sweat like no sweat that comes from working or lying in the sun. My whole body was wet. Then came the rustling noises of corpsmen attending to the wounded, the ammo carriers bringing more ammo to the machine gun, gunners checking their guns for damage or brushing the dirt off with the paintbrushes. It was too dangerous to evac my guys out, so none of the wounded could move off the line. I left them with the gun while I checked on my other gun positions. That is when I noticed again that I had been wounded, not bad but when it's your body, you don't like metal sticking in it. Our machine guns were configured so that they covered the line and flanks. The guns on the flanks had done a great job in holding our line.

A lot of my gunners were killed or wounded, the Chinese made a point of trying to knock out our machine guns. They would go to extreme lengths to knock out our machine guns, including committing suicide. I ran from gun to gun, checking on as many as I could. One of my gunners looked at me face-to-face as I slid into his fighting hole. "Bogey, I thought we were dead. I'm so scared you couldn't drive a needle up my crack with a sledgehammer!"

Well, right there in the middle of all that death and agony, in typical Marine fashion this stupid Marine made me laugh out loud. I looked around that smoky, shell-pocked piece of mud called Bunker Hill and wondered if America had any clue about what kind of heroic Marines were fighting and dying for them. It was around then that some gook yelled out the old standby, "Malinge, you die!"

"Suck a harchi, gook!" came a characteristic reply from some jarhead along the line.

I moved to another gun position as incoming started dropping. The gunners were dead. I grabbed ammo carriers and put them on that machine gun. I made it to another gun position and there was no one manning the gun, all dead or dragged back to the MLR. I grabbed a couple of riflemen just as incoming fire started getting close. We all ducked as I shouted instructions to two very wide-eyed Marines, eager to learn and learn quick! "Listen up! Belt goes here! Pull bolt back twice! And use short bursts or they'll pinpoint your gun and you are dead! In the event you get overrun! Pull this pin and use free gun! But! Only! If you get overrun!" I took off and prayed that God would protect them. I got to another position and there was no one left. I searched for a live body to put on that gun as rounds exploded everywhere, and I found a navy corpsman.

"You! You're now a Marine Corps machine gunner! Put the belt here! Pull back the bolt twice! Use short bursts! Do not lay on that trigger for too long unless you see a thousand of them up close!" He stared back like a madman. "Is that clear, mister!" He couldn't answer. I put the belt of ammo in for him and took off for the next gun. I always wondered if that kid made it.

I don't know what time it was. I found myself back on my gun and drenched again, and then that eerie silence took over and the firefight suddenly seemed to pause for no reason. At that exact moment, out comes a "*yobo* train" from back at the MLR with mail! *Yobo* was the word for the Korean laborers who volunteered to work for the Marines. These little Korean men had powerful legs and they all had these wooden A-frames that they would strap to their backs to carry huge loads—barbed wire, ammo, fifty-five-gallon drums, or anything we needed. The A-frame was two pieces of wood from small trees cut just a bit shorter than the man carrying it. They were brought together to a point at the top and wide at the bottom, hence the term A-frame. About two-thirds of the way up from the bottom were two projecting pieces of wood about eighteen inches long, with a wooden spreader fastened to keep them in position. With shoulder straps a man would lean forward to get the legs of the A-frame off the ground. When he had to rest, he would straighten up, allowing the weight to rest on the ground. They were tough little guys who had walked up and down mountains all of their lives. There were usually five or six of these men together like a mule team, so we called them a *yobo* train. They were not allowed to man gun positions on the line because we couldn't tell them from the Chinese or North Koreans who might sneak in on us disguised as a *yobo* train, so there was always a Marine guard with them.

I couldn't believe this particular *yobo* train walked right into a bloodbath with a mail call. Things quieted down, and the next thing I knew I was deep in my hole reading a letter from my father with a match. With the letter was an article from a Boston newspaper with the headline, THE MARINES HAVE SECURED BUNKER HILL. That was just too good to not share. "Hey, Marines! I just got an article from my dad out of a Boston newspaper that says the Marines have secured Bunker Hill!"

A tired voice came back at me out of the dark. "Hey, mate! The only part of Bunker Hill I know the Marines have secured is the part my bony butt is anchored on!"

When daylight finally arrived, we moved back to the reverse side of the slope as was the norm. We crawled into holes on that side and waited for the usual pounding from mortars or artillery. The corpsman patched me up and told me I was getting a Purple Heart. I felt pretty proud of it. Marines were hard men but they still had those moments when a lump came to the throat or a goose bump showed up on that Eagle, Globe, and Anchor tattoo. Getting a Purple Heart was one of those moments.

We stayed in foxholes on the reverse slope, getting pounded constantly. I mean constantly. My hole had some fence stakes across the top with a row of sandbags. Rounds came in non-stop and you didn't dare stick your head out of that hole. Everybody eventually had to relieve themselves and nobody was making a "head call" outside that hole. We relieved ourselves in C-ration boxes and threw it out. Sergeant Beecher and I shared a hole, he was a section leader for machine guns. C rations are better than no food, but not by much. About 99 percent of the time the one fruit everybody seemed to get was fruit cocktail. Well, we were in that hole and Sergeant Beecher got a can of peaches with his C rats. Like tracer rounds giving away a machine gun position, the smell of those peaches gave away the secret. Marines started crawling down trenches to offer Sergeant Beecher trades or money for those peaches. He set the peaches up on the parapet of our bunker. Shortly after he refused his last sale offer for those peaches, a round came in and blew those peaches to heaven. That was it. Peaches were bad luck in the whole company after that.

Each night was the same routine. We carried our guns back to our fighting holes on the forward slope and waited for the Chinese probes to begin. We sat dead silent, every tiny sound was amplified a thousand times over in your mind. Soon you'd hear rustling in the black night, then digging. A Marine would throw a grenade at a sound that was too close to ignore. The flash of light would steal your vision but give away a row of shadowy figures moving forward and the guns would send out a wall of .30-caliber steel. A Chinese artillery and mortar barrage usually followed, then a full-scale attack that left every man in this strange state of semishock. Then at daybreak we'd pack up our guns and wounded and dead and crawl back over the crest of Bunker Hill to the reverse slope, collapsing into our foxholes.

D Company, 2d Battalion, 1st Marine Regiment spent five days on Bunker Hill. Word came down later that we had been hit by an estimated four thousand Chinese troops. After being relieved we straggled back to the MLR, wide-eyed and haggard, too tired to complain or celebrate living through it. Suddenly I heard something that sounded foreign to me, a sound that was out of place in this scene of weary, filthy, wounded Marines trudging slowly in a long line toward a hot meal and a little sleep. Clapping. Other Marines along the road stood applauding us as we passed. It was a sight I'll never forget as long as I live. They had heard that we held the line against four thousand Chinese. They cheered us. If you looked close at us, there were some misty eyes behind a lot of hardened, shell-shocked faces.

Once we were back in the rear, a buddy came up to me and said they were putting me up for the Silver Star for what I did on Bunker Hill. I only did what every Marine did, his job, but I had never felt more proud in my life. It wasn't our last time on Bunker Hill or Gibraltar or Outpost Yellow. After a year they all sort of ran together. In late February 1953, I was grumbling about crossing the Pacific Ocean at fifteen miles per hour. Troopships were just awful but they sure beat Korea. Arriving in San Francisco was a thrill I'll never forget. There was a beautiful woman in a bright red coat, we hadn't seen many colors in Korea, everything was black and white. She was singing to us as we landed, then the Marine band started playing the "Marine Corps Hymn." I hope I never get over the shivers and the tears when I hear that song. God bless my country and God bless my Marine Corps.

Map by: Patrick A. Smith

6

PFC MELVIN EARL NEWLIN

Medal of Honor

Rank and organization: Private First Class, U.S. Marine Corps, 2d Battalion, 5th Marines, 1st Marine Division (Rein), FMF. Place and date: Quang Nam Province, Republic of Vietnam, 4 July 1967. Entered service at: Cleveland, Ohio. Born: 27 September 1948, Wellsville, Ohio. Citation: For conspicuous gallantry and intrepidity at the risk of his life above and beyond the call of duty while serving as a machine gunner attached to the 1st Platoon, Company F, 2d Battalion, on 3 and 4 July 1967. PFC. Newlin, with 4 other marines, was manning a key position on the perimeter of the Nong Son outpost when the enemy launched a savage and well coordinated mortar and infantry assault, seriously wounding him and killing his 4 comrades. Propping himself against his machine gun, he poured a deadly accurate stream of fire into the charging ranks of the Viet Cong. Though repeatedly hit by small-arms fire, he twice repelled enemy attempts to overrun his position. During the third attempt, a grenade explosion wounded him again and knocked him to the ground unconscious. The Viet Cong guerrillas, believing him dead, bypassed him and continued their assault on the main force. Meanwhile, PFC. Newlin regained consciousness, crawled back to his weapon, and brought it to bear on the rear of the enemy causing havoc and confusion among them. Spotting the enemy attempting to bring a captured 106 recoilless weapon to bear on other marine positions, he shifted his fire, inflicting heavy casualties on the enemy and preventing them from firing the captured weapon. He then shifted his fire back to the primary enemy force, causing the enemy to stop their assault on the marine bunkers and to once again attack his machine gun position. Gallantly fighting off 2 more enemy assaults, he firmly held his ground until mortally wounded. PFC. Newlin had singlehandedly broken up and disorganized the entire enemy assault force, causing them to lose momentum and delaying them long enough for his fellow marines to organize a defense and beat off their secondary attack. His indomitable courage, fortitude, and unwavering devotion to duty in the face of almost certain death reflect great credit upon himself and the Marine Corps and uphold the highest traditions of the U.S. Naval Service.

CPL. THOM SEARFOSS: Me and Bob Bowermaster were stuck in Okinawa together, waiting to turn eighteen years old before they would ship us to the Nam. We hit the bush at the same time and in the same squad. We were put in the 2d Platoon of Fox Company, 2d Battalion, 5th Marine Regiment, 1st Marine Division. We went on Operation Union II in June '67. It was brutal. I was in the paddy that day, June 2, with Anderson, Sugar Bear, Weed, Holloway, Gomez, Lieutenant Shultz was there, Richardson was there, he was humping the radio for the lieutenant. We had "guns" with our squad that day. Hernandez was on the gun, he was a crazy one that had just extended in country for six months. He had just gotten back from his leave, thirty days came free if you extended. We had just moved out of a tree line, on line across a thousand-yard rice paddy. We left our 60mm mortars set up in the tree line. We were about halfway when Richardson yelled out that the 60mm was going to fire a couple of rounds into the tree line ahead of us. One of the 1/5 companies had just moved through to our left. See, we were "sparrow hawk" to 1/5 for this op (operation). *Boom!* About fifty yards ahead of us. "Short round!" Everybody starts yelling at once. Half of us had dropped to the ground. To our immediate front, holes appeared in the paddy dikes. NVA jumped up right in front of me and Anderson, coming out of spider holes. The entire tree line opened up with red and green and blue tracer rounds, zeroing in on Marines all over the paddy. Enemy mortars were being fired from the tree line in front of us and getting closer. We couldn't put our heads above a paddy dike. Weed was hit in the neck, Sugar Bear was also hit in the neck. Lieutenant Shultz was hit in the leg and bleeding bad. Richardson was hit in the head and a chunk of his head was gone, about the size of a silver dollar, but he was alive and functioning. One of the ammo-humpers for Guns was shot in the jaw and his lower jaw was gone. This was only the very beginning of this battle. We killed over seven hundred that day.

The outfit was recuperating and rebuilding from the slaughter of Operation Union II. Casualties had been very high and there were not that many old salts left, so it was a pretty green company. Anytime you got to sit on a hill or a bridge, that was considered R&R for the "grunts." Anything other than setting up ambushes every night or humping through the worst terrain on earth in 115-degree heat or monsoon rains during the day was an absolute vacation.

The coal mine at Nong Son was the only active coal mine in South Vietnam. We were on Hill 351 to set security while a little defoliant was sprayed around the underbrush. The brush was getting real thick and the gooks could sneak right up on top of you. The defoliant was in these orange fifty-five-gallon drums. We had two squads on top of the mountain and one squad on the 105 level, about seventy feet below the top. The 105 area was leveled out and cleared for the artillery and the 106 recoilless. On top were two squads, a couple of 81mm mortars, the command post, and two engineers for the chemicals or defoliant to get rid of the vegetation creeping up the hill.

There was an army team on the top with a jeep that had a big spotlight mounted on it to give them night vision into Antenna Valley across the Thu Bon River. Across the river was Hill 401, or Recon Mountain. At the other end of Antenna Valley was the saddle, two mountain peaks that formed a saddle. The other two platoons were set in the middle plateau of the mountain and around the base of the hill in their bunkers. The bunkers at the base were about two hundred yards apart with trenches and firing holes connecting them.

L.CPL. MICHAEL O. HARRIS: In early June, I was sitting in the EM club at An Hoa combat base, having a few beers and shooting the breeze with some of my buddies from the 81mm mortar platoon. One of the Marines mentioned that it was his birthday. Well, we had a tradition about giving the Marine having the birthday one of our two-beer ration. We were laughing and jaw-jacking, and one of my buddies asked me when my birthday was. "September 27," I said. We were at a big table with Marines from various units.

Somebody yelled, "Of what year?"

I looked around to find a face to go with the voice, and this baby-faced Marine was looking at me waiting for an answer. "1948."

He looked surprised. "Hey, I was born September 27, 1948."

He introduced himself as PFC Mel Newlin, a machine gunner with Fox Company. We hit it off immediately and became friends. He was easy to talk to and a good guy. An Hoa had a shack of sorts where you could watch movies. Mel and me went to the movies and watched reruns of the old television series *Combat* and then we watched *Batman*. It was great seeing anything that reminded you of home. We called back home, back in the World. Nam was so primitive and deadly and we became primitive and deadly, too. Sometimes it was hard to remember what "the World" was like. *Batman* helped.

That night Mel came back to our hootch and Gary Nolan, Harry Marshall, Mel, and me played some "back-alley." That's a card game that the grunts were always playing when they had a few minutes to sit. Mel told me that he was from Ohio and that he was proud to be a Marine. He said that he was proud to be serving his country in Nam. The truth was that even though it was scary, most of the Marines felt that way, even the ones who never said it. Mel was really young, only eighteen just like me, but he looked even younger than eighteen years old. I think he could have passed for a fifteen-year-old. But his pride in being a Marine wasn't young, it was as old as the Corps itself.

The 5th Marines were rebuilding and resting up after the fierce battle of Operation Union II. The 5th Marines took heavy casualties on that "op" but probably killed more than a thousand NVA. I had come in just after the conclusion of Operation Arizona, where I had served as the FO, forward observer, attached to Hotel Company, 2d Battalion, 5th Marines. A week or so after Arizona, I was permanently attached to Echo Company, 2/5, as their FO. We stayed in An Hoa for a few weeks. Mel and I had a chance to become friends and talked a lot about home. Home was everybody's favorite subject. Most of the guys would dream about girls or cars. We gabbed about our families and what we were going to do when we got home. Mel looked at me and said, "I really want to get a college degree."

"Yeah, that's a good plan."

"I hope I live long enough to accomplish that goal."

I told him that he would be just fine. That's the way things went for the next few weeks. We'd go to chow together, play cards, go to the movies at night, or just sit around talking about how homesick we were.

On June 23, Mel and I had chow together at the mess hall and afterward went back to his hootch, and he showed me pictures of his family and friends. We skipped the movies and just sat around jaw-jacking. I told him that I was going to be leaving with Echo Company the morning of the twenty-fourth to deploy to the Nong Son outpost. It was getting late and I told Mel I better be getting back to my hootch in the 81 mortar platoon area. He wished me good luck and we gave each other a Semper Fi.

CPL. DEAN JOHNSON: "Pete" Newlin and I had been in Operation New Castle, Mountain Goat, Union, and now Operation Calhoun. Union II was the worst. We lost our CO,

Captain Graham, two or three weeks earlier in Operation
Union II. He was awarded the Medal of Honor. I was sitting
against a sandbag bunker at An Hoa combat base, sweating
like a pig and talking to Pete. I don't know if anyone even
knew that Pete's real name was Melvin. Pete and I were gunners. He was my best friend and we'd talk about going back
to the World most of the time, just like all Marines did. I
know we all got a feeling every now and then that we
wouldn't make it home. But there was something different
about the way Pete sounded. He looked right into my eyes
and said, "I don't think I'm going to make it back home,
Dean." He wasn't being dramatic, he just seemed to know.

We got the word to move out of An Hoa combat base
about a week later. An Hoa Valley was a maze of booby
traps, and any movement there was always dangerous. We finally reached a river. Villagers from Nong Son brought us
across in little boats, two or three Marines at a time. The hill
was sloped on one side and real steep on the other. Fox Company had a platoon on top and one in the middle and one further down near the base of the hill. I didn't see any Marines
on the steep side of the hill. As machine gunners we got
thrown in with different platoons depending on who needed
us. There were six gun teams to a company, two went with
each platoon. A lot of machine gunners didn't last too long,
that M-60 would draw everybody's attention once you
opened fire. You might be with 1st Platoon one day, and if 3d
Platoon got a couple of gunners killed, then you could find
yourself with 3d Platoon the next day.

PFC DON ROUZAN: Fox 2/5 arrived at the coal mine,
Nong Son, near the end of June 1967. This wasn't that long
after Operation Union II. That was a bloodbath and we took
casualties. I think that was one reason we were put at Nong
Son to guard the coal mine. For grunts, any duty that got you
out of humpin' the bush was considered skate duty. If you
were guarding a bridge or sitting in bunkers on some hill,
that was easy living. A chance to rest, maybe actually get
some sleep. I was with 1st Platoon and we were assigned to

the top of the hill, and 2d and 3d Platoons were assigned below us. There were about four 105mm artillery guns on the hill below the 1st Platoon level. We called it the 105 level. There was a small village at the bottom of our hill.

We were allowed to go into the ville for haircuts and stuff like that. I went into the ville and bought loaves of bread and sodas. Shortly after we arrived, rumors from the villagers started flying around that the VC were going to hit us. Apparently that info was taken lightly because I don't remember any extra precautions being taken.

I'd been "in-country" only about three months at that time and really didn't get to know Newlin that well. Hi and small talk was about it.

L.CPL. MICHAEL O. HARRIS: On the morning of June 24 we deployed to Nong Son outpost. Echo Company arrived via choppers in the late morning hours. I was ordered by Captain Blessing to deploy to the top level with Lieutenant Bertolozzi's platoon. This made me pretty happy because that was where the 81 mortar section was deployed and I had some good buddies there. PFC Harry Marshall was one of my buddies, his dad was a full-bird colonel in the Corps. I also knew L.Cpl. Walt Buschleiter, PFC Ron Reyes, Sergeant Mendoza, the section leader, and my best friend, Cpl. Danny P. Riesberg. Danny had just returned to Vietnam from thirty days of leave in the States. He had extended his tour of duty in Nam for an additional six months.

I stored my gear in the bunker with Walt Buschleiter, on the east side of the outpost. I ran daily patrols with Echo Company and made only minimal contact with NVA and VC. On June 30 a patrol in Ninh Binh Valley was going through thick jungle canopy and the pin on a Marine's grenade caught a tree limb. The pin pulled and the grenade fell to the ground and exploded. It killed two Marines, including one of Echo Company's finest and most experienced squad leaders.

Near or on July 1 our worst fears were realized. Captain Blessing, our company CO, notified us that we were going to be leaving for Antenna Valley on July 2 to conduct patrols there in hopes of drawing large NVA forces out into the open to fight. Once contact was made, a large "sparrow hawk," that's a unit of Marines waiting and ready to join the fight, would be choppered into the valley to engage and destroy the enemy in what was hoped to be a major battle. Intelligence had reported significant movement in the valley by elements of the 2d NVA Division.

On the afternoon of July 1, elements of Fox Company 2/5 (2d Battalion, 5th Marines) were choppered to Nong Son to relieve us of our duties at the outpost. Scuttlebutt was that Fox was being sent to replace us because they were still refitting after Operation Union II in the Que Son Valley. I heard that they had lost somewhere in the area of 46 KIA (killed in action), and more than that number wounded. Those are terrible losses for a single company to suffer. Some companies in Nam had barely eighty men in the first place. Nong Son was considered skate duty because nothing ever happened there. It was a perfect place for Fox to rest and fill in the ranks with new boots.

Fox Company began arriving in the afternoon, and Nong Son became a very crowded place. I was surprised and elated to find out that Mel Newlin's M-60 machine gun crew had been assigned to the top of the hill. Mel and I had a great last day and night at Nong Son. Mel and some of his buddies, and some of my buddies from the 81mm mortar section, started playing cards. We gambled for cigarettes, playing craps. Later that night I went down to Mel's gun position near the road and visited with him while he stood watch on his M-60.

The following morning, July 2, I geared up and said good-bye to Riesberg, Marshall, Reyes, Buschleiter, and Mendoza from the 81 mortars platoon. I left the perimeter on top of the hill with Lieutenant Bertolozzi's platoon. As I passed Mel's gun position, he gave me a smile and a "Kick butt!" thumbs up. I returned the salute and made my way to the bottom of the hill to join the rest of Echo Company, never dreaming that Nong Son had been targeted by an experienced Main

Force Viet Cong sapper attack for July 3–4. It was the last time I would see Melvin Newlin alive.

CPL. DEAN JOHNSON: "Pete" and me wanted to be together, but that isn't the way the Marine Corps works for machine gunners. You might be together one night and separated the next if another platoon loses a gunner. We took so many killed in Union II that most of the company were new men or guys coming back from hospitals. On July 3, Pete Newlin joked about it almost being the Fourth of July and said that the fireworks would begin tonight. Perry Jones from Ellaville, Georgia, was my gun team leader that night. My platoon was put in the middle of the hill and Pete was on top. He was with four other Marines in a machine gun bunker beside the road right near the top of the hill.

CPL. BOB BOWERMASTER: After Operation Union II, I started wondering if I was going to make it home. Me and Thom Searfoss had spent about six months on Okinawa together because we were too young to send into a combat zone. We had to stay on Okinawa until we turned eighteen years old. Now we were the old salts in the company. Like everybody else, I was really glad to be riding on an amtrac out of An Hoa. We had a convoy of amtracs and an Ontos behind us. A Marine Ontos was a tracked armored vehicle with six 106mm recoilless rifles. I took a picture of the Ontos. We had to cross the Thu Bon River to get to Nong Son village. There was a village on both sides of the river and the coal miners and their families lived in Nong Son. We were to guard the only working coal mine in South Vietnam. It was "skate duty."

A narrow, winding dirt road led to the top of the hill, and once we crossed the river on these little boats we were trucked up to the top. I don't know how they got those Marine trucks across the river but I think they had some sort of barge that they pulled across. On top of the hill were some 105s, artillery, at least one 106 recoilless, a half dozen or more bunkers, some 81mm mortars, and an army spotlight

unit. The army guys had a jeep with this giant spotlight on it
that would light up Antenna Valley. We were way up. The
view from that hill was spectacular. I mean beautiful. Across
the river was Recon Mountain, which was even higher than
our hill.

L.CPL. RAY ALVEY: My MOS, military occupational
specialty, 0351, antitank assault, rockets, flamethrower, and
106 recoilless rifle. I was attached to Headquarters Company, 2d Battalion, 5th Marines, Flames. I had been all over
Nam, up on the DMZ and down to Chu Lai and Da Nang. On
the third of July, I found myself stationed at An Hoa combat
base. An Hoa was just a big ring of barbed wire and sandbags near the village of An Hoa. There was a corrugated
steel airstrip big enough for a C-130 to land on, but it was
mostly choppers coming and going. An Hoa had a pretty big
artillery battery there, with 105s and the big 155s. An Hoa
was pretty safe other than an occasional rocket attack or harassing fire, and I could have been comfortable just spending
the war there, though I'd rather have been back in Louisville.
    The lieutenant came into our tent and told us to saddle up.
He told us to bring flamethrowers, we were going to burn off
the side of a mountain at some place called Nong Son. I
never had any idea how high that mountain was, and I never
had any idea how it would change my life forever.

CPL. ROGER HUG: It was July 3 at the coal mines. Just
got back from an all-day patrol and felt really bad. Not just
the normal Nam fatigue that came from humping through
the worst terrain on earth in 110-degree heat with a hundred
pounds of gear hanging off you. My stomach was a mess. I
think I must have drunk some bad water, which was about
the only water in Nam. You never knew what you might be
putting in your canteen. You could fill up in what looked like
a nice, clear stream and find a rotting, dead gook upstream.
It was miserably hot and I may have just had too much sun
that day, sometimes the heat would make you sick even if the
water didn't, but whatever the reason I was feeling lousy. I

was at the bottom of the mountain and had to get up to the middle platoon. I was thanking God I didn't have to hump it all the way to the top.

CPL. BOB BOWERMASTER: On July 3 we had one platoon down near the bottom of the hill near the village and one platoon in the middle and one platoon on top. We really did think it was pretty secure but I kept complaining about the brush on the river side of the hill. It was real steep on one side. There was one part of the hill that really bothered me. The brush there was so thick that I knew the gooks could make it all the way to the top of the hill before anyone would see them. I started griping about it. I don't know where they came from, either trucked in or by chopper, but we had these fifty-five-gallon drums of Agent Orange with sprayers attached to the tops to spray defoliant all around the hill to kill the brush. The drums were up on the very top near a lot of the bunkers. I don't know when they planned to use the defoliant but I guess somebody decided to burn the brush off temporarily because they brought this flamethrower detachment to the top of the hill. I was glad to see that somebody heard my gripes.

CPL. THOM SEARFOSS: We got paid and got a little liberty down the hill to the village that was at the base of the mountain. We got haircuts, shaves, and even some fried rice served on newspaper. For those who were tough there was warm "Tiger Piss" beer. All in all it was a good day. Things were so quiet in the area it seemed like R&R. We started settling in for the night. Everyone on the 105 level was up til about 2300 hours because of July 4 approaching. We went to 25 percent, one out of every four Marines on guard in the trenches, bunkers, and LPs, listening posts.

L.CPL. RAY ALVEY: We left An Hoa real early, walking behind a bunch of amtracs. We carried rifles, and our flamethrowers and gas were aboard the amtracs. We got to Nong Son just before noon or early afternoon. The amtracs brought up fifty-five-gallon drums of gasoline, which we used to mix with our napalm for the flamethrowers. We test-fired them and had orders to burn the side of the mountain off, but it was getting late and they put it off for the next morning for some reason. The hill was really high up, I mean it was like looking down from an airplane. I could see clouds beneath us, actually lower than the top of our position on top of the hill. There were bunkers on top of the hill, and an army unit with a big spotlight mounted on a jeep. Some 81mm mortars and about four 105s and a 106 recoilless sat on a cleared and leveled area near the top. As an 0351, the 106 re-coilless was part of my MOS. That sucker had a serious backblast, and it had to be pointed in such a way that the backblast didn't kill anybody inside your own perimeter. It could be moved around to new positions either by a few Marines picking it up if it was on a tripod or by moving it around on the back of the little four-wheel mules we used to haul stuff. Changing the position of your crew-served weapons was a good idea, so the enemy couldn't know for sure where they were. Machine guns, too.

Around 1600 the paymaster showed up on top of that hill and we got paid. I got about $150 and Jack Melton got about the same. A village was down at the bottom of that mountain, where you could buy drinks, food, and get a haircut. That was a big deal to grunts who were usually in the bush and didn't get their pay sometimes for months, because they couldn't spend it anyway. I guess that since we got paid, somebody allowed a Vietnamese barber to come to the top of the hill to give the Marines haircuts. The next day, after the battle, I heard that we had taken some maps and papers off dead gooks. Word was that we discovered that the barber went down that mountain and made handwritten changes on the enemy maps, showing the changes in Marine positions on the hill. That evening I was taking it easy, cooking up some C-ration hot chocolate and talking about R&R with J. E. Ball and my friend John K. They had both been on R&R and were showing the rest of us their photos. They both had photos of some of the girls they had met in Bangkok, Thailand, and some photos of high school sweethearts. Images of home were about the only pleasant thoughts a Marine in Nam could muster. We'd hear about the war protesters and we hated them. Sometimes it seemed like nobody back home cared about us other than family and close friends.

We finished our hot chocolate as the sun was setting and everybody headed for their bunker. Me and John K. and Jack Melton had a bunker together right there on top of the hill. J. E. Ball was an M-60 machine gunner, and he headed toward his gun position about thirty or forty yards downhill right on the side of the road that came up to the top. He was a machine gunner with a five-man team that included PFC Melvin Newlin. J. E. Ball was one tough Marine. He was real handsome, too. That guy was better lookin' than Elvis Presley. He was a "short-timer." He'd been in Nam for twelve months. Thirty more days and he'd be back in the World. J. E. Ball had been in some of the bloodiest operations of the war and that old boy was a Marine. He was a fighter. He was on Operation Prairie and Union I and Union II and I don't even know what else but he was as tough as he was handsome, a billboard Marine. Those Fox Company boys had just come off of Operation Union II. Captain Graham had won the Medal of Honor there; the men loved him, and when he got killed it affected a lot of the guys. Fox Company had lost so many men in that OP that there were a lot of new "boots," so the outfit was filled with green troops. That's why old salts like J. E. Ball were so important. Young Marines clung close to guys like that.

Jack got the first watch up on top of the bunker while me and John went below to sleep. I took my money and Jack's and stashed it in this little Marine Corps ditty bag to keep it safe. I lay the bag on an ammo box and used it for a pillow. We got eaten alive by mosquitoes and I had a mosquito net that I put over my helmet and tucked into my shirt to cover my face and neck. We felt pretty safe that high up and in those bunkers with a couple of platoons below us, one in the middle and one near the foot of the mountain. That mountain was big, though, and covering the whole thing with one single company was impossible. I put my hands in my pockets so they wouldn't get sucked dry by the mosquitoes and fell asleep.

CPL. BOB BOWERMASTER: They test-fired those flamethrowers but somebody decided to hold off until the fourth, maybe they wanted to fire up something to celebrate. That steep side was covered with brush. We didn't know it, but the gooks had been building steps into the mountain to climb up. They had already placed their weapons and explosives in the brush so they wouldn't have to carry them up. They were there right under us, and if we had burned that brush we would have seen it. Everything, gook flamethrowers, B-40 rockets, AK-47s, and I guess they had machine guns hidden there. They also had satchel charges.

CPL. ROGER HUG: It was dusk now and my platoon was set up in positions in the middle plateau of the mountain. My machine gun team took turns on watch. We had a platoon below us and one on the top plateau of the mountain. I sat and stared into the black jungle like I did every night, until shadows become people. Your mind plays tricks on you at night in the bush.

PFC DON ROUZAN: On July 3, at about 2200 hours, myself, Bob Bowermaster, and Chuck Lloyd went out on an LP, a listening post. On our way out we had to pass Newlin's bunker. His bunker was at the gated entry to the top of the hill, beside the road. We made some small talk with Newlin and his boys and off we went outside the wire. We set up our LP about thirty or forty yards down from the top of the mountain. We found some cover along the side of the road and set in. Not a foxhole but a little cover. The road twisted and turned all the way down the mountain so from where we were beside the road we couldn't see Newlin's gun bunker from our position if we looked back. Bob Bowermaster had the radio.

CPL. THOM SEARFOSS: Bob Bowermaster and me had been together a long time. We had been in Okinawa for six months together just waiting to turn eighteen so we could get to the Nam. We were two of the few that made it through Union II, and Bob was one brave Marine who should have been decorated for heroism. I knew Bob Bowermaster and had worked the radio with him before. About 11:30 I was on because I wanted all my sleep at once so I took the first watch. I was listening to the radio checks going around from the LPs and other positions. Bob and the two new guys with him were below the 105 level and outside the perimeter.

PFC DON ROUZAN: Me, Bob Bowermaster, and Chuck Lloyd were out there for about an hour when we noticed what appeared to be lightning bugs between our position and the hill perimeter. I had been on Union II and survived, so I wasn't total boot, and between the three of us we didn't remember ever seeing lightning bugs in Vietnam. It was common knowledge that Charlie got stoked up on opium sometimes before sapper attacks. We radioed the CP about the lights and got set up for the night.

CPL. THOM SEARFOSS: Bob was about 150 yards away from me. Sergeant Clark's squad was on the 105 level about seventy feet below the top. There was a path up to the east side of the hill running from the 105 level to the top. The 105 level was accessible only through the wire, all three sides were steep and thick with vegetation. Earlier in the day we heard chatter from Recon Mountain across the river saying they had seen movement but it wasn't serious. Recon Mountain had a commanding view of the coal mine and the bend both ways in the river. From the river south was Antenna Valley and on the other side of that was 1/5's area, 1st Battalion, 5th Marines. I heard Bob Bowermaster radio in about the lights, but I didn't see anything from my position.

L.CPL. MICHAEL O. HARRIS, forward observer for 81mm mortars: We had made very little contact in Antenna

Valley on July 2–3. I had called in a half dozen or so close fire support missions in support of Echo Company, but we made no significant contact with the NVA up to the night of July 3. In the early evening of July 3, Echo Company was advised to set up for the night in the village of Ap Ba (4). Accordingly, I radioed Sergeant Mendoza, the 81 mortar section leader back at Nong Son, and gave him a prearranged fire mission for illumination fire should we need it. I gave Sergeant Mendoza the code name Whiskey Echo. If we were to require illumination that night, all I would need to do is raise the 81 mortar section on the radio, identify myself, and give the code name Whiskey Echo. Illumination rounds would be fired in seconds. After a briefing with Captain Blessing, I grabbed my poncho and found a hole for the night.

At 2327 hours on July 3, we were comfortably set in for the night. I was tossing and turning for most of the night trying to keep the mosquitoes and other bugs from eating me alive.

CPL. THOM SEARFOSS: I was still listening in on the radio and still on watch and still staring at pitch black from the CP on top of the hill. Bob Bowermaster radioed in to the CP, "I got movement all around us!" Fred Painter was the CP radioman. The new lieutenant was there, too, with Sergeant Baldwin. Sergeant Baldwin had just come back to Fox Company after being wounded in Union II. Sergeant Hollaway was in the CP on top, he had just returned from being diagnosed with shell shock on Union II, June 2. I liked Hollaway but he was never the same after Union II. Sometimes he would just sit and stare. He was a brave Marine who had seen too much and needed a longer rest.

A path ran up to the east side of the top of the hill from where the 105s sat. We ran back and forth from the top to the 105 level. I told Sergeant Clark that the listening post had movement, and we secured the 105 level and went to 100 percent. I went back to the top. Then Bowermaster radioed in again. "I need ammo! Now! I've only got a couple of magazines out here!" The CP radioed something back as I grabbed an ammo can and started scrambling to load it with all the magazines we could fit into it. The command post radioed Bob again.

"Are you sure?"

Bob didn't answer. He keyed his handset, which gave a static sound. I'd been with Bob since boot camp and knew that if he was keying his handset, that meant the gooks were so close he couldn't talk. I snatched up the magazines and headed for his position. Sergeant Clark closed the concertina wire behind me and my squad. I was the last one out of that side of the 105 level. We headed toward Bob's position. Mike Byrd was one of the Marines with me. Just a few seconds after Bob keyed his set, his LP opened fire with small-arms fire. Bob, Lloyd, and Rouzan were blasting, it sounded like single shot but it was constant and I knew they had some serious targets to shoot at with that much ammo being expended.

About thirty yards out from the 105 entrance a pop-flare went up. My eyes bugged out. The gooks were thick, everywhere, and heading straight for Bob's LP, about 150 yards from where I was. I dropped to my knee and saw several women in black moving away from the wire around the hill. Word was they were dragging bodies away. The M-60 machine gun was working overtime, and Ball and Newlin's gun team were putting out some serious lead, tracers hitting and skipping through the black night like shooting stars. It got real black as the flare burned out.

PFC DON ROUZAN: Those lightning bugs we were watching must have been old Charlie firing up his courage with plenty of dope for the attack, because all hell broke loose. Small-arms fire and explosions everywhere. Loud explosions everywhere that shook your mind for a few moments when they hit nearby. Illumination rounds went off, the place lit up like daylight, and gooks were all over. A lot of them already between us and the top of the hill. The three of us in our LP jumped out of our shallow foxhole and found better cover immediately. We opened fire back up the road.

CPL. BOB BOWERMASTER: Those lightning bugs down and to the right of our position must have been the gooks smoking stuff to build up their courage for the charge because it was like the dam broke. Explosions everywhere, the gooks were throwing satchel charges into the bunkers on the top of the hill. Our foxhole was only three feet deep and we were in a bad position if they fired down on us. We jumped out of our hole and got on the other side of the berm of dirt around it so we wouldn't be in the open as the gooks were overrunning the top of the hill behind us. Me, Lloyd, and Rouzan started firing up the road at the gooks on top. Illumination rounds went off and we had a target-rich environment! I yelled, "Fire single shot! No automatic! Save ammo!"

CPL. DEAN JOHNSON: I nudged Perry Jones, my gun team leader. "Do you see that?" I pointed out at the tops of all these pointed rice paddy hats. They were visible about thirty yards away. Perry said, "Yeah!" We opened up, I laid on the M-60 machine gun while others fired everything else. Somebody showed up and told us to cease fire. They said we had an LP out there. No one had told us we had a listening post out there and I was scared to death I might have killed Marines. Later I heard that a corporal in that LP had been killed. I was sickened over it. But our corpsman assured me that the Marine was not killed by the "sixty" fire. I still worry about it, I'll always worry about it.

CPL. ROGER HUG: All of a sudden all hell broke loose. From the middle plateau of the mountain we could see explosions on top all over from NVA rockets and incoming mortar rounds. They seemed to have every position zeroed in on except Mel Newlin's gun position, and he was taking advantage of it. Melvin's M-60 tracer rounds just covered the plateau, sweeping back and forth, then it looked like he was running around firing from different positions to get control of the situation. I started yelling that I had to get my machine gun team up there. My platoon and gun team were at the bottom of the hill after our patrol. Mules, those little four-wheel jobs that had only a steering wheel, passenger seat, and small platform in the back, hauled us from the bottom of the hill to the top. We went up the road as the battle was going on. We grouped at the middle plateau all within an hour. I was anxious to get there, as it was obvious that the Marines on top were in deep trouble.

CPL. DEAN JOHNSON: Perry Jones was our gun team leader and a good Marine. It was pitch black except for the explosions way up at the top. Everything up on top was exploding and I knew we should be moving out to help, but I never got the word to move out. In the chaos I just never got the word. I knew "Pete," Melvin Newlin, was laying down a lot of fire and he was in it deep, and I had to get up there to help so I took off on my own. I don't know how long it took, but three-quarters of the way up the hill the bullets and explosions were getting closer. It was still pitch black. All of a sudden some Marine shouted from the blackness, "Who goes there!" I knew the next words were going to be spoken by an M-16 and grenades. You never heard somebody talk so fast in your life. I started yelling everything I could think of to convince them that I was a Fox Company Marine gunner. I was told to come on in and we stayed grouped up there til daybreak.

L.CPL. MICHAEL O. HARRIS: At 2330 hours I heard the sound of rockets and mortars as they were fired. I assumed that they might be firing at our position in Antenna Valley and so did some of the other Marines from Echo Company as a few shouts of "Incoming!" were heard around the perimeter. We were seven klicks away from the Nong Son outpost and we could clearly hear the explosions as they resounded through the valley. The sky was set aglow with each new blast. This was the initial attack designed to drive the Marines into their bunkers to take cover from mortars. Then

250 to 300 VC sappers came up onto the hill and began dropping satchel charges into the bunkers where the Marines on top had taken cover. One satchel charge was dropped into the 81mm mortar bunker. It set off the ammo in the bunker and the explosion could be seen and heard and felt by us, seven klicks away. Luckily that 81 position contained mostly illumination rounds. Word reached Captain Blessing that the Nong Son outpost was under heavy attack and Echo Company was ordered to make it back to assist Fox Company.

L.CPL. RAY ALVEY: I heard this loud explosion, then another and I jumped! My friend John K. said, "Let's get out of here! We're being overrun!" As we rushed to exit the bunker, a loud explosion took our bunker out. All I saw was a flash and my face was burning and blood was coming out of my ears, but I could still hear okay. I didn't even have a rifle to shoot back. Outside our bunker was a trench that led to another bunker. The gooks were running right through their own mortar and rocket fire. John led us down the trench line to another bunker where Jack Melton, the Marine who was on watch, had his whole back blown up and was hollering loud. He was covered with dirt, the blast had half buried him.

CPL. THOM SEARFOSS: The top of the hill was getting pounded. I ran to help someone who was screaming. Mike Byrd was digging Jack Melton out, he was covered with dirt and screaming. Mike dug Jack's head and shoulders clear of dirt and Jack wanted a weapon. We gave him an M-16 and a bandolier, then ran downhill to help Bob Bowermaster's LP, as it was getting overrun.

L.CPL. RAY ALVEY: We crawled along the trench to another bunker. There were two Fox Company men in the bunker, one was black and the other one was a Spanish kid, and they were writing letters home! John K. started yelling at them. "We ain't going to a homecoming dance! You idiots!" He turned and yelled at me, "I ain't stayin' here!" And he left. Everything broke loose then. Explosions all over. I took up position just inside the entrance of the bunker and to the right. One of the Marines in the bunker moved to the entrance and opened up with a burst of fire. He must have hit some gooks. The gooks threw a satchel charge. I grabbed a blanket and wrapped it around my head so the explosion wouldn't blow it off. I curled up in a fetal position on a bunch of ammo boxes and just waited to die. The explosion was horrible. I could hear the VC chattering all around us. Then I heard a grenade come into the bunker. I curled up on the ammo boxes and gritted my teeth and waited. It went off and I could feel the steel going into my arms and legs but I didn't scream, I played dead. Marines were screaming in agony all around, boys calling for their mothers. One boy was saying, "Please mom! Don't let them kill us." Then it went quiet and I heard the gooks talking again. They threw in another grenade. I never made a sound. They threw in another grenade and I bit the blanket and didn't scream but I wanted to. They waited and soon another grenade came in. My legs and arms were just getting ripped up but I didn't scream, I didn't make a sound. They threw in ten to twelve hand grenades. I would just count in my mind how long between blasts. It seemed like forever.

After awhile I knew the other Marines in the bunker were dead. I guess I was losing my mind and I seemed to have this out-of-body experience. My whole family was over me in a casket at this funeral home in Louisville. I started praying to Jesus. I just knew this was it. My life was over and I kept thinking how I was only nineteen and it didn't seem right. I could hear Huey helicopters in the distance and I thought it was angels from heaven. I just knew everyone was dead and I started wondering how I would get back to An Hoa. Then I could feel our own artillery coming in on the hill, shells picked me up and slammed me into the ground.

CPL. ROGER HUG: Constant explosions seemed to be blowing the plateau of the mountain off. Enemy tracers green in color were mixing with orange M-60 tracer rounds

8

all around the plateau. Thousands of bullets were being spent. It was quite a show. We were preparing to go topside to help out. There was a backdoor trail to the top that only a few people knew about and we had a point man to take us there. It had been about an hour and a half and we were seeing red smoke from the top, the signal no Marine wanted to see; that meant they were being overrun. We started taking incoming and the gooks were probing the middle plateau. I was gun team squad leader and got word to take my two gun teams up now and hold on for backup that was coming. We made our way up, closer and closer to the fighting, it got louder and louder. At one point I could see Melvin Newlin just working that sweet M-60 and he was doin' the Corps proud. A lot of gooks in Mel's field of fire were gonna be seeing Buddha in hell.

We hit the top and VC were running all around us. We surprised them. One VC went running right by me like he didn't even see me. I shot him with my M-16. Another gook jumped behind the steering wheel of one of the little mules that had a 106 recoilless on the back of it. He took off down the mountain and my number one M-60 machine gun team put a burst into him, a tracer round hit the gas tank and gave him a real ride.

We split up in the trench line around the back of the mountaintop and hoped for backup Marines to start showing up. I could still hear Melvin Newlin's gun working. He was on the other side of the plateau and we put down a lot of fire to cover his backside. The next Marine in my trench line was about fifty feet away. The VC were still coming up the hill and trying to get in. They'd throw grenades and satchel charges into the trench line and we'd jump out, wait for the blast, and then jump right back into the trench. Illumination rounds were going off and we could see the enemy plainly.

Suddenly a gook came running up behind us with a three-foot machete. The Marine on my right saw him and jumped out of the trench and ran at him with his K-bar knife. The Marine knocked the gook flat, stuck him in the eye with his K-bar, then kicked the K-bar with his jungle boot right through the top of the gook's head. Just then another VC jumped in the trench with me and came running at me with a machete and screaming. I was out of ammo so I grabbed my M-16's barrel and shattered its stock across his face. That stunned him, and then I shot him with my .45 pistol. I ran to the back door where we had come up the hill and into the trench and found a VC sneaking up and into our position. I shot at him with the .45 and hit him in the knee. He did a flip and slid down the slope and went behind a bush. I watched and waited for a shot and saw him strike a match and light up on dope right there in the middle of the battle. All those suckers were doped up out of their minds so they wouldn't feel the pain. My number two gunner came running up to me, and I grabbed the M-60 from my guy and turned just as the gook behind the bush came running up at me again with his machete. I shot him right across the waist, don't know how many rounds but it nearly tore him in half.

I tossed the M-60 back to my gunner and searched for a weapon. I found an M-79 blooper gun (40mm grenade launcher) just lying in the dirt on the hilltop. It loads like a shotgun. I ran over and grabbed it up along with a satchel that had a few grenades in it. I got down, snapped it open and shoved in a 40mm round, then stood up. A gook saw me stand up and ran at me. I raised the M-79 and shot him at about fifteen or twenty feet away. The 40mm round hit and lodged in his throat, just below his left jaw. It spun him around two times and went off on him. There was no time to look at anything for long but I'm sure it blew his head off. I ran back and dived into the trench and looked for anything moving that wasn't a Marine.

L.CPL. RAY ALVEY: I don't know how much time went by but I know the gooks were everywhere. I was in a lot of pain from all of those grenades but I refused to make myself known to anyone by yelling. Eventually it got sort of quiet and I could hear "Puff the Magic Dragon" working out and that minigun was kicking some butt. I could hear this horrible noise getting closer and closer. It would *whirr* and *whoosh* and then I could hear Marines screaming in agony. It was a gook flamethrower and it was getting closer and I lay there playing dead with no weapon and praying for Jesus to save me.

CPL. ROGER HUG: I was crouching in the trench when a VC ran across behind us with a gook flamethrower. One of my gunners jumped up and bashed him and took the flamethrower away from him. The gunner lit him up all the way down the hill with it.

L.CPL. RAY ALVEY: I opened my eyes and the three layers of sandbags that used to be over me were all gone. There was a Marine kneeling in front of me with a radio on his back and I could hear the radio going on and off. I heard myself calling out, "Corpsman!" I yelled loud.

The Marine with the radio said, "Shut up!" He pitched me a K-bar and that knife was the first weapon I had my hands on up to that point and for the rest of the night. I could feel the wounds all in my arms and legs and it felt like somebody was putting out cigars in my flesh. I was good enough to crawl, so I crawled out of what was left of that bunker. There were blue and red tracer rounds flying everywhere from our machine guns and theirs. The gooks fired this greenish blue tracer and we fired this orange, sort of red tracer. There were so many machine gun bullets going through the air that the tracer rounds looked like a laser show.

Illumination rounds from Puff and some more being fired from An Hoa lit up the battlefield. I saw a group of gooks remove one of our machine guns from a bunker and bring one of their machine guns into that bunker about thirty yards away. That Marine with the radio had a LAW (light antitank weapon) on him. A LAW is like a small bazooka. It's real light, cardboard and plastic, but it fires a rocket that can stop a tank if you hit it right. That Marine saw those gooks setting that machine gun up in that bunker and he knelt down on one knee, broke the LAW open, pulled off the safety tab, and aimed it with this little site that you pull up. With bullets and explosions everywhere, he just calmly sited in and fired that rocket right into the entrance of that bunker. The gooks who didn't die right away came running out of that bunker screaming, slapping their bodies trying to put out the fire in their flesh, but it was no use, the white-hot stuff that was in their flesh was burning right through their bodies, and they ran and jumped off of the steep side of the mountain to their deaths. They screamed all the way down.

L.CPL. MICHAEL O. HARRIS: After getting orders to move out to help Fox Company, we hastily got our gear together and began a double-time run back to the outpost. We ran so fast that we later learned that our speed saved us from an ambush. The NVA had anticipated our movement following the initial attack on Nong Son, and they set up a two-company ambush on the road leading out of Antenna Valley. We found out later that we came out of the valley a couple of hundred yards ahead of their ambush. No one, including the enemy, had estimated how fast we wanted to get back to that hill to help our buddies. We continued our run through the pitch-black jungle knowing Marines were fighting for their lives and every second counted.

CPL. THOM SEARFOSS: When I passed the gun position on our way to help Bob, Lance Corporal Ball was on the M-60 machine gun. I could see the gun team from my position on the road. We were on the northwest section of the hill. I moved my team to the edge of the road leading down the hill. Guns was starting to cook. We started throwing grenades down the hill at gooks moving. Explosions were getting deafening.

CPL. BOB BOWERMASTER: I think the incoming mortars had stopped or else the gooks were running through their own fire. Now the top of the hill was being blown to bits with gooks running around throwing satchel charges. Gooks were coming off the top of the hill, retreating down the road. The three of us were dropping gooks all over, it was easy pickings but we were low on ammo. I'm not sure why they were coming back down that road toward us, but Puff was dropping parachute illumination and the place lit up like daylight.

PFC DON ROUZAN: When the illumination rounds started dropping it was like broad daylight and the gooks were everywhere. I think they were fleeing. We were shooting them and firing single shot to save ammo. It got quiet, then we heard a noise very close. A wounded gook crawled across the road and right into our original LP hole. He looked over and spotted us. He was in a khaki uniform and maybe a pith helmet but he had no rifle. I immediately jumped up with my M-16 as he reached for a pistol. I don't know who fired first but I was shot in the left wrist and I shot him once and my rifle jammed. I grabbed Corporal Bowermaster's rifle and shot him several more times, this one I know I killed.

CPL. BOB BOWERMASTER: The gooks were falling all around us as they retreated from the top of the hill. Suddenly the new guy, Rouzan, was hit in the wrist. I thought he was going to bleed to death so I grabbed the PRC-25 radio to call for a corpsman. I brought the mike up to speak and saw a flash from a rifle just off my left shoulder. The bullet hit my right ring finger, went through the mike, through my flak jacket, and then through me.

CPL. THOM SEARFOSS: Bob radioed that he was hit and he thought that the others were dead. "There's gooks all around with satchel charges." We propped Jack Melton up with an M-16 and took off as fast as we could. We passed the M-60 and Lance Corporal Ball was firing and Newlin was his A-gunner and they were putting out constant fire and had already repelled one attack from that direction.

PFC DON ROUZAN: Bob was hit bad and I knew it. He was calm and didn't panic a bit. I wrapped something around my wound, stayed quiet, and tried to hold my weapon with what was left of my hand and wrist.

CPL. BOB BOWERMASTER: I thought I yelled out that I was hit and the new guy yelled to shut up so they wouldn't know our position. I thought he and the other new guy, Lloyd, had been killed. Since we were all shot to pieces I wanted to yell back at him real bad, guess what pal, they already know where we are! Then I heard that sucking sound and knew it was coming out of me. I had the classic sucking chest wound just like they taught us in boot camp. I pulled my flak jacket apart and stuck my finger in the bullet hole in my chest. The noise stopped. I pushed this dead gook off of me, maybe more than one. It was getting hard to breathe.

CPL. THOM SEARFOSS: When we got to Bob, Mike Byrd and me put him in a poncho. He pointed to his mouth. I gave him mouth-to-mouth and he was okay. We lifted him, Mike had two corners and I had the other two. We could hear Ball and Newlin's gun cooking out M-60 rounds so continuous that the barrel had to be smoking.

CPL. BOB BOWERMASTER: God, was it good to see Thom's face leaning over me! He gave me mouth-to-mouth, then they put me in a poncho. I felt myself going and reached up and tugged on Thom. They dropped the poncho and he gave me mouth-to-mouth again and it worked. They lifted me up again and headed for the top of the hill. I felt myself going and pointed at my mouth again. They stopped and Thom gave me mouth-to-mouth for the third time and I could breathe. He flat-out saved my life three times.

CPL. THOM SEARFOSS: We were going to hold the top of that hill, so there was only one place to head. We took the smoothest, fastest way to the top, right up the road to Jack Melton's bunker. When we topped the hill, I saw Lance Corporal Ball in a rage as his gun had jammed, the barrel had melted. Melvin Newlin was changing that red-hot barrel

with his bare hands and putting in a new one. We crossed the
trench with Bob in the poncho when an RPG hit to my right,
in front of Melton, and it covered him up again pretty good.
The explosion slammed my face into the bunker. I actually
saw the dirt blowing over Melton as I hit. Bob was still in the
poncho and I still had hold of one corner. Mike Byrd was able
to keep hold of both of his corners of the poncho. We laid
Bob in the trench with his feet sort of up on dirt from where
the trench had been blown in. We got Jack's head out of the
sand and dirt so he could breathe. We had no idea how bad
Jack was hit, he was half buried and firing away and talking so
we thought he was just buried, but he was nearly cut in half.

Ball and Newlin's gun went silent as we were picking targets from the trench. Somebody said Ball had been killed.
Newlin was changing the barrel as the NVA were rushing
toward him. We had so many new guys that I didn't know
Newlin's name, gunners moved from one platoon to another,
so I didn't know if he was a new boot or had moved over
from another platoon. The gooks were closing in on his gun
so fast that they were within five feet when he opened up. He
was able to repel that attack, killed a bunch of gooks, but I
believe he was badly wounded. The corpsman ran to him
with bandages that shined in the light of the explosions and
tracer rounds.

The gooks came back up over the hill with what looked
like about thirty of them. From where I was I couldn't fire as
the gun team was directly opposite me. Guns opened up and
the fire was heavy and accurate, but they could fire only in a
small radius because there were Marines everywhere. The
enemy was inside the perimeter so you couldn't just shoot
wildly. As that group was attacking the gun position, several
enemy sappers were running around on top throwing satchel
charges.

PFC DON ROUZAN: When Thom Searfoss and his squad
got to us, we made our way to the top of the hill. Everything
got sort of foggy. Explosions and machine gun fire. I think
they laid me out with the dead and wounded.

L.CPL. RAY ALVEY: You couldn't lift your head up, there was so much fire. I could hear Melvin's machine gun just working nonstop, he worked the gooks over good and that M-60 sounded sweet. Then it finally went silent. I crawled along the trench. I'm not sure what I was doing, but I stabbed any gooks that I crawled past. I ended up in some blown-up bunker and there were gooks all around. I could hear them. Then I heard this one standing right on top of the bunker screaming orders to the others. I could see him and he was real big, much bigger than the Vietnamese. He wasn't speaking Vietnamese. He was shouting orders in Chinese.

CPL. BOB BOWERMASTER: I was holding my finger in the bullet hole in my chest and I had an AK-47 that I had taken off a dead gook nearby. I had the AK-47 resting between my boots and pointing down the trench toward a blown bunker. I was drifting in and out and praying to Jesus.

CPL. THOM SEARFOSS: After we got Jack propped up, we gave him one of three M-16s lying around in the dirt. The trenches were pretty caved in from all the blasts. I lay down in the trench next to Bob facing in the opposite direction. Bob's boots were up on a pile of dirt from where the trench had caved in, and he had the barrel of an AK-47 resting between his jungle boots. He was going in and out of consciousness. He had a sucking chest wound and it started making that sucking sound and gurgling so I stuck my finger in the hole in his chest and it worked real good. I held my rifle with my free hand and shot any gook I saw. Mike was aiming toward the top of the hill, Jack was pointing downhill, and me and Bob had the flanks down the trench line. We had our own little perimeter.

CPL. BOB BOWERMASTER: I saw this big gook jump up on a bunker, he had a different uniform on, he looked too big to be Vietnamese. I was weak and a little foggy, but then I'd be clear enough to see everything. This big officer saw us and he pointed a pistol down at us. He was close.

L.CPL. RAY ALVEY: I lay still with nothing but that K-bar and stared out of that bunker at gooks running around and this big officer standing sort of above me. I could hear the Huey gunships and good ol' Puff working out from above, and the gooks were taking a real beating.

CPL. THOM SEARFOSS: The big gook was right on top of us when Bob fired that AK. I glanced back. Bob was firing up at him and the gook had an automatic pistol that had jammed. The trenches were pretty well caved in, so Bob's boots were in a natural position higher than his head, worked real good. The gook was just a few feet from us, trying to fire a little black automatic pistol at us, but it was not firing. Mike Byrd ended up with that pistol as a keepsake.

CPL. ROGER HUG: After one of my gunners took that flamethrower away from that VC and burned him, I noticed that for the first time I couldn't hear Newlin's machine gun firing anymore. More Marines were coming in the back door, and we were starting to take the top of that stinking hill back.

L.CPL. RAY ALVEY: I crawled downhill to try to get to Melvin Newlin's machine gun position and found a Marine with no face. I thought it was Melvin. The gooks had cut this Marine from ear to ear after he was dead, then they peeled his face back over the top of his head. I don't know why or how I did it, but I sat there and pulled that boy's face back down and tried to make him look right. I took his dog tags, placed them in his teeth, and closed his mouth down on them so he could be identified. Even as I did this it did not seem real or possible to me. I remember wondering how could anybody be this cruel, and would anyone back home ever understand or care how heroically these Marines were fighting this kind of evil. During all of this it didn't feel like it was really me doing it.

L.CPL. MICHAEL O. HARRIS: We made it back to the banks of the Thu Bon River across from Nong Son at about

0030 hours. We had run the five miles in about an hour with full gear and in pitch-black darkness. Captain Blessing left part of his company with the ARVN (Army of the Republic of Vietnam) unit on one side of the river, and the remainder of the company crossed the river to get to the hill. We made an outpost. We reached the command bunker at about 0115 hours. The company commander of Fox Company, Lieutenant Scuras, had already taken a relief force to the top of the hill to help the battered Marines. The remainder of Fox Company was told to stay in their positions until the arrival of our company, and then they were to proceed with caution to the top of the hill. The lieutenant from Fox Company who was designated to lead the relief force to the top of the hill upon our arrival immediately shouted to his Marines to move out. I requested permission from him and Captain Blessing to go with them. I explained that once on the top, I could turn the 81 mortars on the fleeing enemy forces. I was granted permission to proceed. My best friend Danny Riesberg and many other buddies were up there.

CPL. BOB BOWERMASTER: I lay there with my feet up on the dirt, holding the AK. Thom had his finger in the hole in my chest. I kept asking them which lung had been shot, right or left, because I could feel it filling up with blood and I wanted to roll onto that side so I wouldn't drown from my own blood filling both lungs. Thom looked at the wound. "I can't tell," he said. "It's like right in the center of your chest."

L.CPL. RAY ALVEY: A big Marine from Texas was near me. He told me that he had a record player in his bunker. This gook stuck his hand in and took the record player. He started to play it. The big Texas Marine told me that the gook took the record that was on the player off and reached in and grabbed another record to play. "I couldn't believe it! Right in the middle of this!" the Texas Marine said. "I grabbed him, pulled him inside the bunker, and choked him to death, then ran out of the bunker. Gooks ran right up to me as I exited the bunker and they didn't shoot me! They were all over and none of them shot me. I jumped over the side of the mountain and hung onto a tree."

CPL. BOB BOWERMASTER: Somebody laid me out with the dead and wounded. There was still a lot of gunfire. A corpsman put a shot in me and plugged my bullet hole up. I had a stab wound in my side and didn't know when that happened, but it figured. We shot a lot of gooks and they fell all around us. I remember pushing dead gooks off of me and I guess one of them wasn't as dead as I thought. I could see a bright light and thought I must be dying. After that I drifted in and out of it, but I knew the guys were still fighting, a lot of gunfire. In spite of all of the gunfire, I felt at peace, it was very cool at the time, the peace and comfort.

CPL. THOM SEARFOSS: Women in black were dragging away the dead gooks.

CPL. BOB BOWERMASTER: I could hear women chanting this mournful chant as they dragged the dead gooks away from the perimeter wire. It was really eerie and weird, like some death chant.

CPL. THOM SEARFOSS: Puff the Magic Dragon had flown away to refuel and reload, and for that moment there were no choppers and there was no shooting. It got real strange and quiet. The wind was just right and in the distance I could hear Marines huffing on a full run, crashing through the black jungle valley like they were mad and lookin' for bear. Somebody said it was 1/5 (1st Battalion, 5th Marine Regiment) coming to help, and man they were coming hard. God, it was the coolest thing I ever heard. They weren't even trying to be quiet, they were just determined to get here. It felt real good. Friggin' Marines are crazy, man.

L.CPL. MICHAEL O. HARRIS: I got to the top of the hill sometime near 0200. As I walked into the same perimeter that I had walked out of earlier, I couldn't believe the carnage. Medevac choppers were already landing and picking up the most critically wounded Marines while those who were declared dead were lined up in a neat row in a specified area of the hill near the helicopter landing area. There were other bodies of Marines set aside in another area. These were designated as unidentifiable. I went to Mel Newlin's gun position and it was totally destroyed, but I didn't have time to survey the site completely, there were more pressing matters at that moment. I ran to where the 81 mortar command bunker was located and found Sergeant Mendoza. He was staring wide-eyed and in a state of shock. I looked around and saw an 81 mortar destroyed. Every few minutes an illumination round would cook off and explode from the heat of the fires all around.

I searched the area and discovered an 81 that was still intact and had plenty of HE rounds available. When the VC blew the bunker with illumination rounds, it caused so much smoke that it had concealed the other 81 mortar and all of the HE (high explosive) rounds. I yelled for Sergeant Mendoza to assemble the Marines still alive from his section and prepare for fire missions. He just sort of stared right through me and I knew he wasn't all there. I yelled louder in Marine fashion and he responded in Marine fashion.

For the next hour we fired one mission after another against the enemy routes of egress. I planned the missions and helped the Marines in firing the rounds. I also helped prepare the rounds to be fired. We had inbound choppers so we ceased firing until they came and went. Then we opened up again as fast as we could fire. The barrel overheated so we got cans of water and poured water on the barrel, then continued firing. When we shot off the last round of our ammunition, the Marines around me collapsed from fatigue. I walked over to Sergeant Mendoza and the utterly exhausted group of Marines. I thanked them for a job well done.

PFC DON ROUZAN: I was medevacked out on a chopper along with several others to Chu Lai and later to the USS

Sanctuary hospital ship for two months. Then I went back to the 5th Marines.

L.CPL. RAY ALVEY: I sat watching the horizon as the sun came up, crying. I couldn't believe it had happened, and yet I felt like I had been here before and done this before; it was real strange. I looked around. I looked at Newlin's machine gun position and knew that no one would ever know how heroic people like PFC Newlin were. None of those protesters back home would know how he could have played dead when the gooks shot him and blew him up and ran past him. He could have played dead. You couldn't even lift your head there was so much firing, but he lifted his head again and turned that M-60 on the backs of those gooks and shot 'em down just before they would have opened up with that 106 recoilless on us.

CPL. DEAN JOHNSON: He was "Pete" to me, not PFC Melvin Newlin. When I got to Pete's gun bunker I found him lying dead behind the M-60. He had a bunch of shrapnel holes, but his body was intact. He had a hole near his heart and I figured that was the one that killed him. Pete had no shirt or flak jacket on, only camouflage shorts and boots. Me and two or three other guys carried him in a poncho to the center of the hill and laid him alongside all the other bodies lined up in a row. The 106 recoilless was about forty to sixty yards away from Pete's gun. It was turned around and facing the Marine positions, but the gooks never got a round off because of Pete. There were dead VC near the 106, and one of them had a flamethrower on his back. The only body parts I saw around were all VC.

There was a winding road along one side of the hill. Two or three days later they brought up a truck and we had to gather up all the dead Viet Cong that had not been dragged away. My gun team went back down with the truck for fire support. There was no place to stand but on top of all the bodies in that deuce-and-a-half truck. It was sickening. When you moved, their skin peeled off under your boots. From the heat, I guess. It was filled with whole bodies and body parts. Feet and arms and legs. We took them to the village at the coal mine at the bottom of the hill and dumped them off.

L.CPL. RAY ALVEY: I found Lance Corporal Ball's body. He must have been hit by something big, he had a hole clean through his chest the size of a teacup. It just broke my heart to see him dead. He was a real fighter and I do think he was more handsome than Elvis Presley.

L.CPL. MICHAEL O. HARRIS: I left the 81mm mortar position after we expended every round and headed for Mel Newlin's machine gun position. I was told later that all four Marine gunners in that position had been KIA. I finally found someone who was able to tell me what had happened to Mel. They said he had been killed after furiously fighting off one enemy attack after another. I didn't know at the time what had taken place at the perimeter gun position, but I did know that it was something extraordinary. I knew because there were some forty to fifty enemy soldiers lying around the position who had been cut to pieces by whoever was manning that gun.

I walked to the position where all the dead Marines lay. I didn't know how many Marines were dead, total, but there were about eight bodies that had been identified and were lying in ponchos in a neat row. Next to them were three dead Marines designated as unidentifiable. I walked over to the unidentifiable Marines first. I lifted the poncho off one man's face, then another, and then the last one. I told a corpsman nearby and another Marine who was supervising the casualties that one body was that of L.Cpl. Walter Buschleiter. He had no face. They asked me how I knew this. I told them I'd known him for the last seven months and that he had a tattoo of a big Marine bulldog on his upper right arm. They checked his arm and found it. They tagged him and moved him over to the identified bodies.

I began to check the identified bodies. Under the second poncho that I checked was one of the Marines from Mel's gun team. I lifted the poncho of the third body and it was Melvin Newlin. There was no doubt about it. I felt very sad. The next poncho held PFC Ron Reyes, a friend of mine from the 81 mortar platoon. I sat down in the dirt between Mel and Ron and began to cry. I cried for a while, then composed myself and continued to check the dead. I recognized another member of Mel's gun team and that was it.

The Marines were still working feverishly to get other Marines out of the collapsed bunkers. They did not find many of them alive. One Marine that they did pull out alive died a few minutes later. Once we were positive that we had extracted all the Marines from the bunkers, everyone just kind of collapsed and waited for morning. By that time all of the dead and wounded had been medevacked, some to Charlie-Med and the others to Graves Registration.

It wasn't until first light that we really got a glimpse of the carnage. Nearly every single bunker on the hill had been blown. Both 4.2-inch mortars were destroyed. The 106 recoilless rifle was damaged and inoperable. One of the 81 mortars was destroyed. The lone .50-caliber machine gun was missing. Then somebody remembered that we had LPs still out in the bush. I heard that they had been killed in the initial attack. At least one LP didn't have a chance. They had reported that there was movement all around them. Then a panicked voice screamed that they were being overrun. A detail was sent out and the Marines were brought back into the perimeter. A medevac chopper was ordered back in and the bodies were taken to Graves Registration.

CPL. THOM SEARFOSS: The cleanup the next day was horrible. The huge barrels of Agent Orange defoliant had been blown and the ground had turned into this stinking chemical mush. Pulling all those arms and legs out of it was sickening. I found Sergeant Hollaway in the CP bunker that morning and he was not home. Shell-shocked. I heard that they medevacked him back to the States. He was a good Marine.

L.CPL. RAY ALVEY: They medevacked me by chopper to Da Nang. At the hospital I started to see all these wounded Marines from Nong Son. Each man's story was incredible. My Sergeant Kelly, from flames, was hurt real bad.

John told me that the gooks threw a satchel charge in on three of our buddies. Lance Corporal Hyson from the Bronx lost both his legs and was screaming. John said he fell on top of him to try to help as the gooks ran over them. My other buddy in that bunker had his arm in a cast and had only a .45-caliber pistol with two magazines. A gook ran right up on him after the satchel charge went off and he shot the gook with his .45-caliber pistol. The gook fell on top of him, then the gook started trying to pull the pin on a grenade, so my buddy beat him to death with his cast.

Corporal Hyson died. I felt a great loss. I was in a small building and it was lined with cots. Marines were getting arms and legs cut off. Then the airfield at Da Nang got hit and I started reliving the whole night again.

L.CPL. MICHAEL O. HARRIS: We started to clear the hill of all the dead Viet Cong. I don't know if a precise count could ever be made, the enemy dragged away most of their dead. But I believe that out of the 50 to 70 VC KIA we found, many were killed by PFC Melvin Newlin and his M-60 machine gun. That was so very obvious and was attested to by the fact that most of the VC dead were found in front of his gun position. Whatever happened that night, there is one thing that is so obvious that a blind man could not have missed it. PFC Melvin E. Newlin, United States Marine Corps 0331 machine gunner, performed one of the most heroic and gallant acts in Marine Corps history. In so doing he most definitely saved the lives of numerous fellow Marines. I feel privileged to have known him and even more privileged to have been his friend.

CPL. BOB BOWERMASTER: After I was put on the evac chopper and given a shot, I felt safe and went to sleep. The next time I awoke, I was on a table in the hospital fully clothed, and the nurse kept saying, "Where are his dog tags? Where's his dog tags? I can't find them."

"They are in my pocket," I said. The nurse and others in the room totally freaked out that I was talking. I looked up and a priest was at my head giving me last rites. "You ain't needed yet, I'm going to be okay." I went out again and didn't wake up for five days. I came to and found all these drain tubes in my lung and IVs and a real pain in my back. I asked a nurse what the back pain was and he said it was the bullet wedged between my rib and my skin. So they took me to surgery and gave me a local and took it out. The nurse put it on the table in front of me, an AK round that was bent a little. I went to sleep and when I woke up my bullet was gone. Don't know what happened to it. I really wanted to make a necklace out of it.

I kept thinking about Thom and how he saved my life three times with mouth-to-mouth. The Corps is slow, downright stingy about giving away medals, but I'll tell you right now, that guy's a Marine Corps hero.

L.CPL. RAY ALVEY: Somebody came by and pinned a Purple Heart on me and said what an incredible job the Marines at Nong Son had done.

CPL. THOM SEARFOSS: It was hot and humid on the Fourth of July. It was good to just see the sun come up. I had helped put Bob Bowermaster on the medevac chopper. Jack Melton, too. What incredible Marines. What heroes. And Byrd and Lance Corporal Ball. The stuff legends are made of. I wondered if anyone would ever know what kind of heroic Marines had been on this stinking hill on the Fourth of July.

The Fourth of July. The only difference between this day and any other was the fact that they gave the grunts a treat. Nice surprises came our way in helicopters. They brought us T-bone steak and ice cream and a special mail call and sundry packages. Of course, we ate the steak first as good food was hard to come by. Now the steak was cold, but the flavor was fantastic. To chew it was a major exercise for the jaw, and that just made it last longer. Next we opened the ice cream container with canteen cups in hand. Now the ice cream was just the opposite of the steaks, hot and runny. But it was vanilla and full of flavor, just tasting it made us remember home, the World, it did still exist. We consumed all of it, don't know if everybody on the hill got it, it might have been just Fox Company.

The chopper also delivered cases of Fanta cream soda, and I mean cases. Seems that was all that was left for the grunts in the bush. But being Marines we accepted them gratefully; beat the crap out of muddy, hot rice paddy water.

L.CPL. MICHAEL O. HARRIS: That day as we began the cleanup, I found part of a leg from the calf down. I realized that it belonged to my best friend, Cpl. Danny Riesberg. He had been medevacked out alive, but in grave condition.

I was recalled to An Hoa on July 5 by my platoon commander and gunny. They wanted me to go to Graves Registration in Da Nang to identify my good friend, Danny Paul Riesberg. It was the hardest thing that I had ever done. I arrived in Da Nang on July 5 and reported to Graves Registration. I walked into this cold, dreary morgue and noticed the attendant sitting at a desk eating a white bread sandwich. I told him why I was there. He took me over to a body bag and unzipped it. There was Danny, my buddy whom I loved like a brother, with his eyes wide open. I started crying like a baby. I stroked his forehead. The attendant came over and zipped the body bag back up. I signed a paper verifying that it was Cpl. Danny P. Riesberg, then I walked out and went to find a place where I could get totally drunk. I found a place. The next morning I got up, showered, shaved, got a hot meal, and caught a flight back to An Hoa. I immediately went to the Gunny and told him I was catching a chopper back to Nong Son, which I did.

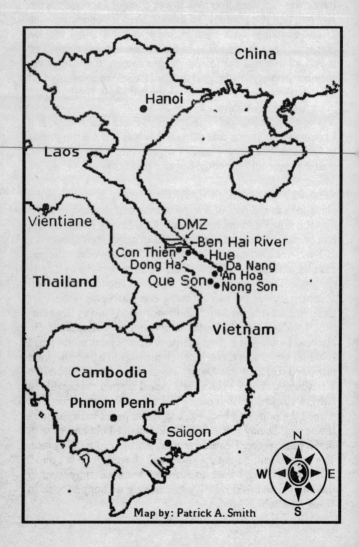

China

Hanoi

Laos

Vientiane

DMZ

Ben Hai River

Con Thien

Hue

Dong Ha

Da Nang

Thailand

Que Son

An Hoa

Nong Son

Vietnam

Cambodia

Phnom Penh

Saigon

N

W E

S

Map by: Patrick A. Smith

7

CPL. JACK HARTZEL

December 27, 1966, I disembarked from the USS *Francis Marion* and into a landing craft. We pulled up onto the beach without weapons, helmets, or even 782 gear. We were whisked away to our respective units aboard trucks. I was attached to MAG-16, as Marine air base security at Da Nang Air Base. It was monsoon season and I had never seen such rain. Our unit was in leaky, ragtag twenty-man tents. I stood bunker watch on the interior perimeter of Da Nang Air Base, watching huge rats go from bunker to bunker searching for food. It was our only entertainment. In the middle of our watch a Marine would bring us out brown paper bags containing "mid-rats," a form of Marine Corps food.

The bag contained cold Spam on dried-up water-base bread. The Spam was right out of the can, covered with that clear gelatin greasy stuff. Nobody ever ate it. One night along came the "mid-rats" guy bringing us that crap. He deposited the bags on the parapet of our bunker so we just left them there and watched. Soon the giant rats crawled over to the bags of Spam sandwiches and apples. They opened the bags like grocery clerks, then proceeded to pull out the sandwiches. We watched in amazement as the rats took both pieces of bread and left the Spam.

After a month or so the gunny asked for volunteers to work security at Phu Bai, home to the 3d Marine Division farther north up Highway 1. We flew into Phu Bai on a C-130. Things were a lot more relaxed in Phu Bai. My bunker was real close to an army quad-50. The army had all the good stuff, as always. I became friends with some army guys who ran that quad-50. They'd been in-country longer than me and knew the ropes. One day the army guys asked me to go to the army EM club with them. The Corps had nothing like this. It was a regular bar with some cute Vietnamese waitresses and real booze. It was heaven. They told me later that I had thirteen Tom Collins drinks, then when I walked outside into the 110-degree heat, my legs collapsed and I went down like a tent folding. They carried me back to my bunker and stood my watch for me.

Two weeks later I did it again, and again the army guys stood my watch for me. This time I wasn't so lucky. The gunny decided to check the lines. I woke up to a torrent of fists just beating the crap out of my face. I came up and tried to defend myself and I guess I did for what it was worth. The gunny wanted to court-martial me and send me to the brig, but the army guys came to my rescue. They told the gunny that I asked them to stand my watch so the lines were never unsecured. Gunny didn't care, he wanted to burn me. He finally gave me a choice of going to the "red line brig" in Da Nang, or I could volunteer to go to "the bush." With no hesitation I shouted, "Send me to the bush!"

I was off to find out how real Marines lived and died in "the bush." I was flown back to Da Nang on a C-130 cargo plane and billeted for the night. I was to take a plane out the next day for Dong Ha and the 9th Marine Regiment. The next day I sat on my seabag at the terminal, waiting for my flight to Dong Ha and just watching all the choppers and planes taking off and landing. You knew they weren't going out on sightseeing tours. My stomach would do a little nervous flip when I thought about where I was heading. I heard somebody calling my name and thought my mind was playing tricks on me. Then Louie Torrellas, an old high school buddy, came running up to me. I didn't even know Louie had joined the Corps. It was a big deal to see somebody you knew back in the World. Louie was waiting for a plane to take him to the 1st Marine Division, someplace south of Da Nang. We had a great time catching up and making plans to get together back in the World. Before either of us wanted it to end, my flight was ready. We said our good-byes, I threw my seabag over my shoulder and headed for the plane.

"Wait up, Jack!"

I turned around and Louie was running out on the tarmac. "What's up?"

"I'm going with you!"

"You can't do that! You got orders. You'll get thrown in the brig!"

"I don't care. I'm going with you, bro."

The maniac was serious. He climbed aboard and we flew to Dong Ha. The first night we were hit by a rocket attack and ordered to man the bunkers. We still didn't have a helmet or a rifle! We both nearly wet ourselves. The next day we caught a convoy to Camp J. J. Carroll, a fire support base northeast of Dong Ha. The drive was about an hour that felt like a week, hot and dusty, and we both felt like sitting ducks the whole way. We still didn't even have a friggin' rifle or helmet. The convoy headed slowly upward, climbing and winding until we reached the top. Here was Camp J. J. Carroll. It was a big compound, hundreds of dust-covered tents, each surrounded by layers of sandbags. The place was ugly as sin, and if you wanted a photo of a Marine firebase, this was it. Sidewalks made of empty artillery boxes and old pallets kept you above the mud during the monsoon rains. Drainage ditches surrounded nearly every structure to help move the monsoon floodwaters. They had constructed crude showers out of fifty-five-gallon drums sitting atop small sheds. Some even had kerosene burners for hot water, but I was to find out that kerosene was rare. We got off the truck and started looking around like men who had landed on another planet, then *Bam!* Marines started yelling.

"Incoming!"

We found our way to the nearest hole and sat clenching our teeth and our fists as NVA (North Vietnamese army) artillery pounded Camp Carroll. The old salts told us the gooks would blast the hill with arty every time a chopper or a convoy came in. That night our big guns opened up on the gooks and I thought the roof of our hootch was going to blow off from the concussion. There were big army 175mm guns and Marine 155s at Camp Carroll. I didn't sleep much.

The next day I searched out the weapons platoon of my new outfit, Echo Company, 2d Battalion, 9th Marine Regiment. I had trained with machine guns back in the States and I just felt safe with the M-60 in my hands. That was really stupid. We were told that a machine gunner is usually killed or wounded about seven seconds after a firefight begins. We didn't really believe it or pay much attention to it until the rounds started flying. I found the machine gun bunker and met my first squad leader. His name was Goodie. I told him I wanted in "Guns" and he directed me and Louie to the gunny's tent.

"Boy. Are you sure you want to be in Guns?"

"Yes, sir, Gunny."

And it was done. He looked at Louie's orders and said, "You really made a mistake coming here, son." Louie just smiled. Gunny gave him a serious look, then crossed out his original unit's name on his orders and wrote in E 2/9. "You're in 1st Platoon, rifleman."

I was quizzed hard about the nomenclature of the M-60 machine gun by Goodie. I was told I was taking over the gun of a guy who was just killed by a sniper. It made me really nervous and I wondered if I had been crazy asking to be a gunner. That night Goodie made me take the M-60 apart blindfolded and put it together again. It was easy for me because the gun was still fresh in my mind from my stint with I 3/2 back in the States.

I was really surprised that they let me carry the gun my first day in the bush. There were a lot of Marines with more experience. I soon found out that after the last gunner was killed, no one wanted to carry the "sixty." One guy told me, "It's like pasting a target on your back, boot. When it hits the fan, you're the first one they call for. Guns Up!, bro."

Because of the insane rules of engagement, the NVA could use the Demilitarized Zone or DMZ as a base of operations, and we were not supposed to touch them. My first trip to the "bush" was a walk into the DMZ on Operation Cimarron. It was the first time I ever saw a dead man. We found a bunch of NVA graves. I didn't see much action, we were a blocking unit for another outfit, but we heard that we really caught the NVA with their pants down because they thought they were safe inside the DMZ.

It felt good to get a little payback after being shelled all the time. It didn't stop the shelling, though. The NVA had artillery batteries across the Ben Hai River in North Vietnam. They could hit us at will, any time or place they wanted. Their Russian artillery pieces had a range in excess of ten miles. Our artillery didn't have that kind of range, so we couldn't return fire. Since we couldn't bomb them or cross the DMZ with Marines and kill them, we just had to live with the shelling. I wondered if the people back home understood how badly we were being handcuffed. Every one of us was hoping that General Westmoreland would eventually turn us loose so we could cross that friggin' river and take Uncle Ho Chi Minh and his boys out for good. Until that day came, our job was to keep them on their side of the river.

On July 28, 1967, we started out on Operation Kingfisher. We were a reinforced battalion with a platoon of tanks, three Ontos, and three LVTEs. Those Ontos were tank-killers; they had six 106 recoilless, three on each side, serious firepower. We started going north on Route 606, heading toward the Ben Hai River. Even some of the "old salts" started getting nervous about the operation. There was no way we were not going to make serious contact this close to the DMZ in an NVA staging area. Echo and Golf companies took the flanks while the main body, along with the M-48 tanks, the three Ontos, and the LVTEs, were on the road. Hotel Company was held back in reserve until the rest of us crossed the river. We had gone quite a distance with no contact when one of the lieutenants suddenly got shot in the helmet. A Marine gunner saw the NVA soldier who had fired from the brush and blew him away with a burst from the M-60. The lieutenant was knocked unconscious but the bullet missed his skull. We came up on an NVA field hospital, and it was obvious the gooks had just left. We started getting a little edgy.

Everyone knew that we were way outnumbered just across that river.

The terrain was thick, it was hard going, and soon the men were forced to use the road, which was just what Charlie wanted. Charlie was the slang name that Marines called the NVA. Charlie knew we would have to leave by the same road that brought us. When we had almost reached the river, A-4s, navy planes, laid down a smokescreen to the west between the high ground and us. Hotel Company was then helo-lifted into the attack zone at the river. We set in for the night. I set my machine gun up facing south, the way we would be leaving.

No place gets any darker than the jungles of Vietnam. A couple of hours into the night my A-gunner and I started hearing noises out there in the blackness. Then a few other Marines heard noises. It sounded as if someone were digging. We gripped our weapons and no one closed an eye through the rest of the night. I sent word to our platoon sergeant, and he came to sit in our fighting hole with us. He heard the noises too and it left us all concerned. We knew we would have to go down that road the next day.

Scuttlebutt the next morning said that Hotel Company was hearing trucks throughout the night. Things were sounding big. They called in artillery but no one knew the results. At first light the engineers in Golf Company checked out the stream crossing the road parallel to the Ben Hai River heading northeast. Engineers said the M-48 tanks would never make it, they'd bog down for sure. Scuttlebutt said that our battalion CO received a message that five NVA battalions were en route to engage us. Our CO called 9th Marine headquarters and informed them that we would be heading out on Route 606. Word was that the NVA were along the river, anticipating that our tanks would bog down and be sitting ducks.

Around 0100 hours we saddled up and moved out. Almost immediately Golf Company made contact with the NVA. Hotel Company was supposed to be the rear guard, but Golf never broke free from the moving battle. Echo Company, my company, took the point, with the 2d Platoon leading. Our progress was painfully slow with so many men and so much equipment moving along that narrow dirt road. About an hour into the march we heard a large explosion that shook the earth. I knew right away that the digging we had heard last night was a booby trap. Corpsmen ran from everywhere. Nearly a squad of Marines was dead. An NVA leaning behind a tree had set off a 250-pound B-52 dud. The NVA soldier who detonated the bomb died with the explosion. Cpl. Bill Underwood came up to me looking sick.

"I was talking to a buddy beside a tank up there. I turned to go back to my squad and the bomb went off. When I went back, my buddy was vaporized. There was barely enough to put in a poncho."

When we moved past the spot, there were entrails in the trees. Marines were busy picking up body parts, heads and legs and arms, feet still laced into jungle boots. Just up the road from that the engineers found another bomb and detonated it. When that second bomb went off, the gooks opened up on us with machine guns, AK-47s, and mortars. They dropped those mortar rounds right onto the dirt road. We dived off of the road to both sides and a lot of men landed on punji stakes. Some Marines tripped booby traps rigged on the roadside.

We moved out again. It became a running battle south with the NVA trying to break us up so they could surround and cut off a company. I grabbed my A-gunner and shouted, "I see gooks on both sides of the road!"

"You're scared. You're just seeing things."

I was staring at a bush as he spoke to me, and I knew I saw that bush move. I lifted the M-60 like a rifle and opened fire with a twenty-round burst. The bush fell over dead and dropped a Russian AK-47 rifle. My A-gunner's eyes nearly bugged out of his head. From that moment on we blew away every bush or treetop that looked suspicious.

Some of the Marines moving along the road started looking to their left. I glanced left and noticed troops moving along our left flank. I looked to the right and there were more troops moving along our right flank. They were wearing flak jackets, jungle utilities, Marine helmets, and carrying M-16s. Then somebody shouted, "We got 'friendlies' on our flanks!"

"We ain't got no flankers out!" another Marine shouted.

"Those are gooks in American gear!"

I turned the M-60 on the gooks to our left and opened up as everyone around me started blasting. We killed at least ten of them and the rest disappeared. There was no time to get a careful body count. The NVA knew that the only chance to survive our supporting artillery and air strikes was to stay as close to us as possible. I could see the small American spotter plane above us and thanked God for that guy. Soon the sweet roar of Phantoms ripped by overhead so low that we could see some of the pilots actually wave at us. The napalm sent waves of unbearable heat across the tiny dirt road, and even when we flattened out you could feel it through your clothes. We got up and moved out again, then the roar of a Phantom swept past overhead and two canisters tumbled toward us. We hit the dirt and I watched NVA running and screaming from a bunker, burning like torches. The stench of burning bodies was awful. I knew I'd never forget that smell as long as I lived, which was starting to look shorter with every step down Route 606.

We moved around a bend in the road and immediately I saw the flash of an RPG let loose on the lead tank. It struck the turret and disabled the tank. An Ontos raced up to help the tank and another RPG hit the Ontos, stopping it. A second Ontos raced forward with machine guns blasting and suppressed the enemy fire long enough to get the wounded out of the tank and crippled Ontos. After that the tracked vehicles flew down that road. Incoming mortars started walking down the road again. My A-gunner and I flattened out just as a forty-ton M-48 tank roared up on us. We were inches from becoming "road pizza." The tanks became a liability. Instead of protecting us, we had to protect them from RPG crews. We used them as ambulances but other than that they were useless. We lost two tanks and two Ontoses. We broke out, but two squads were cut off and pinned down back up the road.

The two squads were from my company. That night our colonel came by and told us we'd be going back in and getting our guys. We liked hearing that. Marines never leave Marines behind. Then I guess the situation got worse. The next thing we knew we were saddling up and moving back down that road in the pitch-black night. Our CO took operational control of 3d Battalion, 4th Marines and a section of tanks. Once we started back in, the NVA knew better than to fight it out. They broke and ran. The young lieutenant, the platoon leader from Echo Company that we were trying to rescue, was all Marine. I heard his last transmission. He told us not to resupply them anymore. He knew that the supplies would end up in the hands of the enemy. "My Marines are fighting so fierce that they'll go to Hanoi!" We halted to keep from getting separated and cut off in the black night. Later we heard what sounded like Marines screaming, but everyone thought it was an NVA trick.

By morning we moved north tracing our route from the day before. When we finally rejoined the rest of the battalion, the NVA were gone. The young lieutenant that we all heard over the radio and several of his men had been caught in the open and captured. The NVA hog-tied them with corn-wire and bayoneted them. They didn't kill them right away. They tortured them with bayonets to make them scream. That was what we had heard during the night. Then the gooks murdered the young lieutenant and the others. They didn't take prisoners unless they were ranking officers whom they could use for propaganda. We took prisoners. But then, Marines are warriors not murderers. We lost 23 KIA and 251 wounded. The enemy lost a lot more than that, but we could have been wiped out; they had everything in place to annihilate us, five battalions against one Marine battalion. I truly believe that God above was watching out for us that day.

In the summer of 1967, I was attached to a platoon that left the barbed-wire security of Con Thien combat base just before light. We were hoping to sneak into the southern

DMZ. We moved as quietly and quickly as possible, hoping that we could make it to the tree line just beyond a cleared out area we called "the Strip." We had a 3.5-inch rocket team attached to the platoon also. The 3.5 rocket launcher is called a bazooka in the army, but it's a 3.5 in the Corps. Our objective was a crossroads on Route 606, about thirty-five hundred meters out, where we had previously destroyed a bunker complex. Our job was to check out the area and get the info back to the 9th Marines without getting killed. We made no contact on the way there.

After setting up a perimeter and dropping our gear, we got word to "Saddle up!"

"What's up, McGee?" I asked.

"A spotter plane just radioed that we got approximately six hundred NVA soldiers moving to engage us."

We got saddled up fast and were humping it back toward Con Thien within minutes. We probably made it twenty-five hundred meters before the gooks opened up on us right in front of "the Strip" of open terrain surrounding Con Thien. Machine guns raked us, then mortars started landing all around us. Our platoon commander yelled for guns and rockets to form a rear guard and hold the gooks off while the platoon made a run for Con Thien.

We laid out, and my A-gunner started linking one-hundred-round belts of M-60 ammo together. The moment the platoon took off, the NVA moved forward. I could see them on line and running toward us, but they probably didn't know we had set up a delaying rear guard. When I opened up with the M-60, they started dropping like bowling pins. Then I heard that *whoosh!* The 3.5 crew had let loose, and when it hit I saw body parts flying. The NVA hit the dirt. Then their mortars started walking rounds closer and closer to us. I shouted, "We gotta move!"

The 3.5 crew got up and darted closer to Con Thien, then jumped into a new position, faced the gooks, and began loading up another round. Me and my A-gunner did the same thing, keeping our distance from the 3.5 guys. We opened up again as the NVA started coming forward and we caught 'em

again and we were "kickin' butt and takin' names." Soon the
mortars were walking in on us again and when the rocks and
shrapnel started singing past our ears, we beat feet again. We
ran another fifty yards toward the wire at Con Thien, then
dropped down and took aim. I couldn't believe they fell for it
again, but they came charging and we cut 'em down while
the 3.5 boys blew the crap out of them with direct hits. The
mortars got real close and we hustled out of a direct hit just
in time. We hit the deck again, and again they ran straight
into a good hundred rounds of 7.62mm bullets and at least
two or three rockets from the 3.5.

The big 155s and 105 artillery batteries in Con Thien
opened up along with our mortars. The NVA scattered like
ants as the earth erupted. It was over and somehow we only
had two wounded, but my knees and nerves were shaking
long after I made it inside the wire. I huddled inside a sand-
bagged hole as the NVA artillery from the other side of the
DMZ pounded us for the next couple of hours. I knew they
had taken a lot of casualties and they were trying to make us
pay for it. I sat in that hole with the earth trembling from incoming rounds and thinking about the people back home
who thought we were the massive American military waging
war against the little North Vietnamese army. In truth, we
were always outnumbered by a crapload. It was common for
Marine platoons to battle it out with NVA companies or even
battalions, and I knew that no one in the States understood
that and it pissed me off. We all knew we could end the war
by invading, by crossing that invisible shield they hid behind
called the DMZ and kicking their commie butts all the way
to Hanoi.

Soon after the shelling ended a group of about ten American soldiers showed up at the wire. They came inside and
talked to our lieutenant for a while. They were dressed like
Recon Marines, camouflaged, but all of their gear was brand-
new. Scuttlebutt said they were Green Berets but I never
knew. The LT told them they should stay inside the perimeter for the night. He told them how many gooks we'd just

made contact with. Their leader scoffed at staying and they
marched off in the same direction the gooks had fled earlier.

The next day we took a company-sized patrol in that same
direction. About three thousand meters out we found those
ten soldiers. Most had been killed immediately but the survivors had been hog-tied with communication wire. They
hung them up by their feet and butchered them. They had cut
the genitals off a couple and sewed them into their mouths
with comm wire. They slashed their stomachs open and let
their intestines hang down. They poked the eyes out of the
others. They did this to guys who were still alive. Our hatred
for the gooks and anger at Stateside cowards who had no
idea what these people were really like was as frustrating to
the Marines as anything on earth.

A week or so later we humped about a thousand meters
outside the wire in a monsoon rain and set up a perimeter.
Guys dug fighting holes that quickly filled with water but we
were so soaked all the time that Marine slang phrase "It don't
mean nothin' " was apropos. We had been wet for so long
that our skin was peeling off our feet. You got real wrinkled.
We put a couple of ponchos together like a teepee in the middle of the perimeter and started a fire. The smoke went out
the top and this was a sure way to draw artillery fire, but you
finally reached a point where you weren't scared, just tired
and mean and you just didn't care. It don't mean nothin'.
Marines would change places on the perimeter to get a
chance to dry their feet out, then go get another guy so he
could dry his feet for a minute. It didn't last long. We got a
radio message to saddle up; 3d Platoon had been ambushed.

We moved about two klicks (two thousand meters) when I
saw an NVA running on our flank, in pith helmet and full
battle dress with an AK-47. I ran at him yelling, "Gook on
the left!" I chased him down this trail through a rain forest.

My A-gunner was from the South and had this wonderful,
slow, Southern drawl. He chased after me yelling, "Jack,
gunners don't walk point."

I stopped and my A-gunner motioned the point man forward. The point man was a "boot." That's one of the many

terms we called Marines who were new guys "in country." I
don't know how the new guy got on point, but it happened.
He looked nervous. He hesitated, then moved past me and
went about twenty meters down that trail. A burst of AK fire
killed him. I probably fired a hundred rounds before the new
guy hit the ground. Rounds were flying everywhere, ripping
through brush with smacking sounds that sent chills through
you. Somehow in spite of the volume of fire my A-gunner
and I put out, that AK kept firing back. The terrain was lush
and thick. The gook had to be dug in to survive all the lead I
was putting out. I was down to about 75 rounds in the last belt.
My A-gunner got to his knees and linked up another 300
rounds, then suddenly another burst of AK fire knocked my
A-gunner down. He was hit in the stomach, and I thought right
away that was it. Stomach wounds are ugly. Somebody rushed
up to us from behind and dragged my bleeding A-gunner away.
A grunt moved up beside me on my left and opened fire with
his M-16. Hot brass ejected from his rifle and burned my face.
I cussed him away from me and opened fire again. I paused,
and me and the Marine with the M-16 heard a thump at the
same moment. We both saw a Chi-Com (Chinese Communist)
grenade bounce nearby and roll toward us, fizzling. It felt like
an hour before we realized it was a dud. We both opened fire
again.

The Marine on my left pulled the pin, rose up, and threw
a frag grenade toward the enemy. But he threw it straight into
a tree! It bounced back and exploded ten feet away, almost
killing both of us. I screamed the appropriate information to
the idiot and opened fire again. I ceased firing, pulled a
grenade off my cartridge belt, yanked the pin, let the spoon
fly, and lobbed it over the small tree to our front. The blast
sent shrapnel slapping through the brush, but the AK kept
firing. I opened fire again, then the gun jammed. It was a
"cook-off." The barrel was white-hot. We were taught to wait
ten seconds before opening the feed cover to clear the jam,
but whoever wrote that rule never had AK bullets whining
past his ears. I lifted the feed cover and *bam!* The round went
off from the heat of the barrel and took my ears with it. I

ejected the spent cartridge and resumed firing. A Chi-Com grenade landed nearby and this time it exploded. I was blown onto my side and so was the grunt beside me.

I was hit under the right eye and bleeding pretty good, but it looked worse than it actually was. The rifleman was hit in the arm but he was okay. We opened fire again and kept firing until the enemy fire ceased. When it was dead silent, me and the rifleman crawled back out of that position. The lieutenant spread the platoon out and we swept the area, Marine Corps style, expecting to shoot the first mosquito that moves and ready to kill in hand-to-hand combat if they're on you too fast to shoot. Every step feels like it can be your last when you're sweeping an area just waiting to draw fire.

We found the NVA soldier who had been firing on us. He lay dead a few feet from an old French foxhole. The French-built foxholes were shoulder-width and up to your neck. It was really hard to hit a man in a hole like that. It was obvious that this dead gook had been holding us off while his pals beat feet out of there. As we swept the area we found blood trails everywhere. No one saw any targets, but it was obvious that we were hitting them as they tried to retreat. We kept moving forward and walked into what had been an NVA camp. They had tents set up, pots on the fire, and food cooking. Every pot and pan seemed to have holes in it, and I knew one thing for sure, we messed up their dinner. The camp was a big one, maybe a battalion-size CP. There were blood trails everywhere and evidence of where they had dragged away dead and dying NVA.

It's hard to calm down after that much adrenaline shoots through you. It took a few minutes to think clearly, and my first thought was whether or not my A-gunner was dead. I smoked a Lucky Strike cigarette and found the Doc. The corpsman said my A-gunner's wound wasn't life threatening and he'd already been medevacked out. Scuttlebutt said that I had hit another Marine, they told me a stray bullet hit him in the helmet but it just knocked him out. You can't think about that stuff too much, but killing another Marine was a real scary thought. I was thanking God he was okay.

I went back to my platoon looking pretty salty. Blood running down my face and the M-60 still smoking hot. I tried to act as cool as I felt, but you don't come down that quick from an adrenaline high like combat. I sat down and started to clean my weapons before some jackass had a chance to shout "Move out!" The gun came first, of course, because it was the lifeblood of every Marine in the platoon. Then I cleaned my .45-caliber pistol. Normally, I would pull the slide back, let it go home, then squeeze the trigger. Then I would put a magazine in and chamber a round. I don't know if my hands were still shaking, but my mind was a little shaky and I was still somewhere else. I did everything backward. Without knowing it, I had already put a magazine in and chambered a round. I aimed at a tree limb about eight feet above my ammo-humper's head and squeezed the trigger, fully expecting a *click,* not a *bang!* We both almost crapped our trousers. I took the magazine out and sat there in a daze. My lieutenant came running up and asked who had fired that round. I mumbled, "I did, sir."

"You'll probably get an Article 15 for having an accidental discharge, Marine."

At that point I didn't give a flip. I was just so thankful that I hadn't killed another Marine. Later that day the captain and some other officers actually set up a little makeshift table and chair right there in the rain forest. I never dreamed that even in the Marine Corps they would have "office hours" right here in the bush. Boy, was I mistaken. My lieutenant was very nervous about it. He came to me and made me find a utility shirt. Marine Corps dress code. Most of the time I didn't wear a shirt, just my flak jacket. I didn't even hear what the captain said as I stood at attention in front of him. I heard my lieutenant, though. "Sir, Lance Corporal Hartzel is my gunner and does his job with zeal and professionalism. He has credit for the only confirmed kill of the day in the battalion." I felt proud. Of course, we all knew we had more than one kill, but we had only one body, so only one confirmed. I still got a ninety-day suspended bust and a hundred-dollar fine. When the day ended, all I could think about was the boot Marine that had been killed. He had only been in-country for two weeks. He had red hair and freckles. 3d Platoon had lost nine Marines KIA.

Con Thien: The Hill of the Angels

Con Thien was actually a cluster of three small hills 158 meters high. It was an ugly, bare patch of mud. Local missionaries called it "the hill of the angels" because so many men had died there. It would accommodate only a reinforced battalion. It was the northwest anchor of what we Marines called the McNamara Line. That imaginary line was actually a six-hundred-meter clearing constructed by the 11th Engineers as a buffer zone from the Laotian border to the South China Sea. "The Strip" was originally constructed for the placement of sensors to detect enemy troop movements. The project was called off and the engineers ended up just fortifying Khe Sanh.

Con Thien was clearly visible from 9th Marine headquarters at Dong Ha to the south. We could see the Gio Linh firebase northeast of Con Thien. If the NVA overran Con Thien and Gio Linh, they had a clear path to the south. It was our job to keep this from happening. We ran patrols and ambushes every day to keep the NVA on the move. We had to make sure the enemy couldn't build fixed positions around the area. It was a hard job. We'd blow up bunker complexes one day and two days later they would be rebuilt. With so few Marines and such a huge area to cover, there was only so much we could do. Without going across the river and stopping the source, it was really like fighting with one hand tied behind your back.

Con Thien was shelled constantly, about two hundred rounds a day fell on that little patch of mud. I don't remember a single day that we did not catch some incoming rounds of some sort. We suffered something that was almost unheard of anywhere else in this jungle war, "shell shock." A lot of men suffered from combat fatigue, but to us shell shock was different. The constant enemy artillery and rocket attacks would make you go nuts. There was nothing you could do but sit and wonder if the next round had your name on it. Echo 2/9 was on a small hill on the southern edge of Con Thien, right next to the LZ and the main gate. We had hardly any protection at all, just holes in the mud. During the month of September 1967, from the nineteenth to the twenty-seventh, we received over 3,000 rounds of incoming artillery, mortars, and rockets. On the twenty-fifth of September alone we took 1,200 rounds. I thought the whole mountain would be blown off the map.

My high school buddy Louie Torrellas got a gift from the Russians on that day. I heard it coming and I heard it hit close by. I looked up out of my foxhole full of water and mud and saw that this big rocket had hit right next to Louie's position. I saw his head come up out of the water-filled hole. He climbed out and staggered like a fighter that had just taken a big left hook. Blood was running out of both ears and his mouth. A corpsman ran to help him. I never saw him again after that day. They threw him on a medevac and a week or so later I got a letter from him. He was on a hospital ship. He wrote that he was going back to the World. I was glad for him but couldn't help wishing it was me. I don't know how God made all those rounds miss us, but I know He did. It was like sitting under a hailstorm and having every one miss you.

We sat day in and day out just getting shelled and unable to fight back. It was driving some of the men nuts. The monsoon rains hit us. I sat in water up to my neck trying to bail it out with my helmet until you heard that freight train coming in, then the helmet was back on the head quick. I had to bail out my foxhole four or five times a day. Everybody got immersion foot. Your feet would just crack and bleed. We were starting to go without food. Choppers couldn't land with so much incoming, but they'd risk landing to pick up the wounded.

One day we started getting hit by barrages of rockets. We stayed in our holes most of the day. I sat listening as one of those huge rockets screamed toward me, getting louder as it got closer and closer until I was sure it would be the last sound I was ever going to hear. Then I was up in the air sort of floating on top of the explosion, above my fighting hole. I finally came down along with a steam shovel's worth of mud that covered me, but I was alive. My ears were ringing but not loud enough to keep me from hearing another incoming rocket. I scrambled back into my hole and huddled deeper and heard the rocket screaming right at me. The wind of the big rocket made a *whoosh* sound as it went just overhead. The splash of it sinking into the mud about forty yards behind me was followed by a single shout but no explosion. Marines all around started peeking up out of their holes to see what had happened. I couldn't believe my eyes. A twelve-foot-long rocket was sticking in the mud. It had hit a Marine but he wasn't dead. No one knew what to do. Somebody shouted that it might be a time-delay fuse. It was scary and everyone was afraid to go near it, but we finally had to go help the guy who was hurt.

A few of us inched up to the thing, expecting it to blow us to pieces at any moment. It was a solid twelve feet long, OD green, and had Russian writing on it. Seeing that Russian writing really ticked off a lot of the guys. We already knew the Chinese were helping the NVA, but this was the first concrete evidence we personally saw that the Russians were getting into the act, too. Unbelievably, the Marine who got hit by the big rocket lived.

More rockets started hitting all around. A CP bunker about twenty-five yards off to my right took a direct hit. Then came the familiar scream, "Corpsman up!" A buddy of mine, Fred, from guns, took off to help. He sprinted through enough shrapnel to build a tank and didn't get hit. He dived into the bunker, where a lieutenant and his radioman were barely clinging to life. The young lieutenant was lying on his back with his guts hanging out. He looked up at Fred, his face ashen and said, "Thank you." Then he drifted off into a coma. Fred quickly tucked the LT's guts back into his stomach and was holding them in with both hands when Doc Dave got there. Doc started working on the wounded, then every other

Marine started screaming for them to get out of that bunker. Just as they finally dragged and carried the wounded out of there and into another hole, that CP bunker took another direct hit. Doc Dave and Fred Gilham just sat in the new hole trembling. They knew that they had been seconds away from dead. Then the Doc realized that Willie Peter, white phosphorous rounds, were lying all around them. They had jumped into an ammo bunker. They sprinted out of there.

That night I lay in the mud trying to sleep, but sleep was impossible. I couldn't help thinking that I wasn't going to wake up. I could hear every sound. Then I heard that dreaded sound of the rockets taking off from the other side of the Ben Hai River, North Vietnam. We were that close, all we had to do was cross that stupid river and knock them out, but that was against the rules. Our artillery and mortars started throwing some serious steel in their direction, then the real big shells started screaming in on the enemy. Naval bombardment. The B-52s started dropping thousand-pounders way too close for comfort. Watching the B-52s do their job was an awesome sight. On one bomb run I watched a giant piece of shrapnel the size of a VW bug fly into the air. We all watched this thing like we were watching a movie as it came straight toward us. It seemed to take forever to reach us, almost like a slow-motion film. It got closer and closer, whirring and whistling through the air. We ducked down in our holes. It sailed right over us, I never saw it hit.

One day I sat on line staring out at the DMZ. A Huey helicopter appeared about a football field outside the lines. Suddenly I realized that the Huey was being chased by an enemy SAM (surface-to-air missile). At first we thought the chopper was crashing because it dropped down so fast, then we realized it was trying to avoid the missile. The Huey landed hard. Then this big, slow SAM missile appeared with a flame coming out of the tailfin section. Out of nowhere this sleek, green Phantom jet appeared low over our heads doing a victory roll in front of the big, slow SAM missile. The missile slowly turned in pursuit of the jet. The Phantom led the big, slow missile away from the chopper and away from our perimeter. We watched that sucker with fire coming out of its tail as it chased our jet and finally exploded against a hill in the distance. It was the coolest thing I ever saw, like watching a movie.

We made a sweep through an NVA bunker complex in the southern DMZ right after a B-52 arc light (bombing) raid. It was obvious as soon as we got near the area that the B-52s had dropped some serious tonnage. You could put a house in some of these craters. Charlie usually got to these spots first and dragged away his dead and wounded. The stench of rotting flesh was so strong, we knew we had beaten Charlie to the site of the bombing. We saw the true devastation of an accurate B-52 strike. The terrain had been physically rearranged. There wasn't a tree left standing in the entire area. I walked up to an NVA soldier sitting against a tree stump with his eyes wide open. The top of his skull, right below the hairline, was gone. His brain was intact and, strangely, there was very little blood on him. It was as if a surgeon had neatly taken the top of his head away to study the guy's brain. Our corpsman Doc Dave came up and dropped his gear. He pulled out a little camera and started taking photos of the guy's brain. I had already worried that the Doc was losing it from being in the bush too long. It happened sometimes. I asked Doc if he was okay. He kept busy with his new obsession, then said, "Purely in the interest of science, Jack."

Doc wasn't the only one acting weird. The carnage was incredible. Body parts everywhere. Pieces of men sticking out of the giant craters like some human garden. One of our squad leaders was looking down into a bunker. There were three sets of bare feet sticking up out of this hole. The feet were black with rigor mortis. The squad leader started talking into the bunker as if someone was hearing him. I looked down and the faces of the dead NVA were covered with maggots and black flies. He pulled out his bug juice, insect repellent, and squirted it on their faces. "Is that better now? You're welcome."

I tapped him on the shoulder. "Hey, are you all right, Corporal?" He laughed. "You're acting shell-shocked, pal."

"I'm not crazy! I'm just clowning around."

I walked away worried about him, but the war and the way we were fighting it, with no effort being made to win, I wondered if any of us would be normal if we got home. Sometimes we were taking the exact same hill four times. We'd take it and Marines would die taking it, fighting like maniacs to win that miserable no-name hill, then we'd pack up our gear and let the gooks move right back in. Our job in this particular B-52 human junkyard was to search the bodies for maps or any info that might prove valuable. I walked toward another crater, past some bloating bodies. The jungle heat would make them swell up really fast and sometimes they'd actually explode. I moved along looking over the mess, with my M-60 at the ready. I rolled a dead gook over to search him. He suddenly sprang up to a sitting position. My heart stopped beating for a full minute. Just about then another dead gook nearby groaned. That was normal stuff, dead bodies do all kinds of weird things as rigor mortis sets in. Even though I knew bodies did things like that, I still was never prepared for it.

We carried all the bodies that we could find and threw them into one of the big craters. We set in for the night as a heavy monsoon rain came down. When daybreak came we were ready to get out of there. The smell was terrible. We got the word to saddle up and engineers started setting the charges. They screamed, "Fire in the hole!" There were four or five loud explosions that covered the bodies with earth. That brought to an end another day in the bush.

We were on our way back to Camp Carroll from just one of a thousand patrols. We had been humping all day long and made no contact with the NVA. The only NVA we saw was a dead one. The Montagnard (hill people) had killed him the night before. They were displaying him proudly as we approached their village. They were amazing. Two of them would go out into the bush at night armed with these little pigmy-looking bows and arrows and some other primitive weapons, and as sure as it would rain in Vietnam they'd come back with a dead NVA. We did all we could to help them.

Our corpsmen would treat any illnesses and the Marines would give them all of our extra chow. Doc finished taking care of their problems and we thanked the chief for his help. We slowly started to leave the ville. We still had to forge the river and there was a long climb back up to the top of the hill.

We made the climb and were almost back to the perimeter of Camp Carroll. We were walking across the rice paddy just outside the wire. Suddenly came that *crack!* We hit the mud. An NVA sniper had waited until the entire platoon was in the middle of the rice paddy before opening up. He got off shot after shot, probably over fifteen rounds. I crawled up on a paddy dike and saw the smoke from his last shot. I turned and shouted, "Lieutenant! I see him! Can I blow him away?" As a machine gunner I couldn't just open fire, giving away the gun position, without an okay.

"No! Hold your fire!"

"Lieutenant, I can blow his head off right now!"

"No! Hold your fire!"

"Sir! Let me kill him!"

"No!"

"But why?"

"Jack! If I let you kill him, what do you think will happen?"

I was stumped. How do you answer that?

The lieutenant shook his head. "If you kill that guy, they will send another sniper in there tomorrow."

"Yes, sir?"

"That gook hasn't hit anyone with fifteen shots! If you kill him they might send in a replacement that can actually hit a target!"

So we let him live. Combat logic, Vietnam.

Marines called Con Thien "the meatgrinder." Not that long after my second Christmas overseas, I finished my thirteen-month tour and was headed Stateside. Our platoon had arrived at Con Thien with 45 men. We left with 12. One of my last memories or at least lasting memories of Con Thien was of a young Marine sitting in a puddle of blood and battle dressings on a poncho with his legs blown off from the waist down. He was numb with morphine and in shock from loss of blood. He was smoking a cigarette very calmly as if nothing had even happened. He was waiting for a medevac. He probably died on the chopper ride back, but for that moment he epitomized just how tough and brave these Marines were.

I got spit on when I got home, called a baby-killer or something like that. I decked the guy and his head hit pavement. I thought he was dead. I really thought I had made it through Nam alive only to spend the rest of my life in jail after my first day home. He was okay, just a concussion that made him a little smarter about spitting on Marines. A couple of days after I got home, I went into a local VFW post. I wore my uniform and they treated me well but said I couldn't join their post because Vietnam was only a police action. I knew that I'd probably seen more combat than anyone in that building. I never set foot inside another VFW until 1984 and only then because Vietnam vets needed the vote to take command of the post.

Nobody wanted to talk to us about Nam. They were bored with the subject. Besides they could watch the nightly news, the news had more deception and lies each night than any drunken Marine could ever dream up. Everybody called us drug addicts. People would come up and ask me point-blank, "How many women and children did you kill over there?" And they actually meant it! They really believed that crap. I was a very bitter man for years. It was sort of a them against us thing. I wouldn't even talk about Nam to anyone who wasn't a Nam vet. The feeling of alienation lasted for years. I hated war protesters and they were in danger around me. I lost faith in everything. I stayed self-medicated for almost sixteen years after I was discharged from the Corps. In May 1986, I decided to commit myself to an alcohol rehabilitation center.

A couple of weeks after I returned home from the treatment center, a veteran friend of mine asked me if I would like to go to Chicago and be in a Vietnam veterans parade. I told him, no thanks, it was way too late for a parade. Our country had blown its chance to treat us well. He talked me into coming along for the camaraderie of being with men who knew the truth.

We departed Wilmington, Delaware, at noon on June 12, 1986. We arrived in Chicago that night and checked into a hotel. The parade was to start at 10 A.M. the next morning. We called a taxi and were taken to Olive Park, where the parade was supposed to begin. There was already a huge crowd of marchers assembled. In my heart I still doubted that anyone cared about us, they never did when it counted, but there was something significant about where the parade started. The park was named after Medal of Honor recipient Milton Lee Olive III. He died in Vietnam, that war that had no heroes, when he threw himself on top of a grenade to save the lives of his buddies.

We were clad in ragged khakis or three-piece suits and it seemed somehow appropriate. We started walking west on Grant Avenue with General Westmoreland and the disabled men leading the way. There were a lot of wheelchairs. There were various veteran organizations marching in the parade and numerous bands playing. People started cheering us. Hundreds of people all along both sides of the street. People were yelling, "Thank you." They ran into the street and shook our hands and patted us on the shoulders as we walked by. I couldn't believe what was happening, it didn't seem real. I noticed that the men were actually in military alignment and in step as if it were still natural. Halfway down Grant Avenue the parade halted abruptly and we ran up the backs of each other like the Three Stooges. It took a minute to figure out what had happened, then I saw this good-looking woman up on the balcony of a building with her top off and screaming, "Thank you, boys!"

We got squared away again and continued to State Street, made a left turn, and went south. People were yelling and screaming and still cheering us on. People started mobbing us as we were walking by, but they mobbed us with love. At some points along the parade route the crowds swelled into the street, overflowing the sidewalks. A lot of the Nam vets were cops and one looked at me and said, "Trust me, brother,

Nam vets own this town today!" He was right. I watched the police turn their backs on people who had open cans of beer along the way. One Chicago cop had a hat on that read, "Vietnam Veteran and Proud of It!" I had never heard the words "thank you" spoken so many times. There were signs in windows that read WELCOME HOME BOYS or WE LOVE YOU BOYS, THANKS!

Guys were breaking down crying around me but trying hard to hide it. We made a left turn down LaSalle Street and I couldn't believe my eyes. There was ticker tape being dropped from every window. It was like a heavy snow. I felt my heart beginning to melt. Up to this point I felt almost suspicious, it was too good to be true. We won every battle and killed the enemy at somewhere between ten and twenty to one and nobody ever cared before, why did they give a crap about us now? Nobody cared when the communists killed tens of thousands of innocent women and children in places like Hue City. Nobody cared when Marines died to take Hue back. Nobody cared about Con Thien and what it cost to hold against overwhelming odds. Why should they care now? It's too late!

Then it happened. A little girl, about five years old, she wore a beautiful white dress and looked like some doll. She came running out into the ranks through the snowstorm of ticker tape with a bundle of red roses, handing them out to the men and saying, "Thank you sir for going to Vietnam for me." She was like a little angel. I started crying so hard I couldn't control it. I had not cried since Vietnam. The anger and hatred and bitterness was just raining out of my eyes and onto the streets of Chicago. I suddenly wanted so badly to share this feeling with all of those wounded brothers who would never be the same physically or mentally.

When I came home from Chicago, people said I was different. I left a lot of tears and anger in Chicago. We had a saying in the Nam. "It don't mean nothin'." When a buddy died you would numbly say, "It don't mean nothin'." If you had to take the same hill for the fourth time and some new "boot" would start complaining, you'd look at him like an "old salt" and say, "It don't mean nothin'." When your own countrymen or women would fly to North Vietnam to help the enemy, you'd say, "It don't mean nothin'." When the nightly news or a Hollywood movie, one and the same, would twist the truth until it wasn't recognizable, we'd say, "Don't mean nothin'."

Well, Chicago, this parade meant something. Thanks.

GLOSSARY

'03—Springfield rifle

782 gear—Marine Corps equipment issued to every Marine

A 1/5—During WWII and Korea the "A" stood for Able Company. During Vietnam it stood for Alpha Company, 1st Battalion, 5th Marine Regiment

AK-47—A Russian assault rifle

ARVN—Army of the Republic of Vietnam

AWOL—Absent without leave

B-40 rocket—A communist antitank rocket

BAR—Browning automatic rifle

Barracks cover—Marine dress uniform hat with bill

BCD—Bad conduct discharge

Betty—Japanese light bomber planes

Blouse—Marine dress jacket or coat

Body bags—Plastic zipper-bags for corpses

Boondockers—Marine field shoes, usually worn with canvas leggings

Boondocks—Rough terrain; jungle

Boot—Slang for a new recruit undergoing basic training or new to combat

Bulkhead—Protective wall; used by Marines to describe the walls of every structure from a barracks wall to the inner wall of a tank or ship

Bush—Vietnam-era slang for the outer field areas and jungle where infantry units operate

Charlie—Vietnam-era slang for the Viet Cong or North Vietnamese army

Chi-Com—Chinese Communist. Also slang for an enemy grenade in Vietnam

Chinook—CH-46 troop helicopters

Choppers—Helicopters

Chow—Food

Claymores—Mines packed with plastique and rigged to spray hundreds of steel pellets

C4—Plastique explosive, forms like hard putty

C-130—A cargo plane used to transport men and supplies during Vietnam War

CMH—Congressional Medal of Honor, America's highest medal for bravery. Also known as MOH

CO—Commanding officer

Concertina wire—Barbed wire that is rolled out along the ground to hinder the progress of enemy troops

Corsair—American single-engine fighter plane flown by Marines in WWII and Korea

CP—Command post, where the CO and radio communications were usually located

C rats—C rations, prepackaged military meals eaten in the field

Cruise—One tour of duty

C-S—A caustic riot gas used in Vietnam

Deck—The floor, also ground; also Marine term for knocking someone flat

Deuce-and-a-half—A two-and-a-half-ton heavy transport truck used for carrying men and supplies

DI—Drill instructor

Dink—Slang for the enemy in Vietnam

DMZ—Demilitarized Zone

Dogface or Doggie—Slang for any U.S. Army personnel

EM club—Enlisted men's club or bar

Flak jacket—A vest worn to protect the chest area from shrapnel

Frags—Slang for fragmentation grenades

Friendly fire—Fire from your own troops

Frogs—Slang name for French soldiers dating back to WWI

Gook—Slang that Marines adopted from the Koreans, used

to describe any Asian person, especially in reference to the enemy

Grunt—Slang for any combat soldier fighting in Vietnam

Gung ho—Chinese saying that means "to work together"; adopted by Marines, used to describe an overzealous person

Gyrene—Slang for Marine

Hatchway or Hatch—Any kind of door, including a tank hatch or helicopter hatch

Head—Any kind of toilet in any location

Ho Chi Minh Trail—The main supply route running south from North Vietnam through Laos and Cambodia

Hootches—Slang for any form of a dwelling place in Vietnam

HQ—Headquarters

Humping—Slang for marching with a heavy load through the bush

I Corps Tactical Zone—The northern five provinces of South Vietnam, called "Marineland" by some

III Corps—The military region around Saigon

Jarhead—Slang for U.S. Marine coming from the Marine style haircut, no hair on the sides

K-bar—A Marine Corps survival knife, bladed on top and bottom for killing

KIA—Killed in action

Klick—One kilometer, sometimes spelled "click"

LAW—Light antiarmor weapon, fired from top of the shoulder like a small bazooka. Also spelled LAAW.

LCI—Landing Craft Infantry; length fifteen feet; can carry over 200 infantrymen

LCM—Landing Craft Mechanized; length fifty feet; can transport 1,200 men, one medium tank, or thirty tons of cargo

Low quarters—Marine dress shoes

LP—Listening post

LSM—Landing Ship Medium; length 203 feet, carries a dozen tanks, vehicles, and cargo of men

LST—Landing Ship Tank; oceangoing ship that carries

smaller craft topside plus numerous tanks, vehicles, guns, and cargo within a tunnel-like hold

LT—Slang for lieutenant

LZ—Landing zone

M-1—Single-shot, clip-fed, eight rounds of .30-caliber ammunition

M-14—A magazine-fed rifle with automatic fire capability used in Vietnam by American ground forces that fired a 7.62mm round, the same round fired by the M-60 machine gun

M-16—Standard automatic rifle used in Vietnam by American forces that fired a smaller caliber round than the M-60 or the M-14, a 2.23 round

M-60—A machine gun used by American forces in Vietnam. Cyclic rate of fire, 550 to 600 rounds of 7.62mm ammunition per minute. Weight: 23.16 pounds without ammo belt. Range: 3,750 meters. Effective range: 1,100 meters

M-79—A 40mm grenade launcher

Medevac—A term for medically evacuating the wounded by chopper or plane

MOS—Military Occupational Specialty

Mustang—An enlisted man who wins a commission

Nambu—Japanese machine gun

NVA—North Vietnamese Army

Ontos—Tracked vehicle designed to be a tank-killer, armed with six 106 recoilless rifles, three on each side

Paramarines—An elite unit of Marines trained to parachute behind enemy lines

PBY—Seaplane; a patrol bomber in WWII

PFC—Private First Class

Piece—Weapon

Pogue—A derogatory term for rear-area personnel

POW—Prisoner of war

Puff—A C-47 aircraft with miniguns, capable of delivering thousands of machine gun rounds in support of ground troops. Known as "Puff the Magic Dragon" due to the enormous amount of tracer fire

Raiders—Elite Marine force trained for action behind enemy lines

ROK—Republic of Korea

RPG—Rocket-propelled grenade

R&R—Rest and relaxation

Sack—Marine Corps bed, also called rack or bunk; could be used to describe an actual bed or the mud you're sleeping in

Sally—Twin-engine Japanese bomber

Salt—A term used to describe a Marine who has been in the Corps a long time or in combat for a significant amount of time

Sappers—Viet Cong infiltrators whose job it was to detonate explosive charges within American positions

Scuttlebutt—Drinking fountain; also, rumors often started at the drinking fountain

Sergeant Major—Highly respected enlisted rank

Short-timer—Someone whose tour in Vietnam or the Corps is almost completed

Slop-chute—Anyplace that serves alcohol in any form

Smoke grenade—A grenade that releases colored smoke used for signaling and also used for covering movement

Survey—Turning in used equipment for new gear; also used to describe a man being discharged, "surveyed out of the Corps"

Swab jockey—Also swabby, or squid; any sailor of any rank

The Island—Could mean any island, but usually meant Guadalcanal

Tiger Piss—Tiger Beer/33 Beer; Vietnamese beer

Tojo—Gen. Hideki Tojo, prime minister of Japan

Top or Top Sergeant—First sergeant; highly respected enlisted rank

Tracer—A bullet with a phosphorous coating, designed to burn and provide a visual indication of a bullet's trajectory

Viet Cong (VC)—The local communist militias fighting in South Vietnam

Web gear—Canvas suspenders and belt used to carry infantryman's gear

White sidewalls—Marine haircut, no hair on sides, also known as jarhead

WIA—Wounded in action

Willie Peter—White phosphorous round that explodes into a white mushroom cloud, usually used to zero in American artillery

Zeke—Japanese fighter-bomber, larger than a Zero

Zero—Single-engine Japanese fighter plane; light, fast, and maneuverable

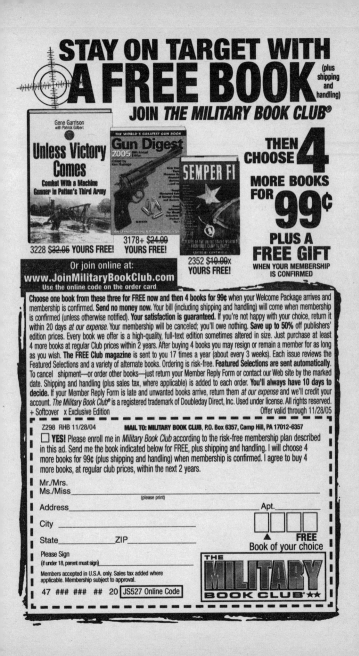